THE CLOUD OF NECTAR

THE CLOUD OF NECTAR

The Life and Liberation of
Nyagla Pema Düdul

YESHE DORJE

Translated from the Tibetan, edited, and annotated by
Oriol Aguilar

© 2013 Oriol Aguilar
Shang Shung Institute
58031 Arcidosso (GR)
Italy
www.shangshungpublications.org
info@shangshungpublications.org

Design: Kasia Skura
Cover photo: Oriol Aguilar

ISBN 978-88-7834-113-5

To the Celestial Jewel

Contents

Preface

✤ The present work is a translation of the biography of Nyagla Pema Düdul (1816–1872), a nineteenth century Tibetan master and well-known exponent of the practice and realization of Total Perfection (Dzogchen)[1]. This translation forms the nucleus of a doctoral thesis[2] addressing the subject of the transmission of knowledge in the lineage of Total Perfection, one of the most ancient meditative traditions in Tibetan Buddhism.

I became interested in Pema Düdul's life many years ago, mainly through listening to the explanations and biographical reports about this master transmitted by Chögyal Namkhai Norbu during teaching retreats. As I listened, my curiosity and admiration for Pema Düdul were fostered by the fact that although he was not an important abbot or tülku raised in the monastic hierarchy, he is considered to be one of the most realized masters of Atiyoga in recent times and a very significant individual in the transmission lineages of this tradition.

Around 1998, my friend the Tibetologist Jean-Luc Achard gave me the biography he had obtained in Chengdu, and I began to translate it. I later referred to the Nyarong xylographic redaction available in the Tibetan Buddhist Resource Center (TBRC). Gradually I developed a thesis based on the biography's translation. Later, at the end of the thesis writing, I went to Nyarong, the region in Kham where Pema Düdul spent most of his life. I had the opportunity to visit Lhang Lhang, the sacred mountain where he remained in retreat for many years, where he discovered his terma teachings, and where he built Kalzang Gönpa, the main seat of his transmission. There I had the opportunity to witness how the spiritual legacy of Pema Düdul as well as the social memory of his life were still very, very much alive among Nyarong's people.

With the biography's translation and the introductory chapters explaining some aspects of the historical, religious and social setting, I am attempting to elucidate the marvelous life of this enlightened teacher. As mentioned above, these chapters were part of my doctoral thesis, but here they are presented in a less academic style. Similarly, the rendering of the biography has been lightened by leaving the Tibetan and Sanskrit words in phonetic transcription rather than in strict transliteration.

Although the namthar of Pema Düdul may offer much information for further analysis in the Tibetological field, I am leaving such scientific elaboration to the future specialist, having chosen here to simply present the biography preceded by some introductory material which serves to contextualize the story.

In the introductory chapters various aspects of this master's life are examined, focusing in detail on his masters and disciples. The historical, regional and cultural circumstances are presented and analyzed, as are the peculiarities of Pema Düdul's biography. A separate section addresses the biographical literature of Tibet.

The main body of this work is the biography, *The Spiritual Liberation of Trülzhig Lingpa: The Bank of Clouds containing the Nectar of Happiness for the Fortunate*[3] written by the disciple Yeshe Dorje. The contents of the teachings revealed by him as spiritual treasures (terma) belonging to the cycle *Self-Liberation which Encompasses Space*[4] are listed in an Appendix.[5]

Interviews were carried out with Chögyal Namkhai Norbu and with other lamas who, through their birthplace or activity are familiar with the life and transmission of Pema Düdul. These include Sönam Tenpa, preceptor (khenpo) of the School of Philosophy at Kathog monastery, who as a native of Nyarong informed me of several aspects of his life, and lama Akha, Kalzang Gyatso, Abbot of the Zhare Gendün Shedrub Phelgyeling monastery in Nyarong Dzong who keeps alive the teachings of Pema Düdul and who is currently overseeing the production of the xylographic edition of the master's works.[6]

I wish to express my gratitude to Chögyal Namkhai Norbu for all his years of work in transmitting the most precious gems of wisdom. Thanks to him and his inspiration, this work has seen the light of day.

I am deeply indebted to my parents who have helped me during my studies and research. I also express my gratitude to many other persons, particularly Verena Stolcke, director of my PhD thesis; Anne-Marie Blondeau who helped me with the Tibetan translation; Peter Guest who did the first English translation; Judith Chasnoff who did the style correction and editing of the text; Joe Evans who did the final proofreading; Khenpo Sönam Tenpa of Kathog monastery and Kalzang Gyatso, abbot of Zhare Gendün Shedrub Phelgyeling monastery, for their kind collaboration; Adriano Clemente who advised me in many aspects and did a final review of the text; Jean-Luc Achard who helped to clarify my Tibetological uncertainties and gave me the text of the biography; Jann M. Ronis who very kindly helped me in Kathog monastery; Artur Skura of Shang Shung Publications for his kind and efficient collaboration; Ramon N. Prats, for initiating me into the Tibetan studies; Riccardo Polveroni, who advised and helped me on so many occasions; Michele Nucciotti, who pointed out some academic procedures, and to all the other persons who through the years have supported and encouraged me in this work.

Oriol Aguilar
Barcelona 2012

Translator's Introduction

The Biography
and the Biographical Genre

THE CHOICE OF NYAGLA PEMA DÜDUL'S BIOGRAPHY

🌸 Nyagla Pema Düdul's biography was not selected at random. This master was one of the great representatives of the heights attained by the Vajrayana traditions in nineteenth century eastern Tibet. His biography provides a clear example of the kind of master who acquires a great reputation without belonging to the hierarchy of a great monastery. His lifestyle was like that of a nomad, as he wandered through the many regions of Kham receiving and giving teachings. But this did not prevent him from building his own temple, Kalzang Gönpa, the seat of his transmission and lineage, on the slopes of the holy mountain of Lhang Lhang.[7]

Another interesting dimension is the revealed nature of many of Pema Düdul's teachings. He was an important discoverer of spiritual treasures, a tertön,[8] and his biography contains detailed descriptions of the histories of the various discoveries. His spiritual treasure, the cycle of teachings *Self-Liberation that Encompasses Space*, is a vast compendium of practices comprising the various methods of the Nyingmapa system. References to the contents of this work as well as fragments of prophetic indications[9] are embedded in the text of the biography. The description of the process of revealing the spiritual treasure, narrated in the seventh chapter, is of particular interest as it discloses many details of the treasure's revelation.

Although the current work focuses mainly on the biography's translation, the historical, religious and even personal context of the protagonist must be explained in order to facilitate understanding of the period's complex social and political mesh. The biography abounds in references to the social and political realities prevalent in nineteenth century eastern Tibet, and in several instances depicts a far from idyllic situation which is portrayed frankly, with no attempt to disguise. The drama of the family circumstances, the various strategies for survival, and the complex political climate are bluntly presented to the Tibetan reader who is already familiar with that society. From the point of view of the transmission of spiritual knowledge, the backdrop of the life of Pema Düdul is especially interesting not only for the great variety of teachings he received, revealed, and transmitted, but also for the absence of sectarian approach. This latter characteristic lends a great diversity in spiritual relationships to his religious activity, involving practitioners and specialists from different fields of all the Tibetan traditions, including the Bönpo.

I must stress that this is not an autobiography, but a biography containing the memories and recollections collected by Yeshe Dorje, one of his most direct disciples. The difference between the two genres may be great, as an autobiography may contain elements that only an author writing about himself could describe. A biography that, as in this case, has been written by a direct disciple may also contain elements that a master would hardly include in his autobiography, such as pious exaltation centered on his person or events occurring after his death that relate to his spiritual legacy.

BIOGRAPHY IN TIBETAN BUDDHIST TRADITION

Biography as a Tibetan Buddhist literary genre has been discussed by many authors, often in comments and analysis accompanying a translation. Here I shall present some key aspects of this genre.

In early Buddhist literature we find that the biographical genre, centered on the Buddha's life, had already achieved a singular importance. When the doctrine was first written down and the Buddhist canon gradually began to take shape, certain biographical elements, particularly stories or anecdotes depicting the four main occurrences in the Buddha's life,[10] were already scattered in the body of writings. Other references were included in the teachings themselves, the sermons that were usually accompanied by information on the place, the circumstances, and the audience to whom they were directed.

The first biographical texts—though not in a strictly historical sense—belong to the mythical literature known as Jataka that relate the previous lives of Shakyamuni. This genre, although secondary, is already significant. The first historical biographies, called *Buddhacharita,* written by Sangharaksha and by Ashvaghosa,[11] were probably a fruit of the Greek influence in post-Alexandrian India. The presence of Greek culture in Bactriana and other regions surrounding the northwest areas of the Indian subcontinent may have fomented the appearance of a realistic representation of the Buddha in both art and literature.

As the tradition meandered through time and history with the consequent proliferation of schools and currents as well as masters, the references to their lives began to be shaped into a type of biographical literature. Although most biographical stories of Indian masters (especially of tantrism) survive only in Tibetan translation, we may be certain that the genre was highly appreciated as a vehicle exemplifying religious values for the faithful while also providing important information for the most advanced adepts. This last is especially true of the mahasiddha biographies in which the transcendent experiences of the crucial life episodes, such as the moment of meeting the guru, receiving initiations and later on, experiencing practice and realization are described, often in the form of songs.[12]

Although some samples of Indian biographical writings have reached us—mainly thanks to Tibetan translations—it must be said that compared to other types of Indian Buddhist literature, the biographical genre is scarce. In fact, many extant biographies of Indian masters were written by Tibetans, such as the life of the mahasiddha Naropa by Lhatsünpa

Rinchen Namgyal, and those found in the *History of Buddhism in India* composed by Taranatha.[13] In the field of autobiography (of which we have good examples in Tibetan Buddhist literature) Indian works are virtually nonexistent. Some have attributed this scarcity to the general lack of interest in historical literature in traditional Indian society and to the cyclic view of time,[14] although future research on the great legacy of Indian literature may challenge this view. Among the various biographies of the Indian Buddhist tradition surviving in Sanskrit, Pali, Chinese, and Tibetan documents, some describe the life of canonical authors, as in Vasubandhu's biography by Paramartha; others are concerned with tantric masters, such as those of the 84 mahasiddhas,[15] that of Krishnacarya,[16] and those of Pramodavajra (Garab Dorje), Shri Simha, and Mañjushrimitra.[17] Most of the tantric materials have reached us in their Tibetan and Chinese versions.

The elements of biographical narrative in Indian Buddhism were generally defined as avadana, 'expression of realization,' but that same word also has a wider meaning. The term vimoksha, 'liberation,' also seems to have been used to refer to the biographical stories which illuminate the path to spiritual liberation. These two Sanskrit terms translated into Tibetan as togjö and namthar[18] are used to characterize the hagiographical genre.

In contrast with the scarcity of Indian Buddhist biographies, the Tibetan tradition contains an enormous quantity of biographical (and occasionally, autobiographical) literature preserving the experiences of the masters of all lineages. The value given to these works is twofold: for the ordinary faithful, reading them is a source of spiritual inspiration and a meritorious act; for the initiate in the practices of the lineage, the inner and secret biographies (two divisions of which I shall speak more below) are a source of precious information, as they document the highest experiences of the subject as well as the birth of the new contributions with which he enriches the tradition.

The above-mentioned values are the traditional values held by participants in Buddhist culture. But the Tibetan biography also provides a series of responses to specific needs and tensions belonging to the Tibetan religious medium. [19] It is first and foremost the description of a life, with all the comings and goings and learning the adept had to undergo to attain the realization qualifying him to be a link in the chain of transmission, which make his life a worthy model for spiritual liberation (namthar). Accompanying all this, the vicissitudes, the obstacles, and the trials suffered by the initiate illustrate the authenticity of his search. Above all, we are shown how the immense soteriological power of the teachings, initiations, and essential instructions is enjoyed by the recipient by virtue of the liberating capacity of the transmission lineage in general and the master-disciple relationship in particular. All this serves to affirm the authenticity of the subject's realization and the solidity of the transmission lineage to which he belongs. When an adept reaches the rank of guru, his spiritual charisma and position in the lineage are attainments that cannot be overlooked in the Tibetan religious arena. Although his status is conferred by the lineage (that is, by the adept's masters who authorize him to act as a lama), the charisma he wields in the social sphere depends on several factors. Even if it is produced during the master's lifetime, the biography can be a powerful tool for fixing his charisma for posterity.

Because he is a discoverer of spiritual treasures (tertön), as in the case of other discoverers, Pema Düdul's biography is also an exposition of the revelation, of the contents, and of the diffusion of these treasures among his disciples. In the Treasure tradition, the biographies of the tertöns serve to validate not only the position of these masters within the transmission lineage but also the relevance of the treasures and the spiritual praxis originating with the discovered cycle.

The Various Kinds of Biography

The contents of the various elements found in Tibetan biographies and autobiographies are often divided into three categories: 'outer,' 'inner,' and 'secret.' There are also 'most secret' ones. [20]

The first (outer) class of biography most closely resembles the Western version. This class presents the major facts, vicissitudes, and ordinary events occurring in a religion-focused human life, with particular emphasis on the subject's early (and often precocious) vocational aspirations, his meetings with masters, his education, practice, realization, and gradual confluence of disciples. To all this is usually added a number of references to the social and political realities of the historical period and to his personal position in the surrounding political and religious environment.

The inner biography usually presents the adept's curriculum, including the masters he met and their lineages, the teachings and initiations received, his progress through monastic training (in the case of monks and nuns), and certain meditative experiences. It is therefore similar to the genre called thobyig and sanyig.[21]

The secret biography, along with the most secret one, depicts the more subjective aspects of the practitioner's life: it is a compendium of all pertinent meditative and yogic experiences, particularly those leading to the achievement of an understanding or realization. Often these are visionary experiences occurring either during sleep or wakefulness, usually containing powerful indicators of obstacles to be overcome, attainments to be achieved, or the stabilization of a level of realization. Also belonging to this category are the meditative and visionary experiences regarding revelation of new doctrines, either in the "pure vision" or the "spiritual treasure" modality. Sometimes second and third personas of the subject may be depicted carrying out paranormal feats, wherein we find ourselves in the social dimension of the marvelous, usually referred to in Western culture as a "miracle."[22]

But these three classes of the biographical genre are not strictly delimited, and often the contents are blended. The biography of Pema Düdul contains elements of all three: the outer, inner, and secret, giving us a full overview of this master's life experiences.

The Gestation of the Biography of Pema Düdul

Leaving aside the autobiographies,[23] in which the author is the prime source of the narrative, the system used by biographers for collecting material is inexorably linked to the nature of the transmission lineage. This is because the biographer is either a direct disciple of the subject or a member the subject's lineage. In most cases the biographer is a direct disciple who, over the years, has collected either in memory or in writing, the personal experiences as told by the master as well as those shared during encounters or periods of living together. Sometimes, although a master may not have written an autobiography, he may have recorded certain experiences in various documents such as end notes to his written works, in the indices of some treasures (if the master is a tertön), or in the Gur,[24] the 'songs of realization' so lavishly composed by some masters, including Pema Düdul.

It is possible that in some cases of biographies containing scant information, episodes remembered from a master's life may have been orally transmitted in one period, then written down later and included in collections of the lineage masters' biographies.

Here we are looking at a biography, not an autobiography. As Yeshe Dorje explicitly states, some of the episodes from the master's life were excerpted from texts written by the master as, for example, from some of his songs, but most of the material is gleaned from the recollections of the direct disciples, including what the master himself told them about his life. In fact, Yeshe Dorje only rarely reports having obtained any concrete information from Pema Düdul's works, and provides few details. Yeshe Dorje was a direct disciple of Pema Düdul and was probably one of the thirteen bearing the name "Dorje" who were considered his spiritual sons.[25] It is probable that the biography was written not long after the death of Pema Düdul, as important events that occurred in later years are not recorded in the text. For example, there is no mention of Lerab Lingpa and his son Chöpel Gyatso residing at Kalzang monastery and providing spiritual guidance there.

The biographical text is followed by *The Collection of Songs*,[26] in which the poems or songs of Pema Düdul are compiled. Some of these lyrical compositions, many of which are spontaneous poems or 'songs of spiritual experience,'[27] are dedicated to his disciples. The songs address the master's inner experiences and are a poetical expression of his deepest realizations. As author of the songs, Pema Düdul assumes the name Nyida Kundze[28] just as in his role of tertön he is known as Khrulzhig Lingpa.[29]

For this translation, I have used the most recent edition of the biography and songs, presented in Western format and not in the traditional Tibetan format of manuscript or xylographic rectangular books of loose leaves, but a printed and bound book[30] as well as the traditional manuscript of the Nyarong redaction, available thanks to the TBRC.[31] The former edition was sponsored by Kunzang Rigdzin, a young incarnate lama of Dzogchen monastery who lives in China, where he has many disciples. He is also a benefactor of the Kalzang monastery, the temple built by Pema Düdul.[32]

The Context of Nyagla Pema Düdul's Life: *Historical and Religious Aspects of 19th century Kham*

History and Society in Kham

🌸 Nyagla Pema Düdul was born during the first quarter of the nineteenth century in Kham, the vast region of eastern Tibet. Buddhism had already been established in the Land of the Snows for more than a thousand years and the various religious tendencies we know today had existed for several hundred. But this master lived during the time of Tibet's last great spiritual movement of the contemporary period, known as the Unbiased (Rime)[33] approach, which had its origin in Kham and which I shall discuss later on.

The area of Kham comprises an extensive natural region limited on the east by the edges of the Tibetan plateau. In contrast to the central, western, and northern parts of Tibet that are composed mostly of highlands surrounded by great mountain ranges and by the valley of the Tsangpo (Brahmaputra) and its affluents, Kham is ridged with a series of tectonic folds, mainly running in a north-south direction, giving it the appearance of a country dominated by mountains. Through these ranges run some of the most important rivers of Asia, such as the Yangtse, the Mekong, and the Salween. It is not surprising that such a rugged country (as large as the Iberian Peninsula) should give its inhabitants their strongest characteristics: a deep sense of independence from their neighbors, a great feeling of clanship, and an assertive character. Sometimes described as a land of warriors and bandits who ransacked the trade routes, this region also produced some of the most outstanding Tibetan Buddhist masters.

Kham is densely populated in Tibetan terms. In many areas, its valley floors do not exceed 3,500 metres, making them lower than those in other parts of Tibet where agricultural and urban land is at a higher elevation. As Kham enjoys more rainfall than central Tibet and is crossed by many great rivers, agriculture thrives on many of its valley floors. Cattle, sheep, and horses are bred, especially in the highlands and plains, and are the main source of income for the clans, the nomadic and semi-nomadic, tribes. Large parts of Kham are covered in forest, although these have been considerably reduced in the last few decades by logging. Westward and northward the climate becomes more continental, extreme, and dry. Conversely, the eastern and southern zones are more wooded and humid.

The people are mostly Khampa Tibetan. This gives them several characteristics that distinguish them from their neighbors, including some morphological features (Khampas are generally taller than other Tibetans, more corpulent, and with more marked facial features, sometimes giving them the appearance of some of the North-American Indian tribes), but above all, a character that has made them famous throughout the Tibetan world. They are admired and feared for their strong, often warrior-like character and independence. (When I was there in 1994, I was surprised to see the number of men openly carrying daggers, pistols, and bandoliers over their traditional dress, not a common sight in the Peoples' Republic of China). Traditionally, the Khampa have been reluctant to accept domination by anyone but their traditional chiefs, be they Tibetan or Chinese. Because of this, the central Tibetan government had to send reinforcements several times to overcome leaders or nobles from Kham who rebelled against their authority. Further, it was the Khampa who offered the strongest resistance to the Chinese invasion and led the rebellion against it.[34] In the regions bordering China we also find Tibeto-Burman peoples like the Kyang, the Gyalrongpa, or the Nakhi, all of whom have been influenced by Tibetan culture to a greater or lesser extent.

Little is known of ancient Kham, although it doubtlessly belonged to the Tibetan Empire from the seventh to the ninth century. According to the annals, after the disintegration of the Empire, different branches of the imperial family retained power in western and central Tibet,[35] but the situation in Kham is obscure. Later, the succeeding kingdoms of central Tibet that tried to unify Tibetan territories claimed to have dominated the region,[36] but it seems likely that the real circumstances were similar to those in later times, of which we have a clearer picture. However, some historical facts are known, such as the consolidation of the Derge kingdom in the fifteenth century centered in Derge Gönchen.

After the unification during the seventeenth century under the fifth Dalai Lama, Kham was part of the kingdom, and there is no doubt that initially it was largely under the control of the Lhasa government. Gushri Khan, the Mongol leader who conquered almost all Tibet only to offer it to the fifth Dalai Lama, finished off his task by overwhelming the Bönpo kingdom of Beri, in Trehor. But as the Tibetan government became weaker—due to inner conflict, raids by Mongol tribes, and the political intervention of the Manchu Empire— parts of the Kham lands came to be governed by local powers such as aristocratic families, nomad chiefs, or great monasteries. In fact, the Tibetan government bore no resemblance to the modern model of a nation-state but was a complex network of exceptions: within the kingdom of the Dalai Lamas there coexisted several states which, while subordinate to the Lhasa government, were almost entirely self-governing.[37] This was especially so in Kham, where several kings and chiefs governed their territory while recognizing the Lhasa government's authority. Some territories in the region were directly controlled by the central government through local governors, while other states were in the hands of the great monasteries.

From the eighteenth century, the Manchu (Qing) dynasty of the Chinese empire burst onto the Tibetan political scene, taking advantage of an invasion by the Dzungar Mongols in central Tibet. In exchange for help in expelling the Dzungars and in supporting Pholhane, the leading figure on the Tibetan scene, the emperor arranged to permanently install in Lhasa two representatives of the Manchu empire, the ambans, who from 1728[38] interfered in Tibetan politics through the eighteenth, nineteenth, and early twentieth centuries. At the same time during this period the Territories of eastern Tibet (Amdo and Kham) suffered intermittent raids from the Chinese military and chiefs, as well as the governors of adjacent Chinese provinces' campaigns to extend their dominion of these Tibetan lands. In the eighteenth century, Amdo fell into Chinese hands, and in the nineteenth century some parts of Kham were increasingly dominated by Chinese armies. However, the submission of Central Tibet came to an end in 1912 with the fall of the Manchu empire and expulsion of the ambans from Tibet, marking the beginning of full independence that lasted until the invasion in 1950 by the troops of the nascent China of Mao. Until the final invasion, Chinese efforts to annex the eastern parts of Kham had never ceased.

Pema Düdul lived during the nineteenth century when the far eastern territories, nominally under the aegis of the Dalai Lama, were often coveted by governors of the closest Chinese provinces, especially of Sichuan. This was not the only cause of conflict. Also to be taken into account were the intermittent litigation among local chiefs and aristocrats, as well as banditry, whose leading exponent was Gönpo Namgyal. Namgyal was a local Nyarong chief who become a bandit and organized an army big enough to dominate a large part of Kham for years, sowing terror to such an extent that thousands of refugees emigrated to central Tibet. This chief was devoted to Pema Düdul, and although the biography does not mention him by name, there is no doubt that allusions to the acts of an often bellicose chief of Nyarong refer to Namgyal.

Most of Pema Düdul's biography is set in the district of Nyarong. The toponymic epithet 'Nyagla' is indicative of the subject's origin, being a contraction of 'lama of Nyarong.'[39] The Nyarong Dzong county (ch. Xinlong Xian), watered by the river Nyag,[40] is in eastern Kham, in the Province of Sichuan. The land of Kham was divided between Tibet and

China in the Treaty of Simla in 1914, which established the upper course of the river Dri chu[41] as the frontier between the two countries.[42] The eastern half of Kham—where Nyarong is found—became part of China, with a short period of Tibetan government domination in the 1930s. From 1950 on, when China could really dominate the region in its expansion into all of Tibet, it became part of the Province of Sichuan, under the name of the Autonomous Tibetan Prefecture of Garze. The other half of Kham belongs to the Tibetan Autonomous Region, and its capital is Chamdo.[43]

The River Nyag runs through upper and lower Nyarong, in a southerly direction, before joining the Yangtse. The current capital of upper Nyarong is the town of Barshok, also called Rinang (ch. Rulong Zhen); the lower part of Nyarong is the county called Nyagchuka.[44] The towns here are small, particularly in comparison with the populous plain of Trehor to the north with its capital Kardze, a real city in Tibetan terms. In comparison with the surrounding regions, Nyarong, a region considered in earlier times as a refuge for bandits, is off the busier routes and lacks important population centers. It is also one of the regions of Kham with the greatest presence of Nyingma and Bön orders, although none of the great monasteries are located there. The most important was that of Chagdü, destroyed during the Cultural Revolution but nowadays restored.

During Pema Düdul's lifetime the Nyarong region, like the other parts of eastern Kham, were still nominally part of the Dalai Lama's kingdom. Nevertheless, powerful local chiefs who in some cases held the title of king (gyalpo) wielded a large portion of the power in Kham. This was the case in the areas of Derge, Nangchen, and Mili, whereas in other areas the local chiefs or nobles wielded the same authority without holding the title. Lhasa, the capital of Tibet (a two month journey) was too far away to hold sway in the region. The lands held by monasteries suffered the same fate. In several instances the biography describes conflicts among the chiefs, especially in the area of Nyarong, and the suffering this strife caused for the local people. Chapter five is especially explicative and opens with the description of the struggles between upper and lower Nyarong. Pema Düdul never regretted having been taken to Bugta with his mother by the chief of Nyagke, a situation which turned out well for the young man, as it was during this time that he met the great Do Khyentse Yeshe Dorje, one of the most important masters of the period.

On another occasion, the chiefs of Derge and Lithang joined forces against the chief of Nyarong (probably Gönpo Namgyal), causing a massive exodus of religious practitioners to Bugta; in this instance, Pema Düdul's exile lasted for two years. These episodes show the great political instability of the area, increased no doubt by the reluctance of the Khampa people (especially their chiefs) to submit, and facilitated by the rugged terrain consisting of many valleys separated by high mountains.

The warlike conflicts appear most markedly in chapter nine. Several regions in Kham rebelled against the central Tibetan government that after defeating the rebels, condemned many chieftains and their sons to death. After helping them in many ways, Pema Düdul intervened to save them from this fate. The role of peacemaker and interceder is commonly seen in Tibetan biographies, even in those of masters like Pema Düdul who, though lacking a hierarchical position in an important monastery, was still able, thanks to his own religious charisma, to successfully intervene.

The Sacred Geography

Pema Düdul's childhood home of Khangtseg, in which the family held an important position, is near a significant holy place of eastern Tibet: the mountain sanctuary of Lhang Lhang. Its importance is such that Pema Düdul's biography begins with a florid description of the place's sacred attributes, as well as a concise mention of the masters and great yogis who were born, meditated, or achieved realization there. Holy places, sanctuaries, and places of power, called ne,[45] are extraordinarily important in Tibetan spiritual practice. This stems both from Tibetan animism, where the natural environment—particularly the mountains with their deities—plays an important role, and from esoteric Buddhism which always considers the relationship with nature and its energy. The selection of a temple site involves a meticulous geomantic study[46] in which the tectonic energies and the prevailing guardian spirit that dominates them are identified. A series of rites designed to pacify these forces are carried out. In this context the preferred locations are precisely the ne, the places of power associated with significant telluric forces, powerful tectonic spirits, and in many cases, places where great adepts have practiced contemplation. The latter would be an important criterion for the location of a spiritual retreat center. Many sanctuaries enjoy all three characteristics. This applies to the rocky mountain of Lhang Lhang, which presides over many passages in the life of Pema Düdul. Traditional Tibetan cosmology considers places of power as the neuralgic points on a network comprising the energy 'skeleton' of the visible universe. Thus, the telluric energies in these locations lend great spiritual significance to the topography. Certain mountains, caves, rocks, lakes, and promontories can be ne, but so can temples, chapels, or monasteries which housed important masters or lineages. Sometimes an entire country is considered to be a place of power. This includes the many beyul, 'hidden countries,' which due to their special characteristics were concealed by Padmasambhava to be later discovered by one of his disciples' reincarnations. Such hidden lands served as places of refuge and practice in difficult times, which is reminiscent of the practice of concealing the spiritual treasures until surrounding conditions improved and they could be uncovered. Another such case is the land of India which, as the birthplace of the Buddha and his doctrine, is considered by Tibetans as the Holy Land *par excellence*, particularly those places associated with events in the life of Shakyamuni.

After he received the highest teachings of the Total Perfection from the adept of Tsophu, Gyurme Chöying Rangdröl, Pema Düdul asked him if it would be propitious to begin a pilgrimage to the holy places of Buddhism in India and China. The master, in an angry tone, replied that although a pilgrimage is a meritorious action, in this case it would be much more important to stay in a suitable place and realize the practice. The place recommended is precisely the rocky mountain of Lhang Lhang, and it was here that Pema Düdul spent long periods in meditation. Similarly, it was in this rocky place that he discovered most of his spiritual treasures and built Kalzang, the temple that housed his community.

Relationships with the local nature-deities, *genii loci,* occur throughout the biography. The 'black demon' who manifests in several of Pema Düdul's dreams and causes such unpleasantness in the area is finally identified as a spirit of the mountain. After causing an avalanche, the spirit is finally subjugated by the yogic power of the young adept.

In several other passages, local deities express their intention to protect him, and Pema Düdul exhorts them to act for the benefit of all beings while promising to compose offering-rituals for them. Although Tibetan cosmology is rich in classifications of the supernatural, including many classes of spirits and guardians of nature, the biography does not supply any specific indication of a deity's link to any particular group. The tradition classifies spirits or demons of nature—especially telluric—into various groups, including Sadag, Teurang, Tsen, Nyen, and Tenma.[47] Because these are mundane spirits, they can demonstrate a variety of attitudes toward adepts, ranging from aggressive to submissive or protective. Tibetan religious history contains many passages on rites of subjugation directed at these types of beings who, because of their strength and power as guardians of the earth, may either be formidable allies or enemies. The most spectacular of these tales is that of Padmasambhava, whose ritual pacification and subjugation of the tectonic divinities in his quest to prepare the Tibetan ground for Buddhism is the prime example of such rites.

The spirits of the underworld and of the element water, the naga, also appear in the biography and are given considerable importance, for it is in their palace that the 'water treasures' are found, revealed by Pema Düdul in two forms: the 'water treasures,' and the 'water treasures of Dzambu.'

In consonance with this spiritual geography, the biography also refers to the temple of Samye, one of the most important cult centers of Tibetan religion, especially for the Nyingmapa. This temple was built by order of the emperor Trisong Deutsen in the eighth century and was the first Buddhist monastery on Tibetan soil. It is also an especially significant place for the Nyingma order because of its association with Padmasambhava.

When the dakinis tell the child Pema Düdul that he will build a temple, they compare it to Samye, the Glorious Site (chapter 2). On another occasion, the rock in the cave of the dakinis where he lived for a long time practicing the Absorbing of Elixirs[48] was compared to a stupa,[49] the relic container representing the illuminated mind, a common architectural element on the Tibetan landscape. Such comparison of physical places is common in literature on the treasures, where physical locations may seem to be endowed with the attributes and even with the essential nature of paradisiac sites. Since these are places of power and sanctuaries of the tradition, the attribution of supramundane qualities means that the site is considered similar to a zhingkham, a pure land for spiritual development.

Similarly, in the dream state the appearance of places as well as their nature can be transformed, revealing dimensions or aspects of the place which are ordinarily invisible. In chapter 3 for example, a mountain appears inside the black demon's hat, containing a dimension of darkness. In the same chapter, the dream state reveals Makhog, a visionary land that appropriates the entire harvest of Nyarong, causing famine stemming from the collective karmic debt incurred by this part of eastern Tibet. Thus the visionary world, either during sleep or waking, generates in the Tibetan cosmology a kind of amplification of the symbolic view of reality, where the consonances, subtle relationships, compensatory relationships, and true qualities of places and dimensions are revealed to the adept.

SPIRITUAL TRADITION IN EASTERN TIBET

As in the other regions of the Land of Snows, the various orders and lineages actively expanded in eastern Tibet over several centuries and some important monastic centers were established. But in Kham the assignments to the various orders by local authorities was, and still is, somewhat more complex than in other regions. This is due to the great number of influential benefactors among the local aristocracy who throughout the ages have patronized the various Tibetan religious traditions.

In the imperial period, Vairochana—one of the most important precursors of the Total Perfection tradition—was exiled to one of the far eastern regions of Kham, called Gyalmo Tsawarong, the 'Hot Valleys of the Queen.' There he established his Dzogchen doctrine transmission line through his local disciple Yudra Nyingpo.[50] Tradition also holds that Padmasambhava's disciple Lhalung Palgyi Dorje settled in Kham after bringing about the fall of the Tibetan dynasty by murdering the last king, the apostate Langdarma. This king, considering the Buddhist church as a hindrance to the prosperity of the country, closed the main Buddhist monasteries and eliminated their religious influence in the kingdom. Following Langdarma's murder, in the ninth century the monastic tradition of the vinaya was reintroduced into central Tibet. The monastic rule had been conserved in the region of Amdo by the monk Gewa Rabsal during the period of Langdarma's persecution of Buddhist institutions. During the following centuries many masters in central Tibet had Khampa disciples who, returning to Kham, established monasteries and meditation centers of all orders. Some of the most important lamas came from the area, including Aro Yeshe Jungne, one of the leading eleventh-century masters of the Nyingma order, and in the twelfth century Düsum Khyenpa, the first Karmapa of the Kagyü order, and Drigung Kyobpa Jigten Gönpo Rinchen Pal, founder of the Drigung Thil monastery.

Due mainly to the fragmentation of political power—a dominant factor throughout most of the country's history—a diversity of patronage was common in Tibetan society. During periods of political unity, we see the central power promoting the currents and doctrines favoring its own position and limiting those seen as a threat to its control. Such doctrinal domination is very evident at two points in time: in the imperial period of the Yarlung dynasty and in central Tibet during the period of the Dalai Lamas. In the first case, the Tibetan emperors limited the distribution of certain tantras through edicts prohibiting them; during the second, the reign of the Dalai Lamas assured that political power was coordinated by the Gelugpa order in central Tibet, leaving the other orders somewhat weakened in this region. Although Kham was part of the kingdom of the fifth Dalai Lama,[51] as mentioned above, due to the presence of a deeply rooted local aristocracy, to the activity of some local chieftains who controlled extensive regions, and, particularly from the the nineteenth century onward, to the increasing pressure from the Governors of the Chinese province of Sichuan (bordering Kham in the east), effective control of the region was not complete. The remoteness of Lhasa's political influence meant that the Gelugpa did not achieve the same preponderance in Kham as in other regions, especially central and western Tibet. The advent of the regime of the Dalai Lama on the one hand spelled the end of secular conflicts among the aristocracy—conflicts which overlapped with the patronage of the various orders—but on the other, gave rise to uniformity derived from the order's institutional control, which certainly benefited the Gelugpa. In the Cabinet of the Tibetan government (the Kashag) the religious personages occupying a ministry were exclusively Gelugpa, and from the seventeenth century we can observe a tendency in some sectors of Tibetan society to regard the doctrines and dogmas of this order as the unique religious orthodoxy.

This circumstance meant that Kham was, from the seventeenth century onward, a region with great diversity of religious orders and lineages. At the extreme eastern limits of the country, at Gyalmorong, the Bönpo order enjoyed the patronage of the local nobility. To the west, in the Trehor region, the government of the fifth Dalai Lama built five great Gelugpa monasteries, thus making it one of the areas controlled by the "official" church. Further west in the kingdom of Derge, important centers of the Sakya, Nyingma, and Kagyü orders flourished, including some of the most important monasteries of their respective traditions in all Tibet.[52] In this kingdom, the institutional order was the Ngor suborder of the Sakya tradition, as it was in the kingdom of Nangchen. In the remainder of Kham we come across circumstances similar to those just described.

The rich variety of religious currents was not limited to monastic Buddhism dependent on the structure of the orders and their hierarchies. In Kham there thrived, as is true today, an intense yogic life centered in both lay and monastic communities. These communities could be linked to monastic compounds—the meditation centers associated with the monastery—or they could be independent, revolving around a charismatic master who was often a layperson. The community of disciples that grew around Pema Düdul is a good example of this. Although they founded Kalzang monastery, the community of disciples often followed the master's lifestyle: the itinerant life of the adept who visits sanctuaries, monasteries, and hermitages to bestow teachings on monks, nuns, and lay people and to receive initiations from the most celebrated masters and yogis.

Such a great variety of religious currents did not always make for peaceful coexistence. Patronage from the local powers and Khampa aristocracy sometimes caused conflict among orders, aristocrats, and benefactors. Conflicts related to religious affiliation and patronage, especially when mixed with strategic dominion from the political side, occurred if not constantly, at least in delicate moments of Tibetan history. In the nineteenth century, in response to such conflict that was chiefly sectarian in character, some prominent spiritual masters of Kham initiated the non-sectarian movement, known as Unbiased (Rime). The factors favoring this approach may be many, but without a doubt these lamas felt a strong need to put an end to such conflicts in the religious field that sometimes led to political and military battles.

In this regard, what occurred during the reign of the royal dynasty of Derge at the end of the eighteenth century, in addition to being paradigmatic, has been considered a precursor of a new way of viewing sectarianism. During the last quarter of the eighteenth century, the dowager Queen of Derge Tsewang Lhamo became a fervent disciple of the celebrated Nyingmapa lama, the Knowledge Holder Jigme Lingpa.[53] This great master of the doctrine of Total Perfection and tantric traditions of the ancient order revealed the spiritual treasure which would become the most widely utilized among the Nyingmapa adepts throughout the whole of Tibet: *The Heart Essence of the Great Expanse.*[54] The Queen travelled to Tsering Jong, Jigme Lingpa's residence in Central Tibet, and on returning to Kham, supported several projects favoring the Nyingma tradition and Jigme Lingpa's works.[55] One of the most important works she patronized was the edition, realized in the Parkhang of Derge, of the *Collected Tantras of the Nyingma,*[56] a multi-volume collection of the canonical tantras of the ancient order. This project was directed by the most important Nyingma lama of Kham at the time, Getse Gyurme Tsewang Chodrup.[57] Traditionally, the house of Derge patronized the Ngor order that held the most important monastery of the country, Derge Gönchen. The question of allegiance and patronage of other orders may have created difficulties for the Queen, even if she managed to maintain good relations with the Ngor order throughout her life. At the end of her life, she suffered military aggression from northern tribes, but this was apparently not motivated by religious concerns.

The son of Tsewang Lhamo,[58] having witnessed his mother's suffering from the troubles of war, renounced the throne on coming of age and entered the religious life. He wrote the historical annals on the Derge dynasty in which he expressed the need for tolerance among the various orders, stating that the religious policy of the country should be based on support for them all. As E. Gene Smith states, this episode is a harbinger of the appearance, shortly thereafter, of the non-sectarian tendency[59] that was later known as the Unbiased, or Rime movement.

This tendency within Tibetan Buddhism, which manifested fully in mid-nineteenth century in Kham, was generated by masters of all traditions who were all adepts of the doctrines of Total Perfection. The new tendency was distinguished by the upholding of the entire spiritual tradition of Tibet, without the sectarian restrictions and political interference that had figured so prominently in the conflicts between the orders. In those conflicts, doctrinal disputes of a philosophical nature had often been mixed with political and territorial conflict, creating a perverse dynamic in which the motives for disputes fed on one another. Another purpose for the Rime movement was to ensure permanence: to keep alive the tradition of teachings and doctrines of all lineages, some of which were in danger of disappearing. All doctrinal, philosophical and religious approaches were respected in this non-sectarian vision, each being situated in its context and tradition. There was therefore no attempt to synthesize a new doctrine or religious approach or to create a new order. The major members of this movement retained their respective monastic affiliations (if they had any), but their view was extraordinarily wide.

As well as being great masters of the Total Perfection, the protagonists of Rime were eminent scholars knowledgeable in the exoteric and esoteric doctrinal currents treasured in Tibet. Most of them were individuals of great spiritual charisma. Perhaps the person most responsible for galvanizing the non-sectarian tendency was Jamyang Khyentse Wangpo,[60] considered one of the 'Five Tertön Kings,' a designation for the five most important discoverers of spiritual treasures.[61] He was recognized as a body-emanation of Jigme Lingpa, one of the major gurus of the Total Perfection in the previous century. Jamyang Khyentse Wangpo spent part of his life traveling around Tibet, collecting initiations and instructions on an enormous quantity of teachings, some of which had all but disappeared. He also discovered a large number of spiritual treasures, some of which had been discovered by previous tertön but whose transmission had been interrupted. Thus he became known as a Knowledge Holder of the Transmission of the Seven Currents.[62] These transmissions are:

1. The canonical tantras, both the ancient ones (Nyingma) as well as the modern ones (Sarma, post tenth century). He received them from both masters and from divinities during his visionary experiences.
2. Spiritual treasures hidden as "earth treasures."[63]
3. Earth treasures that had been discovered previously.[64]
4. Mind treasures.[65]
5. Previously discovered mind treasures.
6. Teachings stemming from pure vision.[66]
7. Oral transmission received through pure visions.[67]

Jamyang Khyentse Wangpo belonged to the Ngor order, chiefly sponsored in Kham by the aristocracy of the kingdom of Derge. But this did not limit his encyclopedic knowledge of Buddhism. In fact, as most members of the non-sectarian movement, his main practice was Total Perfection, and he was a holder of most of the tantric cycles belonging to the ancient tradition (Nyingmapa). Another important master belonging to this movement was Jamgön Kongtrül Lodrö Taye[68] who worked with Jamyang Khyentse Wangpo on the task of conserving the various traditions. This great scholar compiled a large part of the Treasures that had not been included in the canonical cycles, and he edited *The Treasury of the Precious Discovered Teachings,*[69] the encyclopedia of the terma ritual tradition. Born into a Bönpo family and known for his exceptional intelligence, he was compelled to enter the Karma Kagyü order at the monastery of Palpung in Derge. He became one of the great thinkers and writers of the age and, thanks to the prestige he gained, was given free reign to practice and investigate all traditions.

Many more prominent lamas of this period participated in the Rime movement, including Chogyur Lingpa[70] and the great Dzogchen master of the Bönpo tradition, Shardza Trashi Gyaltsen.[71]

Concurrently with the spread of this non-sectarian view, another noteworthy phenomenon spurred religious practice in nineteenth century Kham, especially among the Nyingmapa and practitioners of the Total Perfection. This was the extremely successful circulation of the treasure cycle *The Heart Essence of the Great Expanse,* revealed by the Knowledge Holder Jigme Lingpa. As explained above, the relationship between the royal house of Derge and Jigme Lingpa furthered his teachings in Kham. But it must also be noted that several of his most important disciples came from eastern Tibet. Prominent among them was Jigme Trinle Özer—the first Dodrubchen[72]—born in the Golok region located between Kham and Amdo. This disciple was the main recipient of *The Heart Essence of the Great Expanse* cycle and his activity was crucial to the diffusion of the cycle throughout the whole of eastern Tibet. These teachings were transmitted during the nineteenth century by various lineages, all spiritual descendants of Jigme Lingpa, as well as by three emanations of Jigme Lingpa himself.

One of these, the eminent Jamyang Khyentse Wangpo, was mentioned above. The other two emanations, Do Khyentse Yeshe Dorje[73]

and Dza Paltrül were also very active transmitters of the cycle and con-
tributors to the spiritual revitalization of nineteenth century Kham. The
former, Do Khyentse Yeshe Dorje, considered an emanation of the mind
of Jigme Lingpa, was an extraordinary yogi who led the life of a tantric
practitioner, refusing all the high monastic posts offered to him by the
Derge aristocracy. The latter, Dza Paltrül Orgyan Jigme Chökyi Wangpo,[74]
an emanation of the voice of Jigme Lingpa, was a charismatic ordained
master and great scholar who often led a wandering lifestyle similar to
Pema Düdul's. His works on the theory and practice of the Total Perfection are greatly appreciated.

Pema Düdul met and received teachings from both Do Khyentse
Yeshe Dorje and Dza Paltrül. In the biography these meetings are treated
as highly important, due to both the singularity of these practitioners
who possessed great charisma in the Nyingma order, and to the teachings
and advice they gave to the young yogi. All the above-mentioned masters
were their contemporaries, and those mentioned here are but a few of the
many tantric masters who flourished in eastern Tibet at that time. The
extraordinary abundance of qualified gurus living during this period is
clearly represented in the biography.

The Life of Nyagla Pema Düdul: the Path of the Adept

🪷 The progressive evolution of the protagonist is described in detail in the biography. Although his commitment to Buddhist practice is stressed from the beginning—we should remember that the author Yeshe Dorje is a direct disciple of Pema Düdul—and although his birth is distinguished by a series of prophesies and portents auguring the arrival of a special being (that is, a reincarnation) his infancy and adolescence were marked by circumstances far removed from the contemplative life. These vicissitudes: the death of his father and sudden descent into poverty, being repeatedly robbed, suffering severe illness, being reduced to begging, experiencing the death of his brothers, enduring social exclusion, and so on, although doubtlessly real, are all part of a formulaic set of experiences leading to the renunciation of worldly life as featured in the 'stories of liberation,' the biographies of Buddhist saints. This has been a recurrent theme since the onset of Buddhism, beginning with Shakyamuni's experience of revulsion towards samsara brought on by the sufferings witnessed during his escapes from his father's palace. Clearly, special emphasis is given to experiences of social alienation, the progressive distancing of the individual from his environment. Although the setting for these experiences is nineteenth century Khampa society with its unstable social and political reality, this is neither the focus of the biography nor is it described in any detail. What is described of course, is the spiritual life superimposed on the nuanced backdrop of the social reality. This becomes very apparent from the point at which the youthful Pema Düdul begins the gradual process of becoming an adept. The following lines attempt to explain some of the most important aspects of lay and religious society and their impact on his life.

The Family and Social Context

The biography makes it very clear that Pema Düdul was born into a family rich in land, livestock, and resources. It may be that his father Khangtseg Gönpo[75] was a chief or public official in his village (Shanglang Dragkar, in Khangtseg district) or region; his name in the biography could indicate that this was so. Even if we don't know if it is a given name or a patronymic title, because it means: 'Protector of Khangtseg', it is clear in the text that he was known for his riches and power. As with many Tibetan families, work was divided between caring for the land and the livestock, part of the year being devoted to nomadic life with the flocks in the pastures. Pema Düdul's birth may have occurred during one of these nomadic seasons because at that moment his parents were living in a tent at a place called Delong Gyalnya Thang.[76]

The paternal line[77] counted among its ancestors Tagla Pema Mati,[78] an important lama from the monastery of Kathog. This master was an important transmitter of certain Nyingmapa doctrines in seventeenth century Kham, and affiliation with his line (the kinship system in Tibet is patrilineal) certainly gave prestige. Many passages in the biography depict the relationship between Pema Düdul and his uncle Karma Palden who held a position in the hierarchy at Tagla, the seat of the spiritual lineage descending from Padma Mati.

His mother belonged to the Serzang family of the Akarbu clan. Affiliation with extensive clans is often cited in Tibetan biographies. These great clans were especially significant in ancient times as indicators of identity and belonging, particularly among aristocratic families (kudrag)[79] holding power in a state or territory. Though notably present in the dynastic texts of the seventh to ninth centuries, the influence of the great clans declined over time. As this social structure was supplanted by the new kingdoms, principalities, and religious settlements with their extensive land holdings and associated administrative systems, new modes of social ascent became possible. Nevertheless, even in modern times clan affiliation still has meaning, particularly in the aristocratic lineages and in areas such as Amdo with an abundant nomadic population.

Pema Düdul's life changed dramatically at age seven when his father died and, along with his mother and brothers, he was thrown out of the family home. This reminds us of the well known biography of the eleventh century mystic and poet Milarepa, one of the most celebrated meditators in Tibet who also saw his childhood happiness destroyed in similar circumstances: after his father's death, his paternal uncle casts out Milarepa and his mother, stripping them of all their possessions. Although unlike Milarepa, Pema Düdul did not wreak vengeance through the violent exercise of black magic, his circumstances drove him to resort to begging and occasional thievery in order to survive. Although these circumstances certainly ring true, the vivid frankness with which the biographer portrays them is surprising. The difficulties encountered at the beginning of spiritual life are often described in biographies, as we have seen in the case of Milarepa. Many obstacles, such as losing wealth through the arrival of covetous relatives, are presented in some detail in the lives of other great masters. But in this biography, particularly in the first three chapters, they are presented repeatedly and dramatically. As the text itself makes clear, this is done to demonstrate the implacable law of karma to which Pema Düdul seems to offer no resistance, stoically accepting its blows. The many songs he sings to console his mother seem to be directed at the reader, to convince him of the infallibility of the law of cause and effect and the necessity of attending to one's own actions. Here we see two important functions of the Buddhist biography: to stimulate reflection on the various doctrines expounded and to provide an example for the practitioner of the correct attitude to adopt when faced with adversity.

Throughout the first chapters which are devoted to the periods of poverty, we see an almost constant tension in group solidarity. On occasion it seems that the mother and sons are totally isolated with no support at all and are driven to begging. In other passages some relatives or neighbors help them, offering goods, utensils, and food. Tibetan society was largely composed of crop and animal farmers engaged in a variety of social contracts. There were landowners[80] who paid taxes to the governors or chieftains in their region—generally a percentage of the harvest and some manual labor—and tenant farmers or itinerant workers[81] who owned no land but enjoyed more freedom of movement without the landowners' heavy tax burden. In the case of the landowners, the families' association with a house and farm holdings gave them the status of drongpa,[82] full members of the community. The assignment and inheritance of goods was through the paternal line. This made it easy, in the case of the death of the father, for his brother or sister to appropriate a large part of the widow's inheritance even if she had sons. Although not many examples of such cases have been documented, the fact that this is said to have happened to Milarepa and is known to have happened to Pema Düdul suggests that it did occur, in extreme cases, in Tibetan society.[83]

As we have mentioned, eastern Tibet was only rarely controlled by a single political power. During the nineteenth century even the definition of the lands ascribed to the Tibetan Government and the Chinese Empire was thrown into confusion by the claims of both parties; in reality, large areas of Kham were *de facto* independent and ruled by kings, chieftains or powerful abbots. This political fragmentation gave great power to the local chieftains, who were often at loggerheads with one another. The Khampa aristocracy was not only belligerent toward its political opponents but could be hostile even toward religious authority. On two occasions in the biography[84] Pema Düdul and other lamas are challenged by nobles who accuse them of being impostors and defy them to manifest their supposed yogic powers. In chapter nine even the king of Nyarong accuses Pema Düdul of being a charlatan, propelling the adept to manifest a terrifying vision that cures the king of his pride and converts him into a disciple and benefactor. The king's conversion is interesting in that it encapsulates several elements defining an act of 'spiritual submission.'[85] Since the one who submits is already Buddhist, spiritual submission does not imply conversion to Buddhism but rather the development of a genuine devotion or motivation to practice. The king's declaration begins with the recognition of Pema Düdul as a siddha, followed by the expressed intention to subsidize his ascetic practice. It continues with the generous donation of material gifts—suitable for a king—such as fertile lands, cloth, and equipment for a religious settlement. Finally he offers a consort, who in his refusal Pema Düdul compares to any other mundane offering (such as a thousand ounces of gold), and therefore insignificant.

His relationship with his mother is given special mention and is dealt with in some depth in the early chapters. Full of the pathos that colors the experiences of poverty, loss, and sickness, the relationship with his mother almost seems to show us another side to Pema Düdul; her voice might almost be his if it were not for the particular forbearance with which he accepts his troubles. The voice of his mother is the human voice of lament, trapped in its limited vision and identified with concrete circumstances. The dialogues between mother and son are the juxtaposition of an ordinary human being's lamentations with the response of wisdom emerging from a Pema Düdul who increasingly realizes the inexorability of cause and effect. At the same time, the relationship between the two is an example of the symbolic value Buddhism accords to the first bond experienced by a human being. In the analytical meditations for developing love and compassion toward all beings, one of the most common reflections is that all beings have been our mother at one time or another during our countless previous lives. The fundamental teachings on compassion thus begin with contemplation of the extreme kindness of the person with whom we have the first karmic relation in our current life: our own mother. On the other hand, the mother represents our desire for the socially acceptable things, for the goods and needs which control us, and she also stands for our mind which is tortured by disappointment and dissatisfaction. It is to this mind that Pema Düdul addresses his songs and advice, and by doing so he addresses all beings, all those who were once his mother.

Integration into the Religious Milieu

Pema Düdul's biography follows a pattern that persists in the life stories of realized beings. In most of them, from infancy there arises a clear attraction towards the spiritual life. Many of them describe the protagonist's suffering due to negative environmental factors often related to family circumstances, or to other obstacles that temporarily distance the young person from religious practice. From a certain moment on, often coinciding with the appearance of the 'root' lama, the disciple's inner life suffers no further deviation from the spiritual. This process, involving years of receiving initiations and teachings, studying and practicing them, and attaining realization, is usually crowned by religious and social recognition, sometimes involving the construction of a monastery sheltering disciples and teachings.

While the biography describes the social medium in which Pema Düdul moved—although it sometimes takes much for granted and omits more detail than we should like—and the scenes it depicts give us a clear, unaltered view of the everyday reality, the true media supporting the major relationships are the religious circles.

His first activities in the religious field occur during his nomadic period in which he sang and recited the stories related to the *jokhor*.[86] This object is a large prayer wheel, similar to but much larger than those the Tibetans spin by hand. Associated with Avalokiteshvara, Lord of Compassion—*jokhor* means 'the Wheel of the Lord (Avalokiteshvara)'—it was this Bodhisattva who appeared in his dreams saying that this practice would be an excellent way to help all beings. Spinning the prayer wheel, the wandering yogi expounds the foundations of the doctrine or tells the lives of saints and masters.

From the fourth chapter on, as his yogic experience grows Pema Düdul is increasingly accepted by the great lamas. This recognition is usually accompanied by the lamas' recollections of the special characteristics and prophecies surrounding his conception and birth. When, in Butong, a benefactor tries to stop Pema Düdul from sitting among the assembly to receive teachings from the lama of Chagdü due to his beggarly appearance, the lama Namdag from Chagdü makes him stop and think, stressing the extraordinary circumstances surrounding Pema Düdul's birth—which he himself had witnessed—and concludes with the affirmation that Pema Düdul is a reincarnation. Similarly, when Pema Düdul asks the master Gyurme Gyatso a question on the nature of mind, the master advises him to persevere in his practice, thanks to which he will undoubtedly obtain the fruit he desires, reminding him of his special birth and the numerous prophesies referring to him. Undoubtedly, two of the meetings occurring in his youth were especially important. One was with Pema Gyurme Sangye who gave him the name Pema Düdul and confirmed his own recognition as a reincarnation, listing a series of great masters of whom Pema Düdul was an emanation. The other, which occurred during his captivity in Nyagke, was the meeting with Do Khyentse Yeshe Dorje, one of the most prestigious masters of Dokham.

Throughout the text meetings with masters are described in the greatest detail. It is important to note how these meetings, especially after the latter part of the third chapter, gradually integrate Pema Düdul into a parallel society where power is not necessarily derived from political or aristocratic affiliation, but from spiritual charisma, a force of enormous importance in Tibetan society. The progressive reception of teachings— drawn mostly from the nucleus of Tibetan esoteric Buddhism—the recognition of Pema Düdul as an extraordinary adept by several lamas, and his discovery of his own treasures will consolidate him as a guru, a 'superior' person (lama) capable of transmitting the deepest teachings. To all this must be added the yogic experiences—especially the dreams, both his own and others' that refer to him—which, although kept discretely secret, could be told to masters and adepts and thus contribute to the authentication of his spiritual status.

Of great interest is Pema Düduls mother's response to his explanation of a dream in which Mahakaruna (Avalokiteshvara) exhorts him to practice the *jokhor* for the good of all beings. His mother reminds him that such experiences should not be openly talked about, as they could easily be mistaken for the declarations of charlatans. The process through which yogic and visionary experiences come to be validated is similar to other processes of integration into the spiritual lineage: recognition by masters who assess and interpret them, giving a reading corresponding to the disciple's situation. We can see that the various masters' consideration of Pema Düdul is conditioned by experiences of this kind, such as the dreams that some of them had before meeting him. These include the Bönpo lama Yeshe Özer's dream just before he met Pema Düdul, in which a blazing sun shone on millions of people, and Pema Gyurme's above-mentioned dreams of previous incarnations. Another interesting phenomenon is the visionary perception of some disciples, such as that of lama Orgyan Norbu who in chapter seven sees Pema Düdul as having three eyes (the third being the eye of wisdom), or of the Sakya lama Palden Chogkyi Langpo, who on meeting Pema Düdul has visions of him as Padmasambhava.

Gradually the lamas begin to exhort him to teach, that is, to act as a lama. For example, the reincarnation from Tromde, Namgyal Dongag Tendzin, after giving him deep spiritual advice, asks him to begin to sow teachings. At the beginning of chapter seven, lama Thegchog asks him to go to the temple at Chagdü to expound the Dharma to monks and laypersons, as this would be of great benefit. Even before these events, Pema Düdul makes it clear to his mother and brother that he has no intention of occupying a hierarchical place in a monastery or of becoming the lama-yogi of a village and carrying out exorcisms. His aim is clear: to continue the life of an ascetic practitioner, devoted to going deeper into the essence of the teachings received. In the beginning we see a certain tension between his wish to live a life of ascetic practice and the necessity to begin his life as a teacher, with all the travel and variety of social contact that this role requires.

The request to begin to teach, above all coming from great lamas, implies acceptance into the rank of guru. But there is a further consideration: the prophetic statements[87] about him that appear in various terma texts, including the cycle discovered by Padma Düdul himself, and in the declarations made by different masters in his presence. In Buddhism, 'empowering through prophecy' is especially important. This is not a reference to the good omens interpreted as allegorical prophecies, such as the ones occurring at his birth. Here the statement is direct and un- ambiguous, and its function is to give a blessing or empowerment which, due to the law of karmic interdependence, will configure the future in the prescribed manner. We find this principle operating in the most ancient forms of Buddhism, as in the case of doctrines prophesied by the Buddha Shakyamuni, considered to be authentic because he predicted their future appearance and promulgation by a particular Bodhisattva. Accordingly, in the *Prajñaparamita* and other Mahayana sutras, the Buddha prophesies the period in which Bodhisattvas reaching the rank of Buddha will ap- pear, and the names by which they will later be known, and he does this in their presence. When a great master announces that a certain disciple will attain a certain state or fruit of the practice in the future and does this in the disciple's presence, he is acting in accordance with this principle.

One of the fundamental criteria for the recognition of Pema Düdul was his discovery of the spiritual treasure, *The Profound Doctrine, Self-Liberation that Encompasses Space*,[88] as well as the water treasures and the golden water of Dzambu. These discoveries of spiritual revelation confirm his growing capacity as an esoteric master, above all of the teachings derived from the Nyingma order and related to Padmasambhava of Oddiyana. Many of the important Nyingmapa masters are tertöns, revealers of treasure teachings most of which originated with Padmasambhava. *The Profound Doctrine, Self-Liberation that Encompasses Space* cycle was accepted as legitimate by many of the great lamas of Kham, as evidenced by the insistence with which they requested teachings and initiations of this cycle from Pema Düdul. When an adept in the Tibetan tradition reaches a certain level of spiritual development—especially if he manifests as a treasure finder—he can confer initiations and transmit doctrines to his old masters, and often there is an exchange of teachings. Pema Düdul's name as tertön is Trülzhig Lingpa,[89] and it is this name that appears in the biography's title. However, throughout the biography he is usually called "The Lord."[90]

Regarding the acceptance of Pema Düdul in Nyingmapa circles, some disciples of the great Mipham Rinpoche who had doubts about his realization of the Rainbow Body at his death, asked their master about the authenticity of this claim. In their understanding, the attainment of the Rainbow Body was virtually impossible to achieve in this epoch, especially by someone like Pema Düdul who lacked the social recognition based on religious status. Mipham's answer, directed at his disciples' own lack of understanding, demonstrates his high regard and respect for Pema Düdul.[91]

Another important factor was the building of the temple of Kalzang[92] on the slopes of the mountain-sanctuary of Lhang Lhang. Built in the spirit of the non-sectarian movement, the temple contained depictions stemming from all transmission lines of India and Tibet, as well as the symbolic elements (mandala and divinities) from Pema Düdul's own treasure. Although he never accepted a hierarchical role in any of the Tibetan Buddhist orders and refused the role of tantrika performing rituals for laypeople, the founding of a stable center for the development of his lineage and its teachings was inevitable. The biography informs us that, since his infancy, Pema Düdul had foreknowledge of the temple's construction. Although praised in the text, the building was not a great monastery but a religious seat of modest dimensions, adequate as a center for the spreading of the traditions treasured there. The master and tertön Lerab Lingpa, who lived in Kalzang in the period immediately after that of Pema Düdul, may have enlarged the building. It has since been made even larger.[93]

The progressive recognition achieved by the master in religious circles is reflected not simply in the number of monks and laypersons who gathered around him but also in the wider framework of everyday society. Numerous passages of the biography detail the warm reception given by local chieftains. On various occasions, Pema Düdul acts as mediator—or sends emissaries to carry out the task—in the armed conflicts shaking the country of Kham. Only a lama of great charismatic power could carry out this type of action, and he undoubtedly possessed it, at least among the chieftains of Nyarong and its surroundings. However, his most interesting political relationship was with Gönpo Namgyal, the powerful chieftain who subjected large areas of eastern Tibet to his rule. The biography is especially interesting on this point because it adopts a position considered politically incorrect in modern Tibetan historiography. Gönpo Namgyal is portrayed as little more than a well-organized bandit, illegally dominating an area and committing acts of cruelty. The fact that this chief was a disciple and benefactor of Pema Düdul is openly stated in the biography, and the master's sadness at the chief's death through the burning of his fortress in Nyarong is well described (although details of the burning do not appear in the text itself).

The progressive arrival of disciples, many attracted to his presence by premonitions they received in dreams, is the fruit of the whole process described in this book. It must be remembered that in addition to monks and laypersons of all social rank—from beggars to kings, men and women—many great lamas from Kham asked Pema Düdul to confer initiations and teachings, thereby placing him in the position of spiritual guide. Another characteristic that doubtlessly makes our subject an attractive person for the lamas is his lifestyle, which coincides so closely with the classic traditional profile of an esoteric master.

THE SPIRITUAL ROLE ADOPTED BY PEMA DÜDUL

Although profiles or characterizations of esoteric masters have survived and been passed on through biographies, above all they are preserved through the living examples of tantric gurus. Because the tradition contains a live, uninterrupted transmission, the *exemplum vitae* is not simply a literary argument or image of collective piety: it is present, personified, and incarnate in actual, contemporary individuals.

Just as a disciple must possess certain qualities in order to be accepted by a tantric master, so the lama must possess certain characteristics recognizable by the prospective disciple as indicative of a high level of spiritual development: compassion, few mundane desires, experience in the various soteriological vehicles, and total dominion of the process of initiation, yogic instructions, and practices. Attainment of the experiences characterized as the fruit of the various meditative stages is another indispensable requirement for a guru.

Something that is not described in detail through the orthodoxy expressed in the texts but that does emanate from the biographies and the extremely rich font of orally transmitted anecdotes is the singularity and abundance of paradoxical situations within the master/disciple relationship. A good example of this is the biography of Milarepa[94] where his stormy relationship with Marpa of Lhodrag is well documented; another, in the same transmission lineage, is the relationship between Tilopa and Naropa as described in the latter's biography.[95] The role of master means more than pre-eminence over the disciple based on mastery of the knowledge to be transmitted, as in the kind of relationship which existed in medieval European universities. Because the transmission is soteriological and because the guru embodies the principles of the highest wisdom, his superior rank is not simply based on his position in the hierarchy or his possession of knowledge. The master's actual being is considered to possess a supramundane, in fact, a super-human nature because, if worthy of the title, he is no longer conditioned by human karmic vision. Perceiving the guru in this way is fundamental to esoteric transmission, and not only in Buddhism.[96] The emphasis on this phenomenon, together with the great wealth of methods and doctrines combined in esoteric Buddhism, gave rise to the recognition in Tibet of several kinds of vajracarya.[97] These may be roughly divided into two categories: lay masters and ordained masters. But this division is considerably more complex and nuanced than it seems at first sight because, over the last thousand years, Tibet has tenderly collected and preserved the various currents of Buddhism generated in India, its land of origin.

The teachings promulgated in both Hinayana and Mahayana sutras provided the basis for monasticism, the canonical texts originating from the historical Buddha and the Bodhisattvas, as well as an elaborate philosophical tradition. In this context, the monk-preceptor who guides the monk-disciple in study, in the correct holding of the vows, and in meditation, is paramount. But the tantras and the esoteric currents additionally carried an initiatory knowledge strongly linked to the figure of the guru. The tantras do not expound a path limited to monks; in fact, the ideal tantric adept is not a monk, but a yogi who is subject to commitments that differ from those of a monk. These two models were already unified in India with the integration of tantrism in many Buddhist monasteries and universities after the seventh century. This unified model was fully adopted in Tibet, where the integration of both roles was further emphasized.[98] The ideal spiritual role embodied in this Tibetan synthesis is that of the practitioner who, having taken the monastic vows, cultivates the ethic of Mahayana (the Bodhisattva vow) and practices tantrism as a path of knowledge and liberation, accepting the commitments[99] of that path. This is characterized threefold as the external practice (monastic vows), the internal practice (the Bodhisattva's intention to save all beings), and the secret practice (tantric methods).

Underlying all this is the contradiction between monastic vows, one of which is celibacy, and the process of tantric initiation and practice which, in the anuttarayogatantra, includes experiences of sexual union as a yogic method. The resolution of this contradiction and the integration of the higher tantras (which include this practice) into monastic orthodoxy was achieved by transforming these processes, including sexual experiences with a consort, into processes of creative imagination through visualization. However, this *tour de force* was not universally accepted, and some tantric masters considered that the yogic practice of the supreme tantras, especially that of the yoginitantras, was not intended for monks but meant only for lay yogis and yoginis.[100]

This synthesis of the various approaches within monastic communities did not mean that the lay adept ceased to exist. Particularly in those orders such as the Nyingmapa that were not reformed by Tsongkhapa in the fifteenth century, there continued an important tradition of non-ordained adepts. One way of compliance with orthodoxy for these lay practitioners is the assumption of certain vows, especially those of the lay practitioner. Often known as 'mantra practitioners,' or 'yogis,'[101] these lay practitioners frequently lead a life consisting of both secular and religious activities. They are often responsible for performing rituals locally to ensure good harvests and the welfare of livestock and to exorcize negative influences and malignant illness.

However, other non-ordained adepts and also certain monks lead ascetic lives, far from mundane or social activities. These are the hermits residing in solitary places or small communities of practitioners. Others lead a nomadic existence, wandering with small tents from sanctuary to sanctuary and from place to place performing rituals such as Cutting[102] or the recitations associated with the practice of the *jokhor*, both of which are very present in Pema Düdul's biography. During his own life, Pema Düdul spent many long periods traveling through valleys, to monasteries, sanctuaries, and places of pilgrimage, as well as to nomad camps and small settlements. However, he also spent long periods in retreat—generally solitary—in caves and hermitages where he practiced the teachings he had received as well as those of his own cycles of revealed treasures.

The biography does not mention whether Pema Düdul had a consort. It certainly never states that he took monastic vows or entered a monastery as a monk. However, in chapter five Pema Gyurme Sangye calls him 'young monk,'[103] and so we might suppose that he took the vows of a novice at some point.[104] Also, in the same chapter he remains for a long period in a monastery with his uncle Künzang Düdjom whom he serves as a scribe. Despite this indirect allusion to monastic vows and the fact that he spent time in the monastery, it is currently believed that Pema Düdul was never a monk. Sönam Tenpa,[105] preceptor (khenpo) from the philosophical school of Kathog, told me that Pema Düdul never took the vows, adding that he was a tantrika, although no one knew of his having had a consort.[106] During his youth he banished the sexual desire that troubled him for a time, and, from the warnings he gave his disciples regarding, "young women who do not keep their promises," it seems that he advised against promiscuity. It is also possible that because the biography was intended for a diverse readership, any reference to a consort may have been omitted. It should be remembered that the sentimental and sexual sides of life are considered very secret in religious circles and, although we are dealing with a mainly esoteric medium, such matters are delicate where masters are concerned. The fact that biographies are intended for a great variety of religious readers could favor the omission. However, it is also true that in numerous biographies, the female consorts—and the male when discussing female adepts[107]—are explicitly evoked, and are on occasion essential to the subject's spiritual development. Often the consort or wife is considered to be a dakini who aids the adept's process of liberation, specifically through practices of sexual yoga, considered in the higher tantra as the meditative method capable of undoing the knots in the chakras of the inner channels.

Pema Düdul's ascetic and nomadic existence, combined with his reputation as a tertön and the special characteristics of his birth and youth, gave him a profile similar to those of the siddhas of the past as transmitted by tradition. The great masters he met were perfectly aware of this and did not hesitate to give him teachings as well as the above-mentioned prophetic empowerment consisting of recognition of his high nature and his valuable activity as guru.

As did other masters of his time, Pema Düdul personified the great adept of tantric Buddhism: he was free to move around and free of hierarchical positions in monastic establishments; he led the life of a hermit-yogi; he was a master of the deepest doctrines and a spiritual-treasure finder. From this point of view, far from being heterodox, his way of life was a further sign of his authenticity for other masters, especially those of the Nyingma order and followers of doctrines like the Total Perfection. Besides conforming with the characteristics transmitted by the siddha tradition, this adept's profile also illustrates liberation from factors conditioning the spiritual path, factors that can be pernicious, such as the seductions of the desire for religious power and most importantly, of the intellectual approach to spiritual practice. The latter point is a defect often cited by the followers of tantric paths as being particularly harmful to the practitioner, and is considered to be a typical characteristic of those who have followed a strictly philosophical training (sometimes identified with monastic training).

Another trait of this kind of guru is the abundance of paradoxical situations I mentioned at the beginning of this chapter. Although an antinomian attitude is not exclusive to tantric traditions—the behavior and surprising actions of the Ch'an and Zen masters is well known—Tibetan lamas have often behaved in ways far removed from what would be considered appropriate for a master from an exoteric viewpoint. Although this is true in the apparent sense, for those who understand the characteristics of tantric life, to behave in a paradoxical manner or one contrary to social convention may actually be a sign of having achieved great realization and having transcended such conventions. Pema Düdul's behavior described at the beginning of chapter ten is a good example: he would play with children as one of them; sometimes he would cover himself with a single coverlet, sometimes he would appear naked; he would spontaneously burst into spiritual song, and so on.

He never hesitated to be energetic in his advice, especially regarding the correct attitude towards life and spiritual practice, advising behaviors surprising in their severity, such as hitting oneself on the leg or mouth as a remedy for becoming distracted during contemplation by the desire to get up or to speak. He harangued his disciples on meditative practice in similes of lyrical beauty, comparing the bliss of realization to that of a dancer, or evoking visions of pure dimensions.

On other occasions, the manifestation of miracles—contraindicated by Buddha himself—is justified as leading unbelievers to develop faith. In chapter seven for example, when the chieftain challenged him to show his powers, Pema Düdul multiplied a quantity of medicinal pills; in another passage he materialized a dragon before the proud king of Nyarong. Several acts of this kind appear in the biography, and manifestations of such paranormal powers abound in other Tibetan biographies. Some such acts have a protective function, such as the meditative self-generation of the wrathful deity Palchen Pema Dragpo (a wrathful manifestation of Padmasambhava) to protect his companions and himself from the meteoric iron of the thunderbolt, or the self-generation of Dorje Drolö (another wrathful manifestation of Padmasambhava) to subjugate a mountain demon who caused avalanches.

Each one of these episodes shows us Pema Düdul's progressive development as an adept in accordance with a series of paradigms belonging to tantric tradition. From the beginning of his life—the prophesies at his birth and the prodigious circumstances surrounding it; the suffering and illness, poverty, and robbery due to the maturing of karma; the spiritual awakening through dreams, visions, and teachings received; the deep spiritual experiences in solitude and discovery of his own treasures, crowned by the consolidation of a large group of disciples, including some eminent lamas—he followed a route fully coinciding with what is expected of a master of the esoteric principles, a 'Lord of the Secrets.'[108]

Up to the present day the oral tradition, especially in the district of Nyarong, has preserved the memory of many anecdotes from Pema Düdul's life. In this region, the land where he was born and where he carried out most of his activities, Pema Düdul has acquired the charisma of a 'cultural hero,' a person who epitomizes a series of profiles indicating a high level of spirituality and power, a kind of beneficent thaumaturge whose memory has prevailed in an atmosphere of admiration and mystery. This is common to many tertöns, whose memory remains and is built on over time in the regions where they acted as masters and treasure finders. I present below two stories told to me by Sönam Tenpa, khenpo of the monastery at Kathog.[109]

On one occasion, Pema Düdul was at a certain place in Nyarong, giving initiations to a group of disciples. Among them was a strikingly beautiful woman. He called her over and said: "Live long! You are like a temple blessed with four columns." Lama Taye, who seems to have served as a kind of filter of the people surrounding the master, particularly the young women, was afraid that Pema Düdul would be distracted by the woman's beauty, and removed her from the group. But later on this woman gave birth to four important adepts: the tertön Drime who revealed four volumes of treasures, the khenpo Atho (Gyaltsen Özer) from Kathog, Özer Dorje (one of the thirteen disciples of Pema Düdul having the word dorje in their name), and the lama Ade. Pema Düdul's statement on the four pillars was later interpreted as a prophesy.

On another occasion, Pema Düdul visited the village of Netho (birthplace of the khenpo who told me these tales). For months the area had been in the grip of a famine due to a grain shortage. On arriving, Pema Düdul predicted that from then on, the mill would never stop grinding, as the shortage would soon be over once and for all. According to the khenpo, since then the mill has never stopped turning.

Without a doubt, one of the characteristics that has most colored his memory is the attainment of the 'Rainbow Body,'[110] the supreme fruit of the practice of Total Perfection. This event is commemorated by a stupa located in the very place where Pema Düdul pitched the tent in which he attained the 'Rainbow Body'. The place is known as the 'Place of Attainment of the Rainbow Body,'[111] and every day many of the faithful visit the reliquary to perform circumambulations.

The Transmission of Wisdom

🌸 The following chapters comprise the central matter of this study, the biography itself. Our last introductory section provides some analysis of the various aspects of the transmission, with special emphasis on the masters and disciples as well as the teachings mentioned in the biography.[112]

MASTERS AND DISCIPLES OF PEMA DÜDUL

Regarding the transmission of knowledge, one of the first impressions one receives from reading the biography of Pema Düdul is of the great number of masters from whom he received (and on some occasions, with whom he exchanged) teachings and initiations. Although it is unlikely that he would have practiced all of them, the simple act of receiving them is considered precious, a moment during which a series of sacred principles come into play. The tantric initiations possess the power to drive the adept's 'maturation,' while the consecutive instructions facilitate his 'liberation,'[113] and the two merge into a single process within tantrism, where spiritual development is defined as 'maturation and liberation.' The adept's contact with the master, enhanced by the principle of guruyoga in which the enlightened mind is epitomized in the guru's realization, is fundamental to the esoteric paths. Through this process the disciple is introduced into the practice lineage preceding him and is readied to receive the 'waves of blessings'[114] accompanying the transmission of wisdom. It is this initiatory process that authenticates and empowers the meditation practice undertaken by the disciple.

Looking at the long list of masters and yogis from whom he received teachings and initiations, in the spirit of non-sectarianism that blossomed in nineteenth-century Kham we find lamas of almost every school and current that would have been accessible to Pema Düdul during his lifetime. Although the Mahayana texts and the pledges of the tantric path do set limits on the amount of time a practitioner may remain with followers of the "lesser" or "inferior" Buddhist vehicles and on the activities he may share with them, individual freedom to choose personal masters was not unknown. And in Tibet, where all orders belonged to the same level of soteriological path—the Mahayana and Tantrayana—such exclusionism did not generally occur. The only exception might be the Bönpo tradition, but along with some other masters (especially of the Nyingma order) Padma Düdul seems to have respected them and accepted their teachings. We must not ignore the fact that in principle, since ancient times in India and Tibet a yogi's freedom of spiritual request was not subject to restrictions, particularly from masters belonging to the Buddhist vehicles. The progressive consolidation of the philosophical currents, monastic schools, exegetical traditions, and esoteric approaches of India as well as the later monastic orders of Tibet with their philosophical and ritual preferences, certainly facilitated the appearance of sectarianism. But the absence of a unitary hierarchy recognized as the one voice of orthodoxy and authority has allowed a certain spiritual freedom to exist in the Buddhism of Tibet, particularly in comparison with other religions.

Apart from the above-mentioned characteristics of Buddhism in general and of the non-sectarian tendency in particular, there is another factor favoring the extraordinary freedom enjoyed by Pema Düdul to meet with spiritual guides: he neither belonged to a monastic congregation nor held a hierarchical position in a religious structure. Although several of the lamas he encountered informed him of his identity as a reincarnation, he was never offered anything like an abbot's throne. Later, when his circle of disciples had grown significantly, Pema Düdul built the temple of Kalzang containing pictorial representations of all the lineages of Tibet (reflecting his non-sectarian approach to the doctrine). But he still maintained the lifestyle of a yogi, free from the obligations of a monastic order, free to continue traveling around Kham, and free to choose his spiritual relationships.

Below is an analysis of the lamas and disciples mentioned in the life of this great adept. In many cases the biography does not specify the teachings given, while in others they are named and sometimes even described in some detail.

As we can see in the biography, on several occasions Pema Düdul plays the part of master and disciple at the same time. It is very common that when such lamas meet they exchange teachings, reading transmissions, and initiations, not simply as a mutual recognition but also as an opportunity to increase their own knowledge and receive the benefits of initiation.

Despite the eclecticism of the teachings received by Pema Düdul which covered everything that could be learned about the spiritual traditions considered valid at that time, most of the masters he met and the teachings he received belonged to the Nyingma tradition or to the system of the Total Perfection, Dzogchen. This soteriological path is considered by its followers as the peak, the 'supreme summit' (yang rtse) of all the systems. Traditionally preserved and practiced in the Nyingma and Bön orders, it was also practiced and highly valued by many masters of other traditions, especially the Kagyüpa.[115] This was the case particularly in modern eastern Tibet where many lamas of all orders were and still are adepts of the Total Perfection. These included such important teachers as Jamyang Khyentse Wangpo and Kongtrül Lodrö Taye who retained their hierarchical positions in the Sakya and Kagyü orders, respectively. Thus, most of the teachings that Pema Düdul received belonged to the vehicle of the Total Perfection or to the tantric systems of the Nyingmapa: Mahayoga and Anuyoga, respectively the seventh and eighth soteriological systems of that order.[116]

THE MASTERS

Since the tradition has not thus far named them among those it considers the most significant, I have not been able to identify many of the masters mentioned in the biography. Some of the unidentified masters are probably known under an alias (Tibetan lamas often have more than one name) or may have been active only in Nyarong or other parts of Kham. In the case of Dungral Lingpa for example (who appears as Pema Düdul's master in a visionary dream in chapter three), although I have found no reference to this lama in the texts on Nyingmapa masters, he is named in chapter one of the biography in a description of religious personalities born near Lhang Lhang mountain, where we are told he drew the treasures from the red rock of Drongtül. Khenpo Sönam Tenpa confirmed that this master was a tertön from Nyarong, who was probably alive during the first years of Pema Düdul's life.[117]

One of the first masters mentioned in the biography, Lama Namdag from Chagdü monastery, witnessed the auguries occurring at Pema Düdul's birth. Later, during Pema Düdul's adolescence, this master would be one of the first to recall the adept's identity as a reincarnation, protecting him from rejection by monks and benefactors due to his beggarly appearance.[118] Chagdü Orgyan Ling[119] was the most important Nyingmapa monastery in Nyarong, and possibly because of this it was destroyed during the Cultural Revolution.

Among the best-known lamas present in Pema Düdul's biography are Do Khyentse Yeshes Dorje, Mingyur Namkhai Dorje, Dza Paltrül Rinpoche, Nyoshul Lungtog, the fourteenth Karmapa Thegchog Dorje, the second Kathog Situ, Adzom Drugpa, Kongtrül Yonten Gyatso, and the ninth Palpung Situ. The most important features of Do Khyentse Yeshes Dorje and Dza Paltrül Rinpoche have been described above,[120] and it is enough to mention here that they were considered to be reincarnations respectively of the mind and voice of Jigme Lingpa.

Mingyur Namkhai Dorje,[121] the fourth reincarnation of Dzogchen Pema Rigdzin,[122] was one of the most important Nyingmapa masters of the

nineteenth century in the transmission of the *Heart Essence of Vimalamitra*
[123] and the *Heart Essence of the Dakini*[124] cycles belonging to the Upadesha
section of the Total Perfection. Abbot of Dzogchen monastery, he was a
master who received a great number of teachings in visions—a blend of
treasures (terma) and of pure visions (dagnang)—including one that he
transmitted to Pema Düdul, the *Pure Vision of the Powerful Guru Raksha
Garland of Skulls.*[125]

Nyoshul Lungtog Tenpai Nyima[126] was the most realized disciple of
the great Dza Paltrül Rinpoche and an essential link in the transmission
of *The Heart Essence of the Great Expanse* cycle. He was also a disciple of
many other noteworthy lamas including Gyalse Zhenphen Taye, Mingyur
Namkhai Dorje (mentioned in the previous paragraph), and Jamyang
Khyentse Wangpo.[127] Because he was a direct disciple of Dza Paltrül and
holder of *The Heart Essence of the Great Expanse* cycle, his teachings on *The
Transcendent Wisdom Master* [128]—the instructions on the Dzogchen section
of the *The Heart Essence of the Great Expanse*—were much desired by Pema
Düdul. In the passage referring to this, much importance is given to the
great 'wave of blessing' stemming from proximity to the origin of the cycle's
revelation. In fact, between Jigme Lingpa—revealer of the treasure—and
Nyoshul Lungtog Tenpai Nyima, there are only two other masters in the
line of transmission: Dza Paltrül and Jigme Gyalwa'i Nyugu.[129] Bearing
in mind that Dza Paltrül was considered to be the reincarnation of the
voice of Jigme Lingpa, it is not surprising that Pema Düdul esteemed
as particularly powerful the transmission obtained through his disciple
Nyoshul Lungtog.

Although his name is not mentioned, we can deduce that the Kathog
Situ appearing in the biography is the master of Adzom Drugpa, that is,
the second Kathog Situ Chökyi Lodrö. The Situ of the Kathog monastery
is one of the seven lineages of reincarnated lamas of that monastery.[130] The
title of Situ was a distinction reserved for the great abbot of Palpung, a
large Karmapa monastery in Derge kingdom. At a certain point in history,
one of the candidates for the Palpung Situ reincarnation was not accepted
by Palpung monastery. He remained in Kathog where he was recognized,

thus initiating the Kathog Situ lineage. The Kathog Situ of the biography is precisely the second one, Chökyi Lodrö.

Regarding the fourteenth Karmapa Thegchog Dorje,[131] one of the salient characteristics of this reincarnation lineage is its high rank in Tibetan Buddhism. Considered to be the most important lama in Tibet after the Dalai Lama, the Karmapa is the head of the Karma Kagyü suborder and is seen as the most eminent master of all the Kagyüpa. The initiator of this lineage of reincarnations, Düsum Khyenpa[132] from Kham, was a direct disciple of Gampopa (who was a disciple of Milarepa); later, the Karmapas introduced into Tibet for the first time the tradition of reincarnated masters known as the 'emanated body.' Since, as we mentioned above, the third Karmapa Rangjung Dorje was a Dzogchen practitioner it is not surprising to find that subsequent Karmapas were also interested in this system.

Kongtrul Yonten Gyatso, better known as Jamgön Kongtrul Lodrö Taye, was one of the most eminent lamas of the Rime tradition and the close collaborator of Jamyang Khyentse Wangpo. He is considered to be one of the greatest scholars of the Tibetan tradition and is respected by all orders. Born into a Bönpo family, he received his early monastic education in the Nyingmapa monastery of Zhechen, but because of his intellectual brilliance was later compelled to enter the Karma Kagyüpa order, as his services were required by the hierophants of Palpung monastery. Nevertheless, his prolific written works are oriented more toward the doctrine of the Nyingmapa, and this interest led him to compile the greatest compendium of texts of the treasure tradition, *The Treasury of the Precious Discovered Teachings*.[133] He himself was a treasure finder.[134] The ninth Palpung Situ Pema Nyinje Wangpo,[135] the most important lama at Palpung monastery, was his root lama. In chapter eight of the biography we see how these three masters of the Karma Kagyü order—the Karmapa, Kongtrul, and Palpung Situ—exchange teachings with Pema Düdul, receiving parts of his treasure, *Self-Liberation that Encompasses Space*.

Although the eminence of the masters mentioned here is unquestionable because they were important gurus and because their fame has endured to this day, they were not necessarily the most significant in Pema Düdul's spiritual life. Certainly, the biography stresses the relevance of his meetings with these illustrious masters as, especially in the case of Do Khyentse Yeshe Dorje, Dza Paltrül, the Karmapa, and Nyoshül Lungtog, they were contacts valued very highly by Pema Düdul himself. Nevertheless, we must recall the pre-eminence in esoteric Buddhism of the 'root master'[136], the guru through whose teachings and karmic connection the disciple's doors of understanding are opened, giving him access to the fundamental experience of the vision of reality. It seems that two of these masters played this important role in Pema Düdul's lineage: Gyurme Chöying Rangdröl and Pema Gyurme Sangye.

The first, Gyurme Chöying Rangdröl, known as the great adept of Tsophu, is named in the brief biography of Pema Düdul as one of his most important masters, which is confirmed in the extensive biography presented here. Chapter five, reserved for his instructions and advice, illustrates the great esteem in which this lama was held by Pema Düdul. It is obvious that the instruction of the siddha of Tsophu was decisive in the stabilization of his contemplation and the deepening of his yogic practice, grounding Pema Düdul's understanding in the essential points of the Total Perfection. According to Khenpo Sönam Tenpa from Kathog monastery, Gyurme Chöying Rangdröl was his root master because he transmitted the instructions of Total Relaxation and Direct Leap[137] through the *The Vajra Heart of the Luminous Expanse*[138] cycle; these are the instructions leading to the 'Rainbow Body,' Pema Düdul's final realization.

On the second, Pema Gyurme Sangye, I have not been able to find any information, but it seems that he too was a root master. I say "seems" because although this is maintained in the brief biography of Pema Düdul published by Khetsün Sangpo on the lives of Tibetan masters (in the volume on the Nyingma lineages),[139] the biography I present here does not specify that Pema Gyurme Sangye was his root master. But our biography does contain a number of indications of the special nature of Pema Düdul's relationship with Pema Gyurme Sangye.[140] To begin with, we are told that Pema Düdul, before meeting this lama, experienced feelings of extreme devotion on simply hearing his name. In Buddhist biographies this is generally an indication of a karmic connection generated in past lives. Pema Gyurme Sangye later tells him about his previous night's dream in which Pema Düdul appeared guiding millions of beings to a crystal mountain. Pema Gyurme Sangye also provided clarification regarding the master's spiritual precedence and incarnations. But the most significant indication of the importance of this relationship is that the name by which our protagonist is known—Pema Düdul—was conferred by this master.

Another guru especially relevant to Pema Düdul's transmission of teachings was Dzatrül Rinpoche Kunzang Nampar Gyalwa, 'he of excellent intellect,' who became the Holder of the Doctrine[141] revealed by Pema Düdul. The role of the Holder of the Doctrine is very important in the tradition of spiritual treasures, because it confers the recognition necessary for the acceptance of the revealed cycle. Normally, the Holder of the Doctrine is a recognized master, often an important lama with a hierarchical position. A high lama's acceptance of the role of Holder of the Doctrine for a particular cycle of treasures not only confirms the teachings' authenticity and orthodoxy, but also signifies the lama's assumption of the role of protector and promoter of the study and practice of the discovered cycle.[142] In chapter nine, the author informs us that the paintings at Kalzang temple representing various tantric cycles of Pema Düdul's treasures were done according to the instructions of Dzatrül Rinpoche, precisely because he was the Holder of the Doctrine for the treasures. These paintings were probably done after Pema Düdul's death, and in his absence the Holder, together with the leading disciples in charge of transmitting the treasures, became the major authority on the terma cycle.

On several occasions, the lamas involved in the exchange of teachings with Pema Düdul belonged to the monastery of Kathog. It must be remembered that Pema Düdul belonged to the family lineage of Tagla Pema Mati,[143] who lived between the sixteenth and seventeenth centuries. Tagla Pema Mati, a disciple of Jatsön Nyingpo, Zhigpo Lingpa, and Chöying Rangdröl (three important lamas and tertöns of the time) revitalized the teachings at Kathog monastery, especially those contained in the lineages of the long-standing oral tradition (kama), and also the termas of Zhigpo Lingpa.[144] This monastic center, one of the oldest and most important of the Nyingmapa centers in eastern Tibet, especially treasured the teachings of Rigdzin Longsal Nyingpo,[145] a tertön who lived just after Pema Mati. Most relevant among them is the cycle of revealed treasures *The Vajra Heart of the Luminous Expanse,* which became one of the meditative practice specialties of Kathog monastery. This cycle, containing both tantric and Total Perfection teachings, figures significantly in Pema Düdul's transmission. The biography informs us that he received it on no less than four occasions, including once from Rigdzin Mingyur Tenpai Gyaltsen, the third incarnation of Drime Zhingkyong Gönpo, the most eminent reincarnate lama of Kathog monastery.[146] Pema Düdul transmitted the teachings of *The Vajra Heart of the Luminous Expanse* to his own disciples on several occasions, especially in the early days of his activities as master. In fact, he began 'spinning the Wheel of Dharma' with the preliminary practices of this cycle for the monks, nuns, and laypersons of the temple of Chagdü.[147]

THE DISCIPLES

Once he discovered his own spiritual treasure, the *Self-Liberation which Encompasses Space* cycle, many of the above-mentioned masters exchanged teachings with Pema Düdul and requested the corresponding initiations and reading transmissions of this cycle. Nevertheless, in terms of spiritual heirs, the most important are the closest direct disciples, those 'sons of the heart'[148] who received his teachings. For example, among them are Dampa Tendzin who accompanied him since the beginning, and Lama Taye who became one of his closest disciples and with whom he exchanged teachings, receiving from him the thirteen Putaka (volumes) of the cycle *The Gathering of the Guru's Intention.*[149]

The oral tradition has maintained that Pema Düdul had thirteen especially close disciples whose names contained the word 'Dorje.' I have not been able to discover the identity of these thirteen, but in a fresco at Kalzang monastery apparently completed during the lifetime of Pema Düdul or shortly after his death, the master appears surrounded by this group of thirteen. In any event, both Khenpo Sönam Tenpa of Kathog monastery and Lama Akha, Kalzang Gyatso[150] from Zhare Gendün Shedrub Phelgyeling monastery confirmed that the most direct disciples were Rangrig Dorje, Lama Taye, and Yeshe Dorje, the biography's author.[151]

One of the Kathog reincarnations, Getse Gyurme Tenpai Namgyal, was a disciple of Yeshe Dorje. He later was the teacher of Moksha Rinpoche, also one of the important tülkus of Kathog. Yeshe Dorje himself was considered an emanation of Jigme Lingpa[152].

Standing out from all the others is his spiritual heir Rangrig Dorje, also known as Rigdzin Kusum Lingpa or Rigpai Dorje[153] who we are told[154] appears towards the end of Pema Düdul's life and is recognized by the master as heir to the transmission in a prophecy from his treasures foretelling this disciple's role. Finally,[155] Kusum Lingpa received the posthumous transmission of the master's wisdom by experiencing several visions of the master, empowering him to continue the task of uncovering spiritual treasure. In that epoch the lineage of Mindröling—descended from the great Terdag Lingpa—had no male heir. Rangrig Dorje, considered an emanation of Terdag Lingpa himself, was requested by the Thirteenth Dalai Lama to dispose his son Pema Wangchen to be married to the Mindröling female heir. Pema Wangchen became throneholder of that monastery[156]. Because the union of Rangrig Dorje's lineage with the lineage of Mindroling, this monastery has been one of the main possessors of Pema Düdul's transmission. Later, with the patronage of the Thirteenth Dalai Lama, Rangrig Dorje built the monastery of Lumorap, in Thromge.

The importance of Rangrig Dorje among the disciples is made clear in the later tradition after Pema Düdul's passing: he became known as the 'sun-like son,' whereas Lama Taye was known as the 'moon-like son.' Rangrig Dorje was the principal master of Nyagla Changchub Dorje, the root lama of Chögyal Namkhai Norbu.

In Sögyal, crown prince of the Zhiwa region, Pema Düdul recognized another of his disciples as a reincarnation. In a prophetic announcement proclaiming the young prince as a reincarnation, extolling the excellence of his energy channels and urging others to follow him for the benefit of all beings, he made him his disciple and bestowed several initiations. This young man later became Lerab Lingpa—also known as the Tertön Sögyal—an important master and treasure finder[157] who served as guru to the thirteenth Dalai Lama, Thubten Gyatso. After the departure of Pema Düdul, Lerab Lingpa frequently resided in Kalzang and undertook the work of expanding the monastery, sponsored by the thirteenth Dalai Lama; his son Chöpel Gyatso became Kalzang's abbot. Another disciple recognized by Pema Düdul as a reincarnation was Ngawang Tendzin, later known as the treasure finder Thutob Lingpa.[158]

Adzom Drugpa Drodül Pawo Dorje[159] was one of the most eminent holders and propagators of the lineage of the *The Heart Essence of the Great Expanse*. He was recognized as a reincarnation of Pema Karpo,[160] a great master of the Drugpa Kagyü order. A disciple of the second Kathog Situ Chökyi Lodrö, he began to study and practice Dzogchen and the inner tantra of the Nyingma order. As the biography relates, he met Pema Düdul in his youth, receiving from him the transmission of his own terma, *Self-Liberation that Encompasses Space*. He was also one of the many accomplished disciples of the great Jamyang Khyentse Wangpo and of Dza Paltrül from whom he received, among other teachings, the entire transmission of the *The Heart Essence of the Great Expanse*. He was the only holder of the complete oral transmission of the instructions on *The Transcendent Wisdom Master*[161] and the practices of the channels and winds[162] of the *Heart Essence*. He taught mainly in the settlement known as Adzom Gar, in Upper Trom, where his numerous disciples congregated.[163] Among his vast activities for the teachings was the important task of publishing the texts of the Nyingma tradition to ensure their preservation.[164] According to the Khenpo Sönam Tenpa, Pema Düdul was the root lama of Adzom Drugpa. Throughout the biography, Adzom Drugpa is referred to as Drugtrül Rinpoche[165] and is one of the masters who at the end of Pema Düdul's life would perform the offering rituals and the consecration of the stupa containing the master's relics.

Also among his disciples was Longchen Dorje, better known as Nyagla Changchub Dorje[166] to whom, along with another disciple called Semnyi Dorje, Pema Düdul co-dedicated the *Song of the Energy of Dharmata*.[167] Nyagla Changchub Dorje was an important master of Total Perfection and tertön who gathered a community in Khamdogar, north of Chamdo. As previously said, his root lama was Rangrig Dorje, the main disciple of Padma Düdul. Another disciple was the yogini Ayu Khandro Dorje Paldrön[168] who witnessed the meeting between Adzom Drugpa and Pema Düdul and received the latter's spiritual treasures.[169] It seems that Ayu Khandro received almost all of his teachings. She also received the name of Dorje Paldrön from Pema Düdul as well as the prophecy identifying Semnyi Dorje as the yogi destined to be her consort.[170] Both Nyagla Changchub Dorje and Ayu Khandro were gurus of Chögyal Namkhai Norbu, the former being his root guru. Ayu Khandro transmitted Pema Düdul's terma to Chögyal Namkhai Norbu in their entirety.

To conclude this section on Pema Düdul's masters and disciples, I should like to mention the cases in which the process of transmission took place with practitioners clearly identified as members of orders other than the Nyingmapa. These include Yeshes Özer, a Bönpo lama;[171] several Sakya and Ngorpa (a suborder of Sakya) lamas; the fourteenth Karmapa Thegchog Dorje [172] and the third Situ Rinpoche,[173] both of the Karma Kagyüpa order; Paldan Chogkyi Langpo of the Sakya order;[174] Tsewang (reincarnation of Tromde),[175] the two Gelugpa masters Tsültrim Dragpa and Zigyab Rinpoche,[176] and some masters from unidentified Sakya and Bönpo monasteries.[177] It is possible that other adepts, masters, and monasteries mentioned in the biography whose religious affiliation I have not been able to identify also came from these traditions. I am not including Kongtrül Yonten Gyatso in this list because, although he nominally belonged to the Karma Kagyü order, his activity was generally dedicated to the ancient transmission and the tradition of spiritual treasures.

Translation

The Spiritual Liberation of Trülzhig Lingpa:
The Bank of Clouds Containing the Nectar of Happiness for the Fortunate [178]

YESHE DORJE'S PREFACE TO THE BIOGRAPHY

Namo Mahaguru Vajradharaye

Although he has exhausted the defilements that bind to the net of existence,
He appears as a manifestation of compassionate love.
Although he has entrapped the impure moving [energies]
In the space of the central [channel],
He displays the teaching of cause and fruit in myriad ways.
Although it is free from conceptual limitations,
His mind [abides] in Total Bliss, space, and wisdom
Without union or separation.
The glorious guru, holding the nature of the three secrets,
Enjoys it as the ornament of the wheel of Total Bliss.

The Victorious Ones and their sons [the Bodhisattvas],
Possessing the supreme mind that sees

The manifest dharmata of the natural condition,
Completely overcome disputes—motivated by rivalry—
About the sublime and secret sun of the Vajra essence.
At the proper time, they instantly make manifest
The spontaneously realized wisdoms and bodies
To individuals longing for enlightenment.
May the assembly of the root gurus of the lineage,
The Vidyadharas, protect my entire succession of lives!

Even if it is beyond the scope of ordinary people
To conceive of any of the profound deeds
Of the ardent compassion felt by those
Who have mastered the hundred modes of the many virtues,
I've written this text pretending to present [these deeds]
As a delight for the ears of those people
Who have acquired merit and are endowed with devotion.

As this poem is a brief reverential introduction, regarding this Lord protector of beings, Trülzhig Changchub Lingpa, a manifested great being who was wise, loving, and powerful among the disciples of the Buddhas of the three times and their sons, it must be said that the profound deeds of his life are ungraspable by the limited understanding of ordinary individuals like me. It is like blind people trying to perceive, through their [remaining] senses, the various characteristics of an elephant. Even though the unimpeded compassion born of contemplation by any Bodhisattva fully established in the pure levels of the path is congruent with the relative sense-perceptions of the individuals to be trained, in the real sense, while seated imperturbably on the throne of his displayed body's mandala, [the Bodhisattva] proceeds to the various regions of countless pure realms, meets many Tathagatas and enters the doorway of a hundred samadhis, rises from these samadhis, and benefits numerous beings with form and without form. These profound, inconceivable actions are as difficult to fathom by the mind as it is for children to measure the height and size of the sky.

Furthermore, in general, but even more so in the case of spiritual treatises, one needs to be thoroughly versed in the three aspects of composition—to write properly, disclose the meaning, and use the metrics elegantly—and to completely avoid postulations that affirm what is not, and omissions that deny what is. Superior individuals who possess the eye of the three prajñas can accomplish all this. An individual who exists at the level of the eight worldly concerns and desires to obtain that which does not accord with the above-described values, who is arrogant though unacquainted with any scriptural tradition, or who is ignorant and inclined to be greatly self-satisfied, is unsuitable to write about Dharma.

Accordingly, for what purpose [do I dare to write this text]? If the Teaching—a path whose sole intent is to accomplish liberation—is erroneously taught, this would be a shameful major fault with respect to oneself. In displeasing the sublime beings, it would also bring shame with respect to others.

Nevertheless, those who desire liberation, who recall the precious Three Jewels in general and the grace of their guru and masters in particular, who do not disregard their own conduct and deeds and have developed unfailing faith, these individuals will be able to observe the abatement of their hindrances as soon as they recite the aspiration and supplication prayers linked to the deeds and liberation of the sublime beings. For example, irrespective of their defects or virtues, ignorant male and female householders will generate the immeasurable merit of faith merely by uttering the aspiration and supplication prayers to the Three Roots and the guru.

From the tantras:

Even the dull ones endowed with faith
Are close to the attainment of the siddhi of union.

In accordance with the above, here we describe how the sublime Bodhisattva [Pema Düdul], from the moment his embryo matured into a born body until he proceeded into the sphere of peace, his motivation was focused only on meditation retreats. In order to make it easy to comprehend how such dedication is possible, I have divided the text into twelve parts. The beginning—in chapter one—explains how his place of birth is recognized as auspicious, virtuous, and sublime by the vajra prophecies; chapter two, the apparition of marvelous indications and the manifestation of visions of vidyadharas and dakinis from the moment of his birth; chapter three, how, in order to demonstrate the inevitable fruit of karma, he lived as a beggar; chapter four, how he guided beings using the jokhor following the Great Compassionate One's prophecy; chapter five, how he attended many teachers and achieved deep realization; chapter six, how he practiced the way of yogic asceticism in solitude and requested the authoritative texts of the practice lineage; chapter seven, how he acquired the profound treasures, and the inception of their diffusion; chapter eight, how, having seized the attitude that regards all doctrines as being without contradiction, he established many fortunate ones in maturation and liberation; chapter nine, how he built the temple as a field of merit for the benefit of the teachings and beings; chapter ten, how, having destroyed fixation on illusory vision, he remained in experience free from action; chapter eleven, how he transmitted his spiritual testament in the form of advice, to his vajra disciples; and chapter twelve examines the authoritative texts of the supreme vehicle and explains how he integrated his body into space.

CHAPTER ONE

How His Birthplace, the Virtuous,
Auspicious, and Sublime Realm is
Described in the Tantric Writings.

❧ To begin, [we shall speak of] this great sacred sanctuary to which the saint [Trülzhig Lingpa] came. This place, where in bygone days the Protecting Buddhas of the Three Families, the emanated Dharmaraja Songtsen Gampo and his ministers and the preceptor of Oddiyana Padmasambhava surrounded by Knowledge Holders[179] and assemblies of dakinis miraculously arrived, walked, and bestowed blessings in unimaginable ways is a great sanctuary where the profound sacred treasures—difficult to grasp through the intellect—are hidden.

In the register of great sacred places written by the emanation of Vairochana, the Lord of the Two Doctrines Orgyan Sangye Lingpa, it is said:

The disposition of all sacred places in the pure kingdom of the Land of Snows is like a lotus garden. Lhang Lhang is like [the Lotus] Udumbara since the blessings of compassion given in this holy and excellent pure field are as great as that lotus, and it is a propitious place for obtaining both the supreme and common siddhis.

In the prophecy on the treasures of the Lord it is written:

To the east of the Land of the Snows, in the marvelous southern continent is to be found the land of the great narrow valleys in which the crystalline, orange-colored mountains touch celestial space as though they were swords made of rock or heavenly fortresses of white stone. Lhang Lhang in particular is known as the highest of these jewels. There reside inconceivable assemblies of wisdom deities as well as the protectors of the Three Families and the second Buddha [Padmasambhava]. It is a place to which countless Knowledge Holders and siddhas have travelled, and the variety of signs of realization (which manifest there) is incalculable. Through sight, hearing, touch, and memory, the virtues of the ways and levels of realization are fulfilled, and the heavenly rainbow body is obtained.

Further, Drime Khachö Wangpo and many other realized adepts praised the numberless qualities of this place. Thus, as since remote times it has been a fortunate and propitious place for virtue, the Lord said of its qualities:

In this place was born Chagdü Sherab Gyaltsen who displayed in the skies the standard of victory of the Oral Tradition and the Treasure Tradition. It was the birthplace of Atrug Dawa Togden who, having no fixed place of meditation and constantly wandering from here to there, departed for the kingdom of Khechara. It was likewise the birthplace of Zhagla Yeshe Bumpa who led all who had a karmic tie with him out of the hell regions. Here, Tagla Chödrub Gyatso, who obtained signs of realization including the water of immortality and others, first saw the light of day. Here too was born Akar Chökyi Rinchen, who edited, without exception, the volumes of sutras and tantras from both the oral and treasure traditions. Wachu Mönlam Gyaltsen, who planted the standard of victory (of the teachings) of the Buddha and of Eternal Bön was born here. Gojam Chökyi Tsanchen was born in this place and by the force of his compassion, expelled the Mongol armies. Lakar Chökyi Gyatso was also born here and seeing samsara as illusion, he left to carry out a solitary retreat. The emanation Dungral Lingpa saw the light in this place and it was he who drew the treasures from the red rock of Drongtül. Drubchen Chöying Rangdröl was born here and filled the world with manifestations of the Doctrine of the Three Vehicles.

Thus, many similarly venerable masters were born in this place. Regarding the appearance in this place of the Lord, representative of the Buddha, in the prophetic text of his own treasures it is written:

His clan shall bear the name Gawa Ngatsotag. He shall have parents with the name Nataputyi. He shall bear the signs and marks indicating numerous and complete virtues, such as a freckle on his navel, and the immutable Dharmakaya shall be shown by a mole over his heart. He shall have the yogic ability of a great destroyer of illusion, free from action. Being a great practitioner, he shall show signs of spiritual realization. He shall possess the fortune of opening the hundred doors of profound treasures.

In *The Crystal Mirror for Future Prophecy,* by Sherab Gyaltsen, it is written:

An emanation of the mind of Padma, he of Oddiyana, will surge from the precious rock bearing the name Düdul. Orgyan shall raise the standard of the Victory of the Doctrine in this place.

In the treasure prophecies of Düdul Dorje we find:

In the future, in the rock called Nyag [will appear one] whose name means the renunciation of tea and alcohol and whose lower belly is adorned with moles; to this fortunate being shall be entrusted the mandate of the mind transmission.

According to Rigdzin Tagsham:

*Situ Chöjung, Nyarong Pema, and many others have appeared [at
Lhang Lhang] and most of them have served the Doctrine. Innumerable are the spiritual guides [appearing in this place].*

In the profound words of the treasure discovered by Longsal [Nyingpo],
it is written:

*During the period of the Doctrine, in the land of Kham located
within the borders of Tibet will appear, in the east, an emanation,
a divine prince.*

According to Pema Nyinje Wangpo:

*In the prophecy regarding the lama of Tsokha, Orgyan Norbu [it is
written]: "In the great sacred place in the north of the Country of
the Nobles (India), a mahasiddha will benefit all beings through
the Doctrine. He shall shower them with the teachings of Mahamudra, Dzogchen and Madhyamaka. This will be the time when the
Victory Standard of the Buddha's Doctrine shall be raised. This is
Padmasambhava himself returned. Offer him your prayers!"*

Thus, they praised him with vajra prophesies, [references to] numerous
authentic treasure finders, as well as to many siddhas living in this great
land of spiritual attainment.

On the family lineage, the Lord's father came from the lineage of
Tagla Pema Mati.[180] His name was Khangtseg Gönpo, and he was a rich
landowner with extensive holdings. He went for a prophecy to Gyalse
Pema Namgyal, a descendent of Düdul Dorje, saying, "Which [woman]
will make me happy if I take her as my wife?" The oracular reply was:

*The master of a hundred thousand qualities,
An excellent magical emanation,
[As a] fortunate leaf*

Shall fulfill the great power of the five centers.

He was given a written copy of the prophecy. Further, by some men who were travelling from Nyarong with the idea of visiting Dodrub Rinpoche Kunzang Zhenphen, he was sent a message containing the previous question. The prophecy was:

Meditating on the secret direction,
The freckle-faced one is perfect.
Like the thousand-petalled lotus blossom,
Children of noble lineage will be born.

Thus it was written in the prophetic document. Also, on inviting Chagdü tulku Tenpa Dargye to perform a personal ritual [for the father], he asked the same question. The forecast was:

The omnipresent vajra will expand like the eyes on a peacock's
*   tailfeathers.*

On inviting the emanation of Ase Chophül, also known as Lungtog Tenpai Gyaltsen, to ask him for the ritual of the visualization of Kilaya, he dreamed that on a precious throne of gold was a luminous crystal vase surrounded by thousands of vajras and bells, with all their [special] properties. Also, a prophecy of Gyalse Sönam Nyandrag contained this prediction:

The dream of a white conch shell sounding thrice
[Indicates] the appearance of a son
Who will be renowned for his qualities throughout the kingdom.

Thus, in conformity with the predictions of these masters, he took as his wife a young woman of beautiful qualities whose name was Sönam Kyi, of the Serzang family belonging to the Akarbu clan.

It was a time of great prosperity in the husband's family, so many monks were invited who specialized in the performance of beneficial rituals, and they recited the *Prajñaparamita*, the *Sutra of the Fortunate Eon*,[181] and others, one hunded times. At one point, an expert on the *Prajñaparamita*, the scholar Künzang Chöphel, had a dream in which the Lord's mother danced as she held a shining golden mirror at her heart. On receiving the moon's rays, the mirror illuminated all dimensions in the universe. An expert in the *Sutra of the Fortunate Eon*, the scholar Guru Gyaltsen, dreamed that a brilliantly radiant sun shone on the crown of the mother's head. In the father's dream, a crystal stupa emanated light and transparency, reaching the father's lap; when the sun's rays touched the crystal, its light spread throughout the kingdoms in the ten directions. In the mother's dream, beautiful dakas and dakinis who said they were from Oddiyana, the land of the dakinis, carried a vajra, bell, and text which they gave to the mother saying: "Keep them well!" after which they disappeared into space.

Thus, from the instant his body took its place in the womb, all had marvelous dreams. All this doubtlessly indicated that an emanation was going to arrive in order to convert beings. It is said in the scriptures:

> *Like waves on the ocean, dwelling of the makaras,[182]*
> *The universe has been changing since long ago.*
> *Even so, the Buddhas are prompt in helping*
> *Their spiritual sons [the Bodhisattvas] who convert beings.*

In verses:

> *The Vajra prophecies scattered the blossoms of praises [on him];*
> *The compassion of all Victorious Ones was transformed into a*
>   *continuous dance.*
> *May I be constantly drunk with the elixir of the three secrets*
> *Of the loving holy guru, the only refuge!*

Chapter Two

On the Appearance of Marvelous Signs
from the Moment of His Birth; How He Had
Visions of Knowledge Holders and Dakinis.

The place where he was born was called the plain of Delong Gyalnya. Since this was a period in which his father enjoyed riches and great merit, he commissioned the engraving of the six-syllable mantra ten thousand times on many rocks and was busy promoting the building of a stupa, when, during this year, the Fire Rat Year (1816), on the tenth day of the ninth month, the Lord was born. A five-colored rainbow touched the tent they used as a dwelling. In all directions there was a delightful scent, and many vultures flocked around the tent. When the milk was churned, thirteen small tormas[183] of butter spontaneously appeared. The sounds of the natural elements reverberated beautifully. Three days later, [the child was seen] sitting cross-legged, saying three times, "Ah mi bhi wa," and, "I am an emanation of the mind of Orgyan (Padmasambhava)." At six days of age, when Lama Namdag from Chagdü was blessing him, he struck a dance pose while blinking and saying, "*siddhi,*" seven times. The lama said that the boy was doubtlessly a nirmanakaya who would spread immeasurable blessings. When he was three weeks old the time was ripe for inviting Kathog Zhingtrül Rigdzin Jigme Gönpo who was then traveling through Nyarong. [This master] blessed him and composed these words of prophecy:

This golden chalice of youth possessing the throne and parasol of perfect dominion will epitomize the essence of the treasures capable of bestowing the nectar of maturation and liberation.

When he was nine months old, his paternal uncle Lama Künzang said, "This nephew will be a good lama," and placing a vajra and bell in [the boy's] hands, greeted him in a state of extreme happiness. His uncle then gave him the name of Trashi Döndrub[184].

When [the child was] two years old, while they were in the pastures of the higher mountains in a place called Thangzang before the great holy place of Norbü Drag, a man wearing a white silk turban who said he came from the great holy place (of Lhang Lhang) arrived, accompanied by many dakas and dakinis in the fullness of their youth, and they played [with him] on several occasions.

Thus, the father and mother together with the others, went to the holy place to perform circumambulations and the ritual fumigation of cleansing. On reaching the Plain of Treasures,[185] before the holy place, he saw a multitude of dakas and dakinis who came, singing and dancing, to greet them. Adorned with silk parasols of victory, dressed in monastic robes and carrying cymbals, thigh-bone trumpets, and skull drums, (the Lord) pointed with his index fingers, describing their appearance to the others, to whom they were invisible.

In brief: during his infancy when he played with other children he would only play at conferring initiations, giving teachings, building temples, sitting quietly in a cave in the rocks or at the foot of a tree or staying in retreat, and did not take part in any of the other children's games imitating worldly activities.

He also avoided small negative acts like killing fleas; even the smallest positive acts such as lighting a lamp gave him great happiness. Simply seeing a monk or the written words 'Dharma' or 'divinity' made him extraordinarily happy. When he heard or saw someone suffering, he felt immeasurable pity and went to his parents to ask how the person could be helped. As he was truly of the noble lineage he had clear awareness and a good character.

When he was seven years old, he went to study reading and writing with a lama called Pema. Because his mental clarity was so acute, he understood the whole teaching by simply listening to the lama's introduction, and after four or five repetitions its meaning was established in his mind.

Once when he met the excellent King Gesar [in a dream or vision], he received many of the king's biographical songs, and the king named him "Trashi Döndrub, Bard of all the Songs."

At nine years old, at his uncle Tagla's residence he met Gyalse Dorje Chöwang from whom he received some initiations and reading transmissions. This master told him:

> *Young aspirant, you are an emanation of Longsal Nyingpo and of many other venerable beings. In the future you will labor to benefit all beings and the Doctrine.*

In that same monastery, while he slept he had a dream in which the dakinis predicted the following:

> *In the holy place you will accomplish the building of a temple, Kalzang Sangye Chöling, which shall be as marvelous an accumulation of virtue as the glorious holy precinct of Samye.*

In an instant he saw the temple as it would look once it was built. He said (later) that he had also experienced other pure visions on that occasion. In verses:

> *His infinite accumulation of merit and wisdom*
> *Holds, from the divine sky, the wish-fulfilling tree*
> *Of the most affectionate compassion.*
> *May I be protected by the Glorious Lord Changchub Lingpa,*[186]

Who eliminates the afflictions of cyclic existence
Simply through the hearing of his name!

CHAPTER THREE

How the Condition of Poverty Manifested to Demonstrate the Infallible Law of Cause and Effect.

❧ Then his father Khangtseg Gönpo died. The Lord, his mother, and his two small brothers invited some twenty lamas [to perform the funeral rites] for the father. Together with the monks, they carried out the full rite of forty-nine days.[187] To generate merit for the father, they offered most of the livestock and property they owned.

The Lord explained that his father owned a mansion, a great building, in Khangtseg but on their arrival a paternal aunt called Bodzog refused entry to the Lord, his mother, and brothers. They had to take shelter in a small shed for horses and goats that had belonged to his father. There, they suffered the theft of the female yak, the male and female dzo,[188] until they finally lost all the goods they owned and were scarcely in a position to pay for a packet of tea.

[The Lord] said that at this time the people close to them helped greatly by offering them some goats, pots, sacks, plates, and small receptacles. He explained that from then on because he perceived the defects of samsara as illusion, in his mind he did not feel miserable.

At this time the middle brother died, so they invited some lamas. The Lord and his mother were unable to perform any [actions to serve] as a root of virtue [for the brother] except to offer a piece of good arable land and to model some ten thousand tsa tsa.[189]

Then came the moment when the Lord manifested the illness of smallpox. At that time, while he slept he dreamed that in a past [lifetime] he himself had been an usurious lama who engaged in taxing and giving initiations, thus leading a great multitude who were said to have arrived from Makhog.[190]

Because he had smallpox, after a few days the townspeople took him to a distant, desolate ravine with a man called Gyatso who served as a nurse, as his sole companion. His mother brought whatever provisions she could beg to that place and communicated with him from a great distance by means of signals.

Later, even though the primary cause of his disease began to be dispelled, the provisions ran out so he was thrown into very hard times. Because he had no food, he had to steal a little barley flour, some turnips, and buckwheat from the nomads Gyatso and Ali just to have something to eat. As he himself explained, he also stole some turnips that the villagers had planted so he could eat something.

Finally he overcame the smallpox. He managed to survive by occasionally stealing small quantities of barley flour and turnip flour belonging to a young woman named Achung. Alu, Achung's mother, on discovering these thefts, realized that hoes, ceramic pots, sacks, and so on were also missing. [The Lord] had to spend several nights consuming nothing but a little water, but he never stole anything important.

If he accidentaly killed one of the fallen beings [such as animals or insects] he felt great anxiety, and his feelings at the sacrifice of a large animal cannot even be expressed.

In the presence of any being he would say that its nature was pure suffering, and would shed tears and feel sadness. He said:

No matter how hungry I felt, I would not let myself get carried away by that suffering, and would sing the mani mantra with the vajra melody. I was always reciting prayers. When I saw a wealthy

*person, I never entertained the thought of how I would enjoy being
in his position. Apart from all that, the question arose in my mind:
of what use are all these illusory riches?*

During his illness he dreamed of men sick with smallpox. He knew which
ones would die and which would not, and [he heard voices] explaining
methods of curing the disease, or [describing] places that would promote
their health, saying, "Your health will improve." Similarly, he dreamed of
predictions made by different classes of divinities and protectors.

In the spring, having found almost nothing to eat, the Lord spent
about a month eating any kind of edible root [he could find], such as sweet
potato, lagong roots[191], nimpa[192] and monbu[193] roots, garlic, and so on.
For another month he ate several kinds of ngodum, such as churü and t
sugpa.[194]

Towards midsummer he returned to the village of Khangtseg where,
though mother and son were reunited, they had nothing to eat. An old
woman called Thubpatso proposed that if the Lord would take care of two
leper women who had also caught a disease of "heat" during an epidemic,
he, his brother, and their mother could get a little milk. The Lord had
already shown one or two symptoms of the "heat" disease.

That year, because they had sown no seeds [the family] had no grain,
not even a few pints. That autumn, the Lord dreamt that an extraordinarily
black man as large as Mount Meru was waving a black banner, which
generated a terrifying vision of gathering clouds that produced rainfall.
At this time, the black man caused much unhappiness and all kinds of
suffering [to all beings]. Waving the banner that he held in his hand, he
captured the winds, and immediately the clouds dispersed and not even
a few remained. Then the black man was very happy and laughed aloud.
This was the vision that appeared in the dream. The next night, all the
grain in the area was ruined by frost, which caused the value of that year's
grain to become like that of straw. There was a terrible famine that year
throughout the whole region, as if the sufferings of the hungry spirits had
been transferred to the land of men.

Thus, during the autumn, as there was nothing left in the mother and brother's fields except the exhausted bodies of the vultures, there was nothing on which to live that season, so the Lord had to go begging for turnips. In the spring, with his body scarred by smallpox and his clothes and old mantle of hide—all he possessed—being the remains of what he wore when he was ill, everybody said, "This is the one who was plague-stricken a few days ago."

At first, when he began to beg for turnips in the fields on the plains of the valley floor, from inside their houses cruel people showered him with stones and set their dogs on him. The son of one of the owners said, "Come and look! Here's the one who's got smallpox," and while they were busy insulting him, others started to violently criticize him. Then [the owner's son] added, "He'll bring calamity to the region."

However, some good people said, "Don't go away. We'll bring you some provisions," and they brought a basket with a few turnips and some vegetables. This is what [the Lord] explained. Thus, he returned from the wide valleys and from some monasteries with five sacks of turnips.

At that time, an old, one-eyed beggar was traveling with a group of other people. They allowed the Lord to travel with them and for two nights, greatly honored him by offering him what provisions they had. Just before parting company, [the old man] also gave him a food bag, which was very useful. [The Lord] explained that later on the two would have a fruitful association, begging together.

During the irrigation period in winter, the time for cultivation of enlightenment, there appeared a demon who obstructs the attainment of spiritual awakening. He appeared in fiery form, bent on doing damage. The Lord, who had been paid for his work as a shepherd, went to the other shepherds who were standing in a grassy field. Just then, some of his companions suffered burns from a grass fire. It occurred to the Lord that many mountainsides would be burned, so he leapt forward to put out the fire, burning his hands, feet, and the hair on his head. Thus, he composed the following aspirational prayer:

Fire-demon and inseparable lamas, know this!
Today I have foreseen in the flames the burning death of many be-
ings whose lives have been consumed by fire. May all who take
life be annihilated today!

At that time, the Lord was living in a place that had good, fine quality pastureland. He sold it to his uncle Karma Palden's monastic residence and received in exchange two sacks of turnips, two zho[195] of barley, a goat, and two gyama[196] of butter. The Lord and his mother were more gladdened by this sale than if they had found many silver Chinese coins[197] on a deserted plain. At the moment they were saying that despite the calamities, they would not have to suffer hunger that year, the younger brother, called Norbu, said to his mother, "You and I shall look after the goat. It will have a kid and we'll milk it to make yogurt and [have milk] to drink." At this, the mother began to cry, saying, "Oh son, don't say that! It makes me think of the time when we had one hundred female yaks to milk and now, in our time of suffering, all we have is this old goat. It makes me miserable," and she felt great misery in her heart.

The Lord explained how one day when he was taking the goat to pasture, two thieves gave him a beating, and throwing dust in his eyes they stole the black goat, his clothes, blanket, and hat. At night, going back to the house [in the valley] below, he told his mother what had happened. Her pain was so great that it seemed her heart had been torn out.

One night, two thieves arrived at the house of the mother and sons and took absolutely everything, even the last remaining grains of barley they could see, the only turnip, the pot for boiling tea, and the pots and pans. Come dawn, the mother fainted as if she had lost her mind. On reviving she said, "Did this really happen, or is it an illusion?" Lamenting and crying, she beat her breast. The Lord stood, watching her. On hearing her cries, all the neighbors came. It was as if everything that had been in the house had been swept away, leaving nothing. When the neighbors arrived, the mother was crying bitterly and the old people and some relatives began to lament too. The younger brother began to cry, and when they all started crying it sounded like a swarm of bees. At that moment the Lord said, "Mother, don't cry," and he sang these words:

Mother, don't cry, and listen to my song.
We are an illusory dream.
The thieves, too, are an illusory dream.
Riches, too, are an illusory dream.
Illusion leads to illusion, and we weep over it.
If there are karmic debtors, they have acted!
Because this is an offering, they have returned for the feast.
Feel happy to offer [the things they have stolen].

On hearing this, those present exclaimed, "Corrupt son! An enemy's joy is our sorrow for [the loss of] food!" Then, a white-haired old man called Agön—a really generous person—offered them a plate of flour and a cooking pot, saying:

Orgyan who knows all, [take pity]!
Stand up and lament no more. Fill this pot with water, boil it,
and eat this flour.

They boiled the water in the pot while the mother and sons lamented their anguish, and then other people brought small quantities of kindling, old pots, a few dre[198] of turnips, as well as cups full of barley flour. Then the Lord said, "My younger brother is close to death, so I'll take a little of the flour and leave the rest for you, mother, and especially for my brother." The mother, never ceasing to weep, asked:

Why are mother and sons [living] like insects in a hole, with no protection at all? As the law of cause and effect expounded by the Buddha is infallible, all this must doubtlessly be due to the accumulation of negative karma from the past; but apart from that, in

this time and in this body I have not accumulated negative karma.
Furthermore, when I was under the protection of my ancestors and
your father was alive, I honored the Three Jewels above all, gave
donations to monks, and also offered alms to the poor, trying to be
diligent in any white or virtuous deed I could do. I have avoided
[committing] any possibly black or negative actions. Although it
is the deities who possess the eye of wisdom, and although feeling
desperate is an offensive attitude, this old woman's mind cannot
bear such suffering!

As she cried, she went on:

Your father, who was like a victorious mountain, is dead. Riches
[abundant] as the grass, are gone. I have made all the ceremonial
offerings I can, yet I am poor. I have practiced white virtue, yet I
suffer.

It seemed her mind was being destroyed as she wept, saying:

Although there is no place where your father did not do good, we
have hardly any possessions. Relations and friends scarcely help us.
Apart from all this, the story [predicting] that you will be of the
highest birth has not been actualized. In the past, many venerable
lamas made many irrefutable forecasts, and while you were inside
my body I had auspicious visions and dreams. On the day of your
birth a band of vultures flocked together and the light of a rainbow
flowed over the tent. When you were three days old you assumed the
Vajra posture, and the natural sounds of the four elements might-
ily resounded.. Flowers fell from the sky like rain and you uttered
the word 'siddhi.' Thirteen deity figures appeared in the butter, a
marvelous and unimaginable sign. Nevertheless, what good hopes
can you hold except for the fulfillment of the one hope held in the
hearts of all beggars? At present, no good is manifesting. Haven't you

gone begging? Of course you have! We, mother and children, who in the past seemed like lords, are today in the painful and unavoidable position of having to go out and beg, and thus we have to deal with shame and indifference. We must use anything we can get to procure food. Our very existence is threatened by lack of food. According to the saying, both rich and poor need food. If we don't all want food, why does a white vulture descend on a dog's corpse? In this situation you must carry two stout sticks when you go begging. I myself have to go and sell wood to get food, as if they paid me for carrying it. And if I don't, only death awaits my sons and I.

The Lord of Realization replied:

Mother, in this situation where we have to beg, tell me what would be the best time for it? When I beg, am I not capable of getting a good sack filled with food?

At this the mother replied:

If you are skillful, you'll do it, my son. Wherever you go, live long! We have all become beggars! In our present state of want, I'll consider food obtained through begging as a gift. Apart from having to leave the country, the only thing that hasn't happened to me is being bitten by a dog! Don't lose those two stout sticks!

Weeping, the mother went to the house of uncle Tsedrub and asked him for a sack. He brought one back with a few dre of good rice, saying, "This is a gift," and he, too, wept.

Then the Lord and Tsedrub went to the dwelling of a man called Khuwo Anor who lived among shepherds. On the way they passed about ten dwellings, but in that district, apart from some men who had come from a distance to collect wood or fetch water, nobody dared to beg.

The nomads didn't give them much except for a cupful each of chur, a little butter, a cup of barley flour, and a few turnips. Continuing on their way and approaching the house of Anor, abundant food and drink were offered to them. They sTayed at Anor's house for a day. The next day, Anor told them that if they asked at the [nomads'] dwellings they would get food. Anor himself gave them barley flour, turnips, barley, and good butter. Then Anor, who accompanied them a good distance on their way back, wept for as long as it takes to drink a cup of tea, and on parting company said, "Beware of the dogs!"

The Lord, carrying his load, went home to give it to his mother, who was delighted to have about a month's supply of food. The Lord said, "Regardless of the arising of such suffering, when the mind comprehends the illusory nature of samsara, it is not attacked by sadness."

Then his younger brother Alö died because the food had arrived too late. With his mother in utter despair, the Lord exclaimed:

Mother, do not weep, and listen to my song!
In this world, things are like that.
Who does not suffer death?
Having been our father and mother is the nature of all beings.
Think of the suffering of those in the three inferior states,
Where there is absolutely no chance of happiness.
If you suffer, let it be for them.
If you lament, let it be for them.
Why should you be sad at the death of one man?
Mother, are you not going mad?
This son, due to hostile forces, was unhealthy.
Of what benefit is your sorrow?
[Instead,] attain great happiness by meditating on the illusory
    nature of all things!

At this, uncle Tsedrub shouted, "Ho! Sickening son!" and punched the Lord in the center of his chest, and he too began to cry.

They invited some lamas and offered every part [of the son's body] to the vultures. The Lord went begging every day, but when he did not go he recited [the liturgy of] *The Peaceful and Wrathful Divinities which Procure Self-Liberation of Karmic Inertia,*[199] until the end of the forty-nine days. During this period the mother recited the [purification sutra known as] *The Three-Part Scripture,*[200] the *Vajrachedika,*[201] and the *mani* mantra,[202] and constantly recited prayers of devotion and aspiration.

By then, wherever people met for protective rituals[203] or [to listen to] teachings, there went the Lord uninvited, begging out of necessity. In these circumstances the Lord was admitted, together with many monks and lamas, into the residences of many masters, mostly from nomadic regions. These included the residence of the monastic seat of Tagla, which was that of his own uncle Karma Palden, as well as that of Lama Düdjom. He was also received in the homes of Anye Sönam Rabten in the town of Khangtseg and in those of Chuka Ala, Agön, Atse, Rabten, and Gyushö Achug, as well as in the home of Anor the nomad. These sojourns benefited him greatly.

Arriving during the teachings given in the residence of Jiribö Ala, on his own initiative he went and sat with the many monks and lamas on the house's terrace. At that moment, the benefactor of the residence arrived and, looking at the beggars said, "You! Beggar gazing at the sky, you can't stay here. Go outside!" Since he was rejected and could not stay there, in tearful sobs he made his way outside, looking behind him. Similarly, at the residence of Gyashö Bulu as well as that of Luchug, many benefactors did not allow him to remain among the ranks of practitioners, and threw him out.

In that region it was the custom for lamas and monks to carry with them only the barley flour they needed for their own sustenance when attending assemblies to receive teachings, but because the Lord had no chance to get flour, he stole about three cupfuls from the bag of someone called Anyug. On realizing this, the benefactor punched him several times, telling him that as restitution he should donate [the flour] as an offering for the house. [At this time] he stole many such small amounts of barley flour.

At that time, when the Lord joined practitioners in religious assemblies his only clothes were rags full of holes and patches. To make matters worse, he had fleas and lice, and because he had not been able to obtain any food or drink for some time, he needed a great deal [to fill] his bloated belly. His mouth was enormous, and due to an accumulation of negative factors and their contaminating secondary effects, in the dormitory he couldn't retain his urine. Because of all this, when he went to the end of the righthand row of practitioners, they sent him over to the left; when he went to the lefthand row, they sent him back [to the right]. The Lord has told how everyone threw so many stones, earth, and sticks at him that they fell like rain. The monks, regarding him as a leper, were very hostile towards him. [But] the Lord said:

> *Despite everything, during that time how could I have had even one desperate thought tiny enough to fit inside a mustard seed? Everything that happened was the necessary unfolding of accumulated residual negative karma in need of purification. From the start, all the offerings given by the benefactors were taken by others; I never even got a tiny bit. At that time, I never ate a good piece of meat, but only leg, shin, and hipbones.*

After a while, a man from Khangtseg called Sönam Tsering, shouting insults, hit the Lord so hard that the circulation in his joints was almost obstructed, and the blows nearly stopped his breathing. Then, stumbling and falling to the ground, he made his way back to his mother who was afflicted to see him like this and showered him with tears. At that moment, the Lord sang this song:

> *Mother, do not weep, and listen to your son's song!*
> *All these powerful men are transitory.*

Humble as we are, we too are impermanent.
What difference does it make, powerful or humble? We are all in
    impermanence.
Though in this life we have committed not the slightest negative
    action
[To deserve] the humiliations inflicted on us by these powerful
    men,
To us, humble mother and son,
Are returned the fruit of innumerable lives, as our own actions
    ripen within us.
How can we complain?
Though you lament, there is still a way to work on karma.
If you are incensed with vengeance and hate, like fire,
You become the cause that ignites the coals of hell.
In this there is nothing beneficial.
The patience that takes no heed of injury,
Is the most excellent patience of all.
Meditate on this!
These powerful men were really our benevolent fathers and
    mothers.
Meditate on the knowledge of what they really are, and calm
    yourself!

Thus he comforted his old mother.

The Lord then went to his uncle Tagla's residence to take care of the animals belonging to an old woman called Agongma. During this period, one night as he dreamed, he had the following vision: a strange looking, terrifying black man who said he controlled a myriad of demons appeared, scattering with his hands a shower of weapons such as vajras, wheels, swords, axes, spears, hammers, tridents, daggers, sickles, snares, chains, and so on. At that instant, the Lord's master, the treasure finder Dungral Lingpa, appeared in splendor greater than that of one hundred thousand suns. It was difficult to look at the rays of light emanating from this being's hand, which held a golden parasol that all but covered the entire sky, beneath which the thousand-axed golden wheel [of the Doctrine] was turning clockwise. As it was turning above the Lord's head, the weapons showered by the demons in the sky suddenly became a rain of flowers like those that grow in the water, in the mountains and the plains such as the lotus, the great lotus, the kumutala, and so on.[204] The Lord appeared in the dream with no physical injuries.

The next day, the Lord, feeling somewhat downhearted, took the animals out to pasture, and when he arrived at the beautiful grassy plain below the summit of the holy place of Lhang Lhang, the deities of the four elements manifested simultaneously in the emptiness of the sky, forming a dark cloud in the angry and dense atmosphere. Darkness fell in all directions as the sound 'ro, ro' could be heard. A brilliant lighting bolt descended, so violent and bright that it was impossible to look upon. At that moment the voice of the furious turquoise dragon thundered forth, almost splitting earth and heaven and, at the same time, to the left and to the right there fell particles of the meteoritic iron vajra. Immediately the Lord exclaimed:

Protect me, [Buddha,] Lord of the Wise without equal!
Protect me, King of the Victorious Padmakara!

Saying this, he concentrated on existence and on phenomena as the manifestation of the Primordial Base, and he manifested himself as the flaming wisdom body of Palchen Pema Dragpo,[205] the wrathful form of the radiant nature of compassion. As the Lord remained in an intensely luminous protective circle, not only did the meteoric iron particles not hurt him, but neither his shepherd companions nor the animals suffered any injury.

It is hard for ordinary people [like] us to appreciate intellectually such prodigious events as these, which are signs of realization. Yet if we reflect a little, we can understand that [this apparition] could only be a Buddha primordially emanated out of compassion, appearing as a glorious protector of beings and of the Doctrine. [The ability to understand] events such as these distinguishes a person who is [from] one who is not trained in the higher paths.

Later, when the Lord went down toward the residence of Agongma, the old woman thought:

> *This shepherd who is working for me has very bad karma. When he was very young, his father died. First off, he was high and mighty, and then he turned into a beggar. The fever and the dangerous smallpox have scarred him. On two or three occasions thieves stole the few goods he had managed to keep. Now he's a shepherd, and the meteoric iron thunderbolt caught him on the mountain, and this excellent dzomo has broken her leg. If one thinks about it, it's all bad karma. I think I ought to fire him.*

When she fired him, she gave him some boots, two or three cupfuls of ram flour and a few good turnips, and saying, "You must leave today," she made him leave at once. Then, the Lord went to his mother and offered her the few things he had acquired.

A famine fell over all the land of Kham, and because they had no seed to sow and couldn't get any food, mother and son had to consume stagnant water, wild garlic or anything edible, such as various kinds of ngodum.

They had to go begging in the town of Khangtseg and at Tagla's residence. In this way they managed to survive for some time, getting a little food here and there. However, when the Lord went to the two abbeys of Dzikhugmo to beg, lama Tsognyi Gyatso called to him, inviting him into his home. With tears in his eyes he said:

> *Your uncle and father were prosperous and were also great patrons of the Doctrine. This is not your lot. Some time ago, many venerable and excellent lamas unerringly prophesied [about you], and at your birth infinite marvelous signs appeared. I, too, think about those unequivocal signs of realization you clearly showed, and how well*

they developed. But I tell you that the time has not yet come for these [prophecies] to become manifest.

Uttering these and many other comforting statements, [the lama] offered him a great banquet as well as two dre of barley and a great sackful of red turnips, adding:

Be certain that you shall become a beneficent person. You need not worry! Last night I dreamed of a beautiful procession, so you should not harbor any doubts that things will turn out well.

Saying these things, he made him happy. Also, when [the Lord] went to the monastic residence of Sönam Tsültrim, the lamas spoke to him affectionately and gave him a great quantity of food and drink—such as milk and yogurt—and on leaving they gave him two dre of barley, red turnips, and butter, saying, "Son, although this [miserable] situation will not recur, wherever you go, beware of the dogs!"

They gave him good advice. Finally, he begged from some other monks who were also there, and they all gave him turnips and other offerings in abundance. He took everything back to his mother in Khangtseg. Mother and son enjoyed themselves as if they had found a treasure, and they felt very happy.

The Lord was living in the town of Khangtseg when one night as he slept, he dreamed of a man of terrible and dark appearance with fangs so threatening that it was almost impossible to look at him. His eyes were red and his dark brown hair stood on end and was in flames; his hands and feet were talons of iron. In his hands he held a black hat divided on the inside into nine sections in which darkness gathered. By this power [the dark man] caused a black donkey that was a great distance away, to bray. Offering [the hat] to the Lord he said, "Take this hat. At the foot of this great rocky mountain are all the things you wish for and need, including food, drink, and so on. You should go and live there." At that moment, the Lord, centering himself on the luminous clarity [he had acquired through] his previous practices, could instantly see the high rocky mountain that touched the sky, and the intensely unpleasant and forbidding darkness gathering there. On beholding this vision, the precious Lord thought to himself:

> *This is just like the magic previously displayed by the black demon. On several occasions he has created obstacles to my realization of bodhi, this holy teaching whose aim is to establish beings in the supreme illumination.*

Thus he emerged from the luminous clarity of his dream. The next day he went to tend his uncle Tsedrub's goats and, on reaching the slopes of the mountain called Langag Lungba, his mind was established in the state of Transcendent Wisdom of the primordial nature, free from birth, movement, or disturbance. At that moment, a mountain identical to the one in the previous night's supernatural dream collapsed, precipitating three avalanches. The largest contained rocks the size of horse or yak corpses; the medium-sized one consisted of rocks the size of goat and sheep corpses, and the smallest one let fall stones the size of catapult projectiles and pillar bases. Then, when there fell a shower of stones the size of bowls and dishes, the other shepherds ran off in all directions shouting, "The rocky mountain has collapsed!"

At that moment the Lord, present in the state of the one flavor of samsara and nirvana in which the mind and phenomena appear as inseparable—the dynamic energy of phenomena's incessant fluctuation—generated himself as the glorious body of Dorje Drolö.[206] His hair, flowing upwards, conquered the formless realms. The upper part of his body subdued the realms of form, and likewise from his hair, beard, and eyebrows leapt flames of transcendent wisdom, burning up all disturbing emotions. From the vajra in his right hand there emanated rays of meteorites, and his left hand, in the scorpion mudra, grabbed the king of demons by the throat, preventing the demons from causing further problems. Victorious in this conflict, he set in motion the interdependent conditions that make long life and enlightened actions increase like the waxing moon.

The next day, the Lord's left side showed signs of the impact of the small avalanche. That night as he slept, the Mantra Protectress Ekajati said to him:

> *I am simultaneously present throughout your succession*
>   *of lives.*
> *You, great daka whom I protect and never leave,*
> *Are, since the beginning, the primordial Buddha.*
> *Samsara and nirvana are ornaments of the play of energy*
>   *of dharmata.*
> *In the primordial nature, gods and demons are not separate.*
> *I am the possessor of the final word of the Buddhas*
> *And the custodian of the six million [verses].*
> *I have promised to constantly survey and accompany*
> *The yogis of the Total Perfection who have really manifested*
> *The Natural State of the Primordial Nature.*
> *I am the one who protects the practitioner's entourage from*
>   *defects,*
> *And I protect against obstacles that cause discord.*

As [she] said this, the tremendous certainty and courage of the self-generated transcendent wisdom was born in him, and the ultimate understanding that is the realization of the self-liberated state, totally devoid of reference point, sprang forth in his mind.

From the blow he received during the avalanche, the Lord felt ill for a month.

In times when demonic armies and hosts, motivated by the perverse aspiration prayers they recited in the past, prepare to destroy the wellbeing and happiness of beings and the Doctrine, the excellent Buddha Padmakara manifests among humans as an expert in conversion methods who has the ability to dominate those demons. This moment in time generally corresponds to a period during which the five degenerations[207] are on the rise. Although in this particular [case], being a locale of wicked beings with their corresponding powers, somehow the small avalanche hurt the [Lord's] body, the fact remains that as long as the commitment of the Buddhas and Bodhisattvas to benefit all beings exists, they will never abandon their task. Thus it is said:

> *The sublime beings don't make many promises.*
> *If it happens that they agree to make a difficult promise,*
> *It is just like an image carved in stone:*
> *Even if death arrives, it can't be changed.*[208]

Therefore, in the first place, if one follows a lama possessed of the right characteristics, receives all of the most sacred teachings containing the profound essence, and applies oneself to the austerities of solitary retreat over many months or years, not only does one achieve the realization of dharmata, but because one hasn't any thoughts based on desire, the true identity of the Lord of the Family of Realized Ones—Vajradhara—manifests before one's senses as the miraculous display of a human being who has united the wisdom, love, and power of the final refuge. [The Lord is just such a human being]. As [Vajradhara] is the deity predestined by the flower,[209] over many eons [the Lord] accumulated the two factors [merit and wisdom] in great measure.

Considering the power unleashed from the moment an aspirational prayer is recited, these verses of praise are [appropriate] for this occasion:

> *The skillful acts and conduct that the Buddhas and their sons [the*
> *Bodhisattvas] exercise for [the benefit of] others, are difficult to*
> *understand,*
> *And impossible [to access] through speculative thought,*
> *As when the King of the Wise [the Buddha] manifested an impure*
> *birth [as a human], among other things.*

After these events, the Lord went begging at Khuye, where there were many shepherds from Khangtseg. When, upon his arrival, two dogs bit both his feet, the Lord thought, "Hey! Lama and the three Precious Jewels, look what's happening to me!" Then, many old friends who had played with him in his infancy chased the dogs away and offered him what little butter and churwa[210] they could steal. Similarly, all the nomads there offered him much food and drink, such as meat, butter, churwa, barley flour, and so on. Having obtained all this, he filled the large sack he used as a pillow with the provisions. While he slept that night, he dreamed that two monks appeared saying, "You've owed us a monk's shawl for years. Now, without fail, you must give it back." Then the Lord asked, "When did I take a monk's shawl belonging to you?" They replied:

The debt of the theft of our monk's shawl has generated five hundred rebirths during each of which you must pay, and there are still many left; in any event, you must return it now.

When they made this demand, the Lord answered:

Ho! How could I not repay this debt that is imbued with the truth of the infallibility of action, cause and effect?

In the Sutra of the Hundred Karmas,[211] *it is written:*

The karmic traces of beings who possess bodies will not disappear in a hundred eons. When the time and conditions are right, the fruit ripens.

Saying this, he thought, "How could I not give it back?" and leaving this visionary state, he awoke. The next day he set off at dawn, carrying the sack on his back and two sticks in his hands, feeling happy and thinking, "There won't be anyone as happy as we two, mother and son." When he reached the valley floor of Tsarnag, two thieves grabbed him from each side and, while one at a time they beat him as if they were cutting cane, his mind gradually entered the state in which cognition and phenomena are integrated, and there emerged [the memories of] his succession of past lives. One of these recalled lives occurred in a remote time when he was a great lama in an important monastery in Lhasa. In the monastery were two monks who began to quarrel with a third, and because of this, that important lama had them beaten and took their shawls saying, "Perhaps you'd be better off killing yourselves, you beggars," and other terrible things. It occurred to him that the present attack was the ripening of these actions, and he sang the following song:

A ho!
Infallible, really infallible are the Three Jewels!
Really, really true is the law of cause and effect!
Transgressions, my transgressions, are really negative actions!
Need, need, need produces the true debt!
Some lives ago I beat and robbed,
And continually squandering [the opportunities] of a hundred
    eons,
I designed the form of my own misdeeds.
Now, oh what a surprise! The fruit of all this repeatedly ripens.
It is extremely important to be aware of the infallibility of action,
    cause and effect.
All phenomena are the Three Jewels.
Ho, Protector, stop [what is happening]; protect my life!
It is a great truth that I am in the power of you two,
And though you devour my flesh and blood, there is no other way:
By the power of the root of virtue which is the offering of this
    excellent banquet,
Let the debts that have provoked this beating, the thefts
I committed in the past and their corresponding karma,
    be repaid!

Let both your karmic debts be paid through my offering,
And both your desires be wholly fulfilled!

As soon as the Lord had pronounced these words, after they had talked between themselves the two thieves took a little meat, butter, a cup, and a portion of cheese out of the sack and offered it to the Lord in the cup. Then the Lord said to them:

> *The fault was committed by myself, so I blame you not at all. Not only this time, but in many other lives I have repeatedly had to pay this debt. You should not be sorrowful in your hearts.*
> *May this food be an inexhaustible treasure in your lives! May it become the elixir of immortality! May your desires be fulfilled as they are conceived!*

Thus spoke the Lord and then one of the men—the one wearing a golden earring—began to shed such a flood of tears that they filled his eyes and, speaking insistently to his friend as they moved away, he repeatedly lowered his head. Then the man wearing a silver earring, on reaching a distant spot, kept looking back as they walked away.

Then the Lord, robbed by the two thieves, put what they had left him inside a pair of his old, torn boots, covered it with grass and leaves, and continued on his journey. Reaching Thangzang Chukhar, when he had walked a third of the way across the river, of all his torn clothes it was only his boots and the little food they contained that fell into the river and were carried away. Straightaway the Lord tried to go after them, but then, attaining the mental recognition of the natural state—dharmata— primordially free from its origin, he thought that if he crossed that river and the karmic causes matured, his feet would respond. It was not so. His feet were pulled out from under him by the current, and when he reached a flat and comfortable place downstream, after hanging up his clothes—which seemed more like battered old armor as they were made entirely of patches—he sat himself down, naked, to dry off.

He expressed the infallibility of the law of cause and effect in this prayer:

May the fruit of all nonvirtuous actions such as taking what is not given, committed by all beings that fill space ripen for me [alone]!
May all beings, starting with these two thieves, reach the level of the precious omniscient Buddhas thanks to the merit I have accumulated in the three times!

Thus he dedicated, and having generated bodhicitta which interchanges oneself with all others, he sealed it with a dedication [of merit] without object.

Then, in the mind of the Lord appeared the following:

A Tsi!
The law of cause and effect is subtle and precise!
Having put both boots inside my bag, the little I had was carried away by the water. From now on, I engrave in my mind the promise never to commit any of the ten negative actions—such as taking what has not been given—even if it costs me my life, until I have reached supreme realization, and at the same time I commit myself to learning the meaning of the Sutra of the Application of Mindfulness[212] and the Sutra of the Hundred Karmas.

Later, having dressed, it was time to continue his descent, and he thought:

A kha kha!
My old mother sits placing [a pot of] blue water on the kitchen fire. She will see that I bring nothing but this cup and just one of my old boots.

He went on his way, at times saddened by this thought and at others, closely examining the subtleties of the maturation of karma, and thus he reached his mother at Khangtseg. She was waiting for him and cooking a few turnips. The Lord told her of his dream, of how on his way back, the thieves had beaten him, taking almost all he had, and also of how in the past he had lived as a lama in Lhasa, explaining the story in all its detail. All this caused the mother to feel very happy, giving her a firm conviction in the law of cause and effect. She said, "Oh, no doubt it is thanks to the compassion of the Three Jewels that the two thieves didn't kill you," and mother and son remained together for some time.

[I add] these intermediate verses given to the disciples in praise of the teaching on the infallibility of the law of cause and effect in relation to the wise actions of the Supreme Protector, the Precious Lord of the Siddhas [the Buddha]:

> To illustrate the infallibility of the law of cause and effect to an
>   assembly of disciples,
> And demonstrate the significance of stealing, he explained that
> Due to [the theft of] five hundred karshapani²¹³ by the brahmins,
> [Even] the arrival of [the Buddha,] the King of the Wise was
>   impeded by obstacles.

Later, when the Lord went begging at Dzitritog, [he obtained] from the abbot's house one dre of barley, and inside the entrance where an assembly was celebrating a zur-offering (by burning food), he picked up some of the food and ate it. Previously, he had carried a karmic debt, but from this time on [his deeds] did not lead to accumulation [of karmic debt]. He took a torma and any offering he could find. From the monk Yönten Yeshe he received four balls of dried turnip [paste]; from Namdag Yeshe, a plate of perfect turnips; from the old matron Sadagmen, a cup of tsampa and another of barley; Trashi Phüntsog offered him three cups of cooked turnips; from Khengyal's house he received two dre of good turnips, and from Yaksha's residence, a good dish full of food. At Sönam Gyatso's residence, after being invited to the terrace, they gave him excellent tea with barley flour soaked in tea and butter. But when he reached the door of the residence of lama Gyurme from Gyokyang, the terrifying house dog Gyawo[214] appeared and bit his hands and feet until Karma Tendzin stopped it and invited him in. Lama Gyurme cured his wounds, saying:

> *My mother and I have dreamed that the sun's radiance extended all over [this world,] Dzambu Ling, indicating that someone really outstanding would arrive, and that his fame would reach all the kingdoms.*

Saying this, Karma Tendzin gave him a gilded tin container with two dre of barley and good bone marrow, adopting a very considerate attitude, and accompanied him a long way [on his journey].

When he returned to his mother's side in Khangtseg they lived off the food until autumn.

Then the Lord had a dream of shining light in which a country named Makhog appeared. In the center, surrounded by numerous, immense, rocky mountains, was a mountain that embraced the earth, extending further than the eye could see. It was armored with indestructible rocks, wrapped in a turban of camphor (glaciers) and dotted with many lakes of pure water. A strong current of water [that ran] through the silent canyons reached into the distance, passing the dwellings of nomads and farmers. In the very center of this enormous country of perfect prosperity there were thousands of dwellings in which food and cloth were stored, separated into different kinds, such as silk, brocade, and cotton—the three best kinds of cloth—as well as various kinds of precious materials like gold, silver, and turquoise. There were also many kinds of food, such as tea, beer, milk, and yogurt. All [the houses] were so stocked, lacking nothing. Such prosperity could compete with the five sensual pleasures of the gods. Further, seeing that many storehouses were empty [the Lord asked], "What are these storehouses?" and they replied, "These empty

storehouses are only for the barley arriving from outside our territories."
As they spoke these words, a great variety of grazing animals such as deer,
antelope, wild goats, donkeys, and wild yaks appeared carrying many
loads of wheat and barley. Also, many different species of birds, such as
eagles, peacocks, vultures, and hawks arrived, all calling: "*Ki so!*" and other
cries, carrying loads of barley and other grain on their backs. Once [the
grain] was put away in the empty storehouses, everyone felt something
akin to pure happiness, but when [the Lord] emerged from the natural
luminosity [of the dream], all [the fields] in his country [Nyarong] had
been attacked by blight, hail, and frost. A great famine was certain to be
the result. The thought appeared in the Lord's mind that there is no way
to avoid the ripening [of the karma] resulting from taking something
that was not given.

After a few days the storm clouds gathered and darkened, and suddenly a hailstorm broke accompanied by the furious roaring of the [thun-
der-] dragon, destroying that year's entire rice harvest, leaving nothing.
After that, anything that remained in Nyarong[215] was completely ruined
by frost. The Lord explained that, because there was no harvest, he had
to go to Khangtseg and other places to pick up a few leftover tormas in
order to feed himself during the autumn.

In winter, begging inside his uncle Tagla's monastery, he could only get
a few turnips. Since they had nothing to eat, mother and son went begging
in richer countries, but unable to get any food or drink whatsoever, they
returned to the mother's house. One day when the mother was weeping
bitterly over her sufferings, the Lord sang this *Song of the Impermanence
of Life's Happiness and Suffering*:

> *Mother, stop crying, and listen to your son's song!*
> *Prosperous places are not permanent,*
> *And neither are we two vagrants.*
> *This sadness and happiness are like last night's dream.*
> *What good or bad is there in impermanence?*
> *Everything the rich eat and drink is a cause of suffering.*

The poor food you and I eat is perfect,
The hungry ghosts who, for so many years, never get food and
drink,
Have acquired their avidity by being obsessed [with consump-
tion]!
Not getting mixed up in wrongdoing
Has been praised by the Victorious Ones as the best of foods.
You can be satisfied with these pure foods!

After the song, the mother said: "This is certainly true, my son," and she felt much better. Being afflicted by extreme poverty, they had no clothes for their bodies nor cups [from which to eat], and so they had to use the hollows in the turnips for cups and they slept in the [tall] grass of the plains. Once they came to a dung heap, but were not allowed to stay there.

After this, although he went begging to Dzikhugmo and Dzitridrog among other places, all that year because of the great famine he only got a bit [of food]. He managed to get some torma left over from an offering ritual, and he ate half and took half back to his mother. He also went up and down the valleys and plains, and although he returned to the places where he had begged before, they only gave him a few turnips. Begging in the village of Nyingye, he managed to get some good food, such as turnips. Even though he went to two or three large villages, all that year because of the famine he could get no more than a few cups of flour and about three dre of good turnips. The Lord explained that except for about a cupful of barley flour and a couple of turnips, he saved everything he could lay his hands on, thinking that he must give it to his mother who had borne him, and feeling great loving compassion towards her. Keeping this in his heart, he brought her what little he'd obtained.

When he arrived at the monastic residence of Tsewang Dargye in Butong, [the monks] were consecrating a vase of medicinal pills and, because he had not managed to get anything during the last six days, [the Lord] spent a week with the beggars of Lagthu and other places, as he knew them from the past. In these circumstances he had to live off food thrown away by the other beggars. After six days a great assembly gathered, presided over by the lama from Chagdü called Namdag. When lama Namdag sat on the upper floor [of the temple] he thought that the Lord, too, should sit among the assembly, and said so to Tsewang Dargye [the monastery's benefactor]. He, however, replied, "Impossible!" so on that day [the Lord] was not allowed to enter and remained among the beggars.

The next day, seeing [the Lord] from the terrace, Lama Namdag shared the following reflections with Tsewang Dargye:

> *Benefactor who has faith, listen to me!*
> *The lad who is hanging 'round the door these days is the younger*
> *son of Khangtseg, whose family were great patrons [of the Doctrine]*
> *when they were wealthy. Six days after this supreme incarnation left*
> *the lotus vagina, I myself went and, being next to him, saw how*
> *the tiny reincarnation maintained an unusually peaceful posture,*
> *accompanied by a sensation of delight. I saw how, through a dance*
> *of wrathful gestures, with his mouth he formulated harmonious*
> *vajra sounds seven times. Never in all my life have I met such a*
> *marvelous incarnation possessing such unimaginable virtues. You,*
> *Tsewang Dargye, must now place this sublime reincarnation in the*
> *best row of the assembly.*

At this, the benefactor, a devout man incapable of [ignoring] the indications of the lama of Chagdü, ordered that [the Lord] should be seated downstairs among the rows of the assembly.

Thus, in the biographies of great realized beings, the Buddhas' and Bodhisattvas' wise and skillful activity aimed at strengthening our belief in the infallibility of the law of cause and effect, overshadowed as it is in this degenerate age by the power of ignorance, is difficult to judge with the ordinary intellect. Because they are not conditioned by desire, all these great realized beings physically reveal themselves before the senses [of ordinary beings] as the unification of the powerful, omniscient love of the Victorious Ones of the three times, appearing as the play of a person who has come to convert beings. Furthermore, because they are not ordinary people and display countless, true signs as visible phenomena, I dedicate these lines to my Lord:

> *[From] the single sphere of wisdom, love, and omniscience of all*
> *the Victorious Ones,*
> *With the aim of demonstrating discernment of the infallible law*
> *of cause and effect*
> *To beings afflicted by the devil: ignorance of their own primordial*
> *nature,*
> *[The Lord] appears in the disciples' perception as a human being,*
> *Showing, in several ways, the activities of a worthless beggar.*
> *Removing himself from violent people obstructed by negative*
> *karma,*
> *Although the material goods he enjoyed have been plundered*
> *without exception,*
> *In their great love, his actions are comparable to those of the King*
> *of the Wise.*
> *Thus, he demonstrates this conduct through exceptionally skillful*
> *means.*

Then, while [the Lord] was in the back row of the great assembly, Lama Namdag from Chagdü looked sad enough to cry and, collecting a little barley flour from those assembled, he placed it in the Lord's provision sack. Another lama from Chagdü, Jigme Künzang, offered him some good food.

On that very same occasion the lama taught the mantra, 'A ra pa tsa na dhi,' and the vowels and consonants written in the lantsa[216] script, and immediately on seeing them, the Lord began to whisper, "Sha ra ra." The monks, motivated by pride, cried: "You can hardly feed yourself with what you get from begging! You can't recite from the Indian lantsa writing! How dare you!" and other humiliating words.

The preceptor Shantideva who, as a Bodhisattva, knew just how deep are the abysses of hell said that, according to the Buddha, one should tell the patrons that if they give rise to malevolent thoughts towards Bodhisattvas like the one to which we are referring, they will remain in the hells for as many cosmic eons as the number of their negative thoughts. Accordingly, when those monks who were accumulating the disgrace of the hells told [the lama] what had happened, the lama from Chagdü responded by saying:

> Don't say that, you perpetrators of perverse acts!
> As Jamyang Sapen said:

> "Though you may possess the highest virtues,
> If you dress humbly, you will be despised by all."

And also:

> "Just as the depths of the earth conceal precious gems,
> So those born into poverty possess good qualities."

> Thus, do not accumulate the negative karma that will thrust you
> into the hell regions!

The same lama spoke kindly to the Lord, saying, "You will become a person whose fame shall extend in all directions."

Then, when the assembly was called for the Consecration of the Vase for which they distributed the empowered pills, the Lord left. When he was passing through a wood of tarbu[217] between the towns of Nyingye and Gyashö, two thieves appeared. Grabbing hold of his hands from both sides they snatched away the bag he carried on his shoulder. When they were about to leave, [the Lord remembered] how in a remote lifetime he had been born in Nepal as a man called Alo, who was rich, powerful, and famous. On one occasion, at age twenty he had taken some serzho (coins) belonging to some beggars. The fact that these few coins had been obtained by begging caused the maturing of the act of theft to last for many lives, leading [the Lord] to suffer similar thefts. Thus, realizing that due to the maturing of the karma those two beggars had become the people who were now robbing him, from the depths of his heart he sang this song on the ripening of karma:

> *Protector who shows the infallibility of the fruit of karma, think*
> *of me!*
> *You two [thieves] who are like my father and mother,*
> *Were under the power of a great debt.*
> *[Knowing this], how can I even feel sadness*
> *As negligible as a sesame seed?*
> *If I did, I should be punished by the Three True Jewels.*
> *I am happy that cause and effect are infallible.*
> *I committed bad actions:*
> *In a past life in Nepal I was known as Alo,*
> *And had power, wealth, and elegance,*
> *While you were begging due to your past karma.*
> *No matter how many gold coins I found in the sand,*
> *I gave you only half, keeping the other half for myself.*
> *The maturing of these acts is not yet complete,*
> *And though I have repeatedly made offerings, still I must pay.*
> *You are right and need no karmic debt, therefore:*
> *By the virtuous offering of this excellent food,*
> *In the succession of all your future lives until the ocean of eons is*
> *emptied,*
> *May you completely fulfill the ocean of the two accumulations!*
> *May you enjoy the treasure of this inexhaustible ocean!*
> *May you mature the ocean of beings to be converted!*

When he sang this, the two thieves set the sack aside, opened it, and looked inside to see what was in it. They took about a dre of the cooked food that had been offered at his patron's residence as well as the tea and most of the barley flour and wheat. Placing the sack, a small bag, and a little cup of food in the Lord's hands, the two thieves went off.

Then, setting off for the highlands to beg, he carried what little food he had received from the country people he had met there. Thus he arrived at his mother's, in the town of Khangtseg, and offered her all that the thieves had not taken.

The Lord explained that these were the sufferings shared by mother and son over many years.

In the same vein, a savage thief robbed mother and son their dzomo. When the mother burst into tears, the Lord, thanks to the characteristic clairvoyance of the Noble Ones, clearly stated that the Protectors would bring the dzomo back home, and said to his mother, "Mother, don't cry. The dzomo has now come back." Although his old mother thought it was a lie and did not take it seriously, the dzomo appeared back in its own stable.

There are numerous stories depicting the Lord's endurance of a great variety of circumstances of happiness and suffering and his manifestation of knowledge based on the clarity of his illuminated mind, but in this work all is presented in brief.

In verses:

By walking the three paths of virtuous action,
He adopted the activities of a beggar
In order to teach the law of karma and its fruits
To blind sentient beings who follow rejection and acceptance.
By benefiting whomever I encounter,
May I become like you!

CHAPTER FOUR

*Following the Prophecy of [Avalokiteshvara]
the Great Compassionate One, How He Guided
Beings Through the Practice of Jokhor.*

🌺 At a certain time, during sleep or in some type of vision, the Lord was transported instantly to Khechara where the great secret of Oddiyana unfolds. There was the wisdom-dakini Vajrayogini, wearing her bone ornaments, carrying her drigug[218] and blood-filled kapala[219] and serving as the main deity. Surrounding her was a large assembly of Knowledge Holders bearing heruka implements, as well as an assembly of yoginis similar to the main deity, [appearing] in a manner ungraspable by the intellect. "*Hum*" resounded from all their mouths, and all present smiled radiantly as they said, "Welcome, great daka."

The queen gave him the initiation with the drigug and the blood-filled kapala, and, placing some texts in his hands, together they all said:

*Oh son, you must mentally apprehend the whole of the Doctrine
without exception!
One day, when realization has arisen in your mind, you must
guide innumerable beings!*

On waking from this dream or vision, he had an experience of inexpressible bliss and happiness based on emptiness and luminosity. On other occasions, in dreams and visions [the Lord] knew precisely what the various positive and negative outcomes—in both happiness and suffering—would be like in all countries, particularly in his own, even before they occurred. He explained, in confidence, exactly what would happen to many people whom he met. Others heard about this, and observed by all, they said, "Trashi Döndrub is omniscient!" and this is how he became known everywhere.

At the age of thirteen, the observance of spiritual life and the practice of the Dharma blossomed naturally in him, and his capacity for intellectual knowledge expanded. Similarly, having cleared his spiritual intention of obstacles, he could plainly see both his meritorious karma and his other karma, accumulated over many lives from the remote past. In particular, he vividly recalled a group consisting of king [Trisong Deutsen] and his subjects [the twenty-four other disciples] following the Great Guru Orgyan[220] into the Glorious monastery of Samye. He remembered, never to forget again, the numerous vast and profound instructions of the Great Orgyan. To sum up, he saw only [his] births as spiritual nobility including those as Indian adepts such as the prince and Great Adept Damdzin who was in the presence of Padma. He also [saw his births] as Orgyan Sangye Lingpa, who opened profound spiritual treasures, and as the Sovereign of the Hundred Siddhas, the Dharma Lord Natsog Rangdröl.

Up to this point, this story has consisted of the life he had to lead as a beggar following the death of his father.

At the age of fifteen, from his uncle, the great Knowledge Holder Drodül Ösal Dorje—also known as Künzang Düdjom—who was the miraculous [incarnation] of the translator Palgyi Yeshe, he received the initiation and reading transmissions of the revealed treasure, the complete cycle of the *Heart Essence of Venerable Tara*,[221] and [this master] gave him the following instruction:

> "*From the direction of Nya[rong],*
> *Will appear one who bears the name Düdul.*
> *Whoever enters into contact with him will multiply his virtues.*"

*This statement, to be found in the index of my revealed treasures,
doubtlessly refers to you.*

Progressively, as the instant presence of his contemplation was enormously
sharpened, he began to perform the practices of his own tradition, all the
tantric cycles, the recitations [for increasing] the intellect, musical pieces,
the preparation of food, and so on, excelling among his companions and
causing his erudition to be praised.

At that time, the inhabitants of Nyarong being a horde of igno-
ramuses, to find a master who could explain canonical texts, teach the
preparation of a mandala, make sculptures, or write syllables was as difficult as seeing a star by day. But because Mahakaruna and the Venerable
Tara with their youthful faces had appeared to him, the Lord knew how
to draw divinities and engrave essential [mantras] on rocks using the
Indian scripts lantsa and warthu,[222] which he had never seen. All this
had appeared in his dreams, and having been instructed by the divinities
themselves, he became a great connoisseur of painting as well as smithery
and woodcarving.

Also, the Sovereign of Mantras Mahakala and other guardians appeared to him disguised as monks and were very friendly towards him. At
this time, being among the ranks of disciples of Lama Sönam Tsültrim, he
made the chatröl mudra[223] for the rites of realization of the Three Bodies
which he had never learned, causing great surprise. Then, some stupid
coreligionists entered into the spirit of competition by saying that these
practices were undesirable and unnecessary. Some others, who had pure
vision, said that these were doubtlessly the result of residual karma from
the Lord's past practices, which had become activated, and [on saying
this] they felt even more delighted.

On reaching the age of eighteen he had an experience in which dream
and vision were one, and he saw the immeasurable suffering of the lower
hells. The vision contained the aspects of panic and terror of all dimensions.
In the place where one could hear, "Kill! Kill! Destroy! Destroy! Phat!Phat!"
and, "Hum! Hum!" were the innumerable servants of the Lord of Death

looking like karmic butchers with imposing, nauseating faces. On a high throne covered in brocade, copper, and iron was the Dharmaraja Lord of Death, dark brown in color and of extremely wrathful appearance. Before him were the two princes of karma, one white, the other black, differentiating between virtue and wrongdoing. The wrongdoers were chained and led by various types of servants of the many-headed Lord of Death, toward the infernal cauldrons filled with molten copper. The virtuous were invited to enter the path by many lamas, excellent guides who led them to a white path of pleasant appearance heading upward. Then, thinking, "Although I am not worried about having to go to the copper hell, I feel compassion for those beings with bad karma," as soon as he began to beg the lamas and the Three Jewels, there appeared before him the smiling and peaceful Mahakaruna,[224] the supreme divinity who is a master. [The Lord] asked:

> *My master Mahakaruna,*
> *I feel great pity for those beings,*
> *Is there no way to lead them—my fathers and mothers*
>   *—to freedom?*

Mahakaruna replied:

> *Yes, there's a way. Follow me, my son, maintaining that*
>   *compassion.*

As the Lord followed the master Mahakaruna along a pleasant path resembling a crystal staircase, there instantly appeared a beautiful and exquisite paradise with a wish-fulfilling tree, a fountain of nectar, a garden of many kinds of flowers, birds singing the six-syllable mantra in beautiful tones, and so on—everything possessed of great qualities. In the center of this kingdom was a celestial dwelling made of precious materials, all perfect. There, on a throne of brocade and lotus, the previously mentioned great master [Mahakaruna] shone with intense glory, adorned with the thirteen ornaments bestowing ultimate peace. On his right and left were White Tara and Green Tara; in the intermediate directions were many Bodhisattvas and adepts—male and female—from India and Tibet. [Then the Lord begged Mahakaruna]:

> My compassionate Master, I beg you to show me the way to free
> those beings!

Mahakaruna replied to this by holding in his hand an object similar to the *jokhor* of existence[225] of the human realm of the universe. Spinning it with his right hand, the master and his retinue began to sing the melody of the six-syllable mantra. Finally, after spinning [the *jokhor*] for a long time, he held it in his hand and placed it on the Lord's crown, saying three times:

> Son, guide those beings by spinning a Dharma wheel like this
> one.

Waking from this dream and vision, he was full of compassion for the beings he had seen in the infernal vision and, remembering the Noble Ones he had seen and the pure realms, he felt increasing joy. Thus did these two feelings arise.

The next day, when he told his mother of the vision, she said:

> Although Mahakaruna and the pure realms that you have seen are
> something really positive, you shouldn't tell anybody you've had these
> pure and impure visions. In these decadent times, many say they
> have seen gods and devils, but who believes them?

To which the Lord replied:

> The Noble Mahakaruna prophesied that if I spin the jokhor it
> will be an excellent thing.

The mother added:

That is really good! Last night I—a poor old woman—also had a dream. In the dream, from a mountaintop appeared a sun glowing with intensely bright light, and in the sky, among the colors of the rainbow, were many lamas proclaiming the presence of Oddiyana Padmasambhava and the Noble Avalokiteshvara. They all held a jokhor in their hands and spun it, and finally they gave it to you. By spinning it, you caused the jokhor to send out rays of light as bright as sunlight, lighting all the kingdoms. This must be an auspicious sign.

Therefore, mother and son agreed and within a month they had accumulated everything necessary for the *jokhor*, which they constructed with all its characteristics. They asked his uncle, the lama Kunzang Sonam, to consecrate it. The lama had also had a dream the previous night:

I dreamed that on a great plain covered with many kinds of flowers, there was a white silk parasol sheltering a high throne. You sat on the throne giving Dharma teachings, during which many marvelous signs appeared. This jokhor will bring benefit to beings.

He consecrated it and recited aspirational prayers. Then, [the Lord] met a member of his paternal clan, the monk Tendzin who was greatly interested in the Doctrine and whom [the Lord] had known since childhood. When [the Lord] asked him to be his companion, [Tendzin] felt very happy, and said:

I'll go! This is a very positive connection! Later, we two shall be upholders of the practice lineage and shall benefit all beings by showing them the path to liberation, thanks to the interdependent connection which makes this possible.

Later, on the way to Dzikhog [the Lord] met two men on the road and asked them their names. "Our names are Namkha Tsering and Chödzin," they replied. They said that the night before, one of them had dreamt that suddenly hundreds of suns and moons appeared; the other had dreamt that the sound of the white conch of the Dharma spread throughout the universe. Also, the chief of the nomads Norbu Samdrub and other chiefs invited the Lord and his disciple, paying them great homage. Some people with few karmic impediments said that they had dreamt that in the sky were hundreds of steps made from precious materials upon which several million beings were being carried toward a mountain made of gems. On [hearing about] these dreams, with great heartfelt devotion, monks, laymen, and beggars cried, "The lama with the *jokhor* has arrived!"

The Lord and his disciple were led on horseback all around upper and lower Dzikhog and upper and lower Logkhog. They were accompanied by the melodies of the lotus song of *Salje Drönma* and *Kayig Sumchui Peyang* of the Lord Karmapa, as well as songs from the writings describing the visions of the delog[226] Changchub Senge, as all the while they spun the *jokhor*. The Lord devoted himself mainly to introducing countless people to the methods of accumulation and purification, and with his melodious voice he inspired true faith in the depths of his hearers' hearts, causing everyone in the bustling marketplaces to shed tears of great, sincere devotion, and many were established on the path to liberation.

On one occasion, two dishonest people appeared at the Lord's tent planning to rob them later that night. At that instant the Lord, knowing their thoughts by clairvoyance, said, "You two, take the *jokhor* and everything I own!" Saying this, he took everything out [of his tent]. Immediately—as certainty was born in their minds—the two thieves confessed and offered [the Lord] a ball of butter and one of cheese.

To all the inhabitants of that place, monks and laymen alike, The Lord offered a little of the gift of the teaching on the difficulty of obtaining a human birth, on the certainty of death and impermanence, and on the results of karmic causes, thereby managing to help them by [motivating them to] abandon negative acts and cultivate virtue such as [not kill-ing] defenceless animals like mice or yak's calfs, to save lives [of animals destined for slaughter], give alms to the needy, spread [the Doctrine] of the Buddha, carve the six-syllable mantra on rocks, [recite it] millions of times, and so on.

Then the Lord and his disciple went to meet the precious incarnate Guru Tendzin from Ne. The incarnation very kindly offered them initia-tions and textual authorizations for the *Leu Dünpa*[227] and other texts of the *Treasures from the North*.[228] In this way he responded to signs favoring the request to receive the meditation method for realization from the *Transparence of Samantabhadra's Realization*.[229]

At this time, mother and son had no possessions, and when they went looking for food, they found little. They went back to their own district. Guiding his assistant—his old companion Tendzin—and his younger brother Norbu, they set off for Khyobe. On the way, at a place called Rinang, the lady Yeshe Drölma came to meet them. In this lady's dreams a great silk tent crowned by a golden jewel had appeared, and pleasant music spread throughout all dimensions.

Later they spent about a month in a place called Phülo where they performed prostrations and circumambulations around the three principal relics [stupas, statues and writings]. Then they went with their disciples to a place called Gongtong. There they met the Bönpo lama Yeshe Özer, who had a dream that a young, new sun would emerge from a mountain in the east, radiating hundreds of light rays upon millions of beings.

Then they reached upper and lower Khyobe, and to the rhythm of the lute [the Lord] offered verses and spun the *jokhor*, offering the gift of the Dharma and sowing the good seeds of liberation for rich and poor, for monks as well as laypersons. Also, in that region there was a great river where the inhabitants used to fish. He made them promise to protect the lives of these animals. He got them to recite hundreds of millions of *mani* and *siddhi* mantras[230] and to engrave the six-syllable mantra on the rocks. Thus he labored to benefit all beings.

With the offerings of the devout and those made for the good of the dead, he made a thardo[231] and a nadig[232] of the two precious materials [gold and silver]. He also commissioned the fabrication of all the components of a *jokhor* and, in recognition of his mother's love, he took some red copper objects that had been given to him [as offerings] and returned to his country.

Then in the land of Shanglang Shipa, as above, he offered all the nomads of the highlands and lowlands a little spiritual advice while turning the *jokhor*, bringing benefit to all beings who [on hearing him] renounced their evil actions and cultivated virtue. Also, going to the markets in that nomadic region, he did the same. In summary, while he was spinning the *jokhor*, as soon as he began to speak about the four thoughts that direct the mind toward the Dharma[233] and [toward Taking] Refuge,[234] the laypersons, monks and beggars became inclined towards the Doctrine.

Thanks to the power of his vision of the supreme tutelary deity Mahakaruna and to the prophecy he was given, from the moment he spun the *jokhor*, neither he nor his mother ever experienced the misery of poverty again.

The Lord also explained how he acted for the benefit of all beings and the Doctrine in other places.

At this time, some fifteen fortunate people who had faith and good fortune, such as Namdag, Tsültrim, Lama Tsering, and others, received auspicious signs on meeting the Lord. In fear of writing [too much], I'll say no more about this. Although detailed [explanations] exist on the mode of perceiving the infernal appearances, since many sections of the master's teachings have been scattered, I have not been able to obtain the manuscript [in which these subjects are detailed]. What is written here is enough [to provide] a general idea.

In verses:

Having seen the loving faces of all Sugatas
And the joyful fortunate ones,

He obtained relief through knowledge
Of the arts of taming whoever must be tamed.
May I be reborn at the feet of this guru, the supreme guide!

CHAPTER FIVE

How He Followed Various Masters and Realized the Profound Understanding

🌸 When he reached the age of twenty-one, there was a battle between [the forces of] upper and lower Nyarong, each region considering the other its enemy. The chief of Nyagke, becoming hostile, invaded Khangtseg, the Lord's paternal country, stealing cattle,[235] and three or four people were killed. A half-brother of the Lord, a man called Norbu, guided them. Because the Lord's sibling escaped, the chief of Rinang thought of taking the Lord and his mother to the conflict zone in Nyagke. Consequently, the Lord had to go to Bugta, in Rinang. But by the power of the connection [engendered] by the aspirational prayer [recited] prior to these events, when the reincarnation of the Omniscient Jigme Lingpa, Yeshe Dorje Rölpatsal,[236] also known as Tülku Khyentse Rinpoche, came to mediate and make peace between upper and lower Nyarong, he sTayed among them for some months. Among other things, he taught *The Gathering of the Knowledge Holders,*[237] and gave many initiations and textual authorizations from the *Heart Essence,* such as *Yumka,*[238] as well as instructions on their preliminary [practices]. He also gave other teachings and conferred the reading transmission and brief instructions for *The Transcendent Wisdom Master.*[239] He gave profound special instructions to the Lord, saying [to him]:

Oh my son, if you can exert yourself onepointedly during the practice, you will be able to realize incalculable good for the Doctrine and all beings.

Thanks to the indications of Khyentse Rinpoche, the sibling of the Lord and another seven men were freed from prison by the chief of Nyagked.

Then the Lord returned to his country. Because Gyalse Rigdzin Kalzang Deutsen of Trozur had also come to Lhang Lhang and Shangshi, [the Lord] received from him various initiations and reading transmissions such as *Kilaya*.[240] The lama said:

Oh son, you are a fortunate person with good karma! As you apply yourself to the path, good will come to all beings.

At one moment in time, during a vision, he was transported to Zangdog Pelri.[241] There he found the Precious Guru and Trisong Deutsen together with the twenty-four subjects[242] and an ocean of millions of realized beings from India and Tibet. They authorized him [to teach] and blessed his mind. During the vision he also went to Tushita, and there the protector Maitreya and the unimaginably pure Bodhisattvas of the tenth level—such as the omniscient Tsongkhapa—surrounded him and gave him permission [to teach]. But since I have not been able to find writings detailing this vision, I cannot go into more depth. For a general understanding, this explanation will suffice.

Then, in the presence of his uncle Terchen Kunzang Düdjom he remained in the monastery for a long period, serving as a scribe of the numerous sections of the lama's Dharma treasures that had just been revealed[243] and assisting with the rituals. When the great tertön left to work for the benefit of all beings in different regions, [the Lord] decided to follow him [and serve] as his assistant.

Feeling satisfied with the Lord due to his effective service, the master gave him many oral instructions and much profound advice. The Lord asked him about the genuine mental attitude centered on the Dharma, and the method for realizing the true nature of mind. The lama replied:

> *Oh son, your previous births were noble, doubtlessly of good [spiritual] lineage, and your intellect is clear. If you leave these uncertainties behind, you will undoubtedly bring much benefit to sentient beings.*

Later, spinning the *jokhor* on his way to the market, he met Lama Palden from Dzaka and obtained from him some initiations and reading transmissions. At this time he also met several of the Sakyapa and Ngorpa masters and those from [the monasteries of] Kathog and Dzogchen. In the presence of them all, he received some initiations and reading transmissions. On returning to his home country, the master Wangchen Rabten of the lineage of Rinchen Lingpa[244] arrived, and he received from him more initiations and teachings. Then Lama Gyurme Gyatso who possessed the capacity to attain self-realization in a single lifetime and who had vowed to remain in retreat for thirteen years, on finishing his retreat, went to the hermitage at Dragkar and there performed a ritual fumigation and circumambulation of the place. There [the Lord] sTayed with him, acting as his assistant for about a month. The lama gave him much advice and profound instruction. The Lord asked him what was the mental attitude [required] to realize true virtue, and how does one remain in the natural condition, the nature of mind or Buddha Nature.[245] The lama obliged him, saying:

> *Many masters made prophecies before your birth. At your birth there were also many signs of all kinds. In this place, if you persevere in your practice, you will certainly become a great being, a holder of the Doctrine.*

Later, when the great practitioner left to spread the gift of the Doctrine that limitlessly benefits all beings—the offering of the Jewel—[the Lord] also acted as his assistant in the fields of lower Nyag and all its great valleys, doing unimaginable good for all beings [by expounding on] the abandonment of wrongdoing and the cultivation of virtue.

At this time, back in his country, something occurred that illustrated the Great Preceptor [Padmasambhava's] observation: "When [one is] practicing the Dharma in a pure way, there arise many opportunities for entering the narrow demonic paths." The Lord spoke of a premonition he had had at twenty-four which indicated the appearance of deceptive obstacles appearing [before] sublime beings:

> *The body seemed dressed in beauty, and in my mind there*
> *   emerged the torment of desire.*

In his perfect thought the Lord said:

> *These are not good thoughts. From my youth until today I have*
> *maintained my practice commitment as pure as a crystal sphere.*
> *He who has practiced white virtue in this life is now defeated by a*
> *sinful [thought].*

He composed many songs on this matter. The Lord prayed firmly and fervently to the guru and the Three Jewels[246] and devoted himself diligently to the practice of Pema Dragpo. Concentrating on the profound state of the [integration of] vision and meditation and remaining in that state, in a moment during sleep he had [this experience]:

A seductive girl appeared. From this moment, as his sleep was submerged in the clear light and he realized that this was a spell cast by a gyalpo or demon, he took the girl by the hair, threw her into space and cast her nine times against the earth. Because this was a magical [appearance, the girl] became a red bird. After he had cast down the red bird nine times, it became an owl bearing the marks of a theurang. After he cast down the owl nine times, it turned into a monkey with the characteristics of a gyalgong.

After he cast down the monkey, it became a rat with the characteristics of a sinmo.[247] After he cast the rat down nine times, it transformed into a white "*A*," with the characteristics of liberated consciousness. This condition occurred as a blazing dream in space.

The day after this experience, the demonic spell being pacified, the Lord said he once again felt disgust for and desire to renounce samsara, and he developed devotion towards the Doctrine, and great perseverance.

At the age of twenty-five, he heard that Pema Gyurme Sangye, the great adept renowned throughout all Dokham for his ability to liberate beings through his compassion, was going to Tromkhog. Feeling a persistent devotion toward the lama, he sought an occasion to meet him. He found him giving teachings to a crowd in the marketplace and, on meeting [the Lord, the lama] immediately said:

> *Oh young monk, you are very fortunate, and for many lives you have united the two accumulations and purified obstacles. You are the emanation of many excellent beings. Last night I dreamt that a yogi who told me he was an emanation of Lord Atisha, of the All-Powerful Milarepa, and also of Tsele Natsog Rangdröl was on the immaculate summit of a crystal mountain from which emerged a white path. Millions of beings followed him on that path.*

Then, those who had come to listen to the teachings were filled with boundless joy and faith in the lama. From this master [the Lord] received some initiations and reading transmissions for the *Heart Essence of the Great Expanse* cycle, along with some other initiations. [The lama] gave numerous profound words of advice and prophecies for the future, and gave him the name Pema Düdul. He also said:

> *If you can manage to center yourself solely on practice in the holy place of the rock at Shang Lang,[248] you will produce immeasurable benefit for all beings.*

He also received initiations and reading transmissions from Drodül Tragthung Dorje, who told him:

> *Anyone who acquires a karmic connection with you will certainly be guided to Chamara.*[249]

Returning to his paternal country in the Male Iron Rat year (1840), it so happened that the Lord, cultivating the [non-dual] state of vision and meditation, received a manuscript in the language of the dakinis [containing the list of termas he was to discover]. At this the Lord said:

> *In the spontaneous celestial space of perfect, pristine, primordial purity were the five families of dakinis, the miraculous unfolding of Transcendent Wisdom. Each one of them carried in her hands several manuscripts of symbolic writing. They were very loving towards me.*

Thus, as he explained, being the dakinis of the Buddha, Vajra, Jewel, Lotus, and Karma families, each one carried a manuscript with symbolic writing in blue, white, yellow, red, and green, respectively, all clearly written in the symbolic dakini script. "They gave me those manuscripts," said the Lord.

Then, in the year of the Male Fire Horse (1846), Drubpai Wangchuk Namkha Gyatso arrived with the intention of benefiting all beings. Also [the Lord] went before the Great Adept of Tsophu, Gyurme Chöying Rangdröl whose name resounds as far as the deities' drum which can eradicate the violent suffering of the universe, to ask him about the profound instructions on obtaining irreversible bodhi in this life. The Lord said:

> *I have rejected the pleasures and comforts of this life, and have venerated the profound advice aimed at the attainment of the qualities of the paths and the levels of realization. Abandoning the eight worldly dharmas,*[250] *I have longed for the instructions that cause the emergence of the state beyond meditation. Having renounced the illusory*

experiences of worldly people, I desire the profound instructions for realizing the four visions.[251]

Thus he spoke.

Searching for offerings (suitable to accompany) a request for teachings, he could only find one or two pieces of clothing. His uncle, the great tertön, gave him a packet of tea and two gyama of butter. Then, with some friends who had arrived to receive teachings, he reached the circle of snowy mountains of Sharshingo. When they met him, the lama appeared clearly before their senses as the miraculous aspect of Vajradhara in human form. The lama said to him:

First, it is necessary to receive the initiations that lead to the maturation of the mind, and the general preliminaries of the The Vajra Heart of the Luminous Expanse.[252] *Later, the preliminaries of Total Relaxation and Direct Leap*[253] *[will be] given in detail.*

During the period when he trained in the teaching of the Transference practice,[254] the marvelous signs of realizing this practice spontaneously appeared on the crown of the Lord's [head]. Later, some fortunate people went to find him, and their meeting became a celebration in which the fortunate desire not to return to samsara became settled in their minds. Those people had already been trained in the past.

He practiced the meditations of the profound path of Transference as well as meditations with no characteristics or name, with the aim of entering into the meditation with characteristics; further, using *The Vajra Heart of the Luminous Expanse* text, he perfectly followed the instructions on the channels and energies.

During this time, because he had no suitable provisions, Ane Lhamo—the lama's assistant—often gave him good quality food. Also, in that same place and from several masters he received, in an inconceivable manner, teachings on the *Mother and Son Heart Essence*[255] and on the cycles of [the tertöns] Mingling Terchen and his brother [Lochen Dharma

Shri],[256] of Godemchen, Düdul Lingpa,[257] Longsal [Nyingpo],[258] and of Ratna Lingpa,[259] as well as teachings from *The Heart Essence of the Great Expanse,*[260] all with their initiations and reading transmissions. Several signs of the purification of obscurations appeared, both in dreams and visionary experiences. In particular, his transcendent experiences radiated effortlessly and as a result, all his uncertainties regarding the viewpoint of the natural state were completely resolved. On several occasions he asked the lama about the way to practice with great precision. The lama replied:

> *The essential point is to have numerous profound introductions*
> *[into the real nature].*

Then the Lord said:

> *In order to progress in my practice, I'm thinking of going on a pilgrimage in search of supports (for practice) in India and China, such as [the sacred place of] Wu Tai Shan.*

The lama, furious at this, replied:

> *You, son, [should realize that] the supreme method is knowing how to cultivate the natural state! You who, as I have heard before, are from a good family, are intelligent and clear minded, have had faith in the teachings since childhood, and are an emanation of former pure beings, if you do not persevere in the practice and follow the spirit of the teachings, this frivolous act would be [a provocation] of the gyalpo. This wandering mind is a seductive deceiver. Ruining shoes by walking is a virtue, but more virtuous still is breathing in a single place of meditation. Do not travel to the ends of the earth; explore the limits of your own mind! Now, if you do as I say, you will go to your homeland, to that especially noble place, the hidden land of Padmasambhava and live inside the white rock at Lhang Lhang. If you are capable of concentrating firmly on your practice,*

great benefit will arise for yourself and others. This is the advice of an old monk.

Instantly, the Lord committed himself to doing so, crying:

Kye ma kye hud! How sad I feel! I have obtained this precious human birth, but my mind is unbridled. Having known the nature of mind, if I do not practice, it would be as if I had fallen into the gyalpo's trap. May I continually maintain the vision that does not wander!
If one has known the nature of mind and does not cultivate it, one receives the punishment of the dakinis.
If one has known the nature of the mind and does not cultivate it, the protectors of the domain of action will drink one's heart's blood. One must maintain the vision that does not wander!
The red vein of the path is easily severed. May I constantly maintain the vision that does not wander!

He stated all this as a wrathful promise, taking it to heart. Thus, he sTayed in that place.

Then, from Dose arrived the tertön Garwang Rangdröl Lingpa. From him [the Lord] received many initiations and reading transmissions of this lama's treasures, particularly the instructions on Mahamudra.[261]

From the emanation Gyalse Tenphel who arrived from Tsangshi, he received many initiations and reading transmissions of kama and terma cycles. From the Tsonag circle of mountains came Drubse Changchub Drölma, from whom he received the full initiations and reading transmissions of the Venerable Tara. Thus having completely received the initiations and reading transmissions of numerous kama and terma, sutra, and tantra cycles, he returned home.

At a certain time, the chiefs of the five clans of Derge Torwa and those of the region of lower Dokham and Lithang declared war on the chief of Nyagked. Fearing conflict in the districts of Nyarong, the lamas of the monasteries and the practitioners as well as the religious specialists had to go to Bugta [to seek refuge]. The Lord had to go there, too. Thinking only of stimulating virtue in these adverse circumstances, he persevered in the practice of meditation and kept up his austere asceticism. He also exhorted the others to practice it.

During this period, Gyalse Lama Tobgyal of the Knowledge Holder Chögyal Lingpa's family also arrived in Bugta and conferred [on the Lord] many initiations and reading transmissions from the Dharma Treasures of Chögyal Lingpa. They all had to spend about two years there.

Despite the fact that the Lord possessed clairvoyance and marvelous powers to an unimaginable extent, he concealed them in his mind and only showed them to others on rare occasions.

After [the wars ended], he returned to his native country and established himself there. In the year of the Female Iron Boar (1851), he continually practiced the paths of Total Relaxation and Direct Leap, and having fully trained in the self-originated wisdom of the Nature of Mind, he travelled to countless pure realms, a sign of his evolution. He received many prophecies from the many Sugatas[262] he met there.

During the Male Water Mouse year (1852), he went to the borders of the hidden land of Padmasambhava's profound treasures, the excellent rock at Lhang Lhang, to the right of which the Great Adept Palgyi Dorje[263] had meditated in ancient times. There he obtained the list of Profound Treasures of Padmasambhava, and the mandala of these Profound Treasures was revealed to him. Nevertheless, because he had not received the dakinis' authorization for diffusing them, he kept them secret for a time. Then, due to his yogic capacity, he suddenly developed the ability to leave his handprints and footprints on rock. Nevertheless, he kept this [ability] sealed under a vow of secrecy.

In the year of the Female Water Bull (1853) when the chief of Nyarong invited the reincarnation of Kündün Rinpoche of Tromde named Namgyal Dongag Tendzin, many monks and lamas from all the monasteries in Nyarong convened at the remote retreat site called Bachag. The Lord, too, was present to receive the teachings. The reincarnation gave these transmissions: the *Single Syllable of Black Yangti*,[264] the instructions on Mahamudra, the *The Vajra Heart of the Luminous Expanse, The Heart Essence of the Great Expanse, The Instructional Text of the Red Pointing Mudra*[265] of the Bön tradition, and also initiations of the kama and terma cycles, together with an inconceivably vast quantity of advice and profound instructions.

[The Lord] then shared his deep understanding of the way in which one's Natural State is recognized. The reincarnation said:

> *Noble son, your practice has reached the naked view of the Total Perfection, and you really do seem like a crescent moon among the assembly of Nobles, standing out from ordinary people. From now on you should sow the instructions that will liberate your fortunate disciples.*

During this period when the Lord was practicing the instructions of the Clear Light in darkness in his meditation cell that was sealed with clay, he said to the yogis Dampa Taye, Küngyal, and others:

> *Bring me paper and writing implements. I am gong to write.*

He wrote various songs on the experiences emerging from within him, born of the profound intuition [developed] during the practice, such as the [experience] of the primordially empty Dharmakaya.

Kündün Rinpoche also said:

> *Come, now I will show you the way to remain [meditating] on a cushion to experience the nucleus of the Dharma!*

The others came to see, and he showed them the way to remain [meditating]. At once [the Lord], having ejected his object-free consciousness in the shape of the syllable '*Hum*,' journeyed to innumerable pure realms where he met the most glorious of the Knowledge Holders, the King of

Oddiyana,[266] thus obtaining assurance. These were the unsurpassable acts he achieved to acquire the doctrines of the supreme vehicle.

The minds of master and disciple merged into one. Following this episode, the Lord went back to his native country.

In verses:

As the sun, friend of the lotus, matures the beauty
Of the fortunate Udumbara flowers,
The sacred spiritual friend [the guru]
Wears the fragrance of the perfect fruit of ten million virtues.
May I emulate the deeds of this supreme guide!

CHAPTER SIX
*How He Practiced Solitary Asceticism
and Requested the Authoritative Texts
of the Practice Lineage*

The Lord said to his mother and younger brother:

> *Now I am going away to a ridge on some lonely mountain. I have
> decided not to do anything—such as heading a monastery, being
> a town's local lama-yogi, or getting rich by accumulating religious
> goods—other than practice [the meditation] that brings enlighten-
> ment in this life. So, Mother and brother, do not worry about me!*

The glorious and venerable Dragpa Gyaltsen has said: "Friends and relations are like people passing in a market, and even loving friends are like
a dream." [The Lord] said:

> *If you renounce attachment to friends, this is good. Should I not
> meditate alone with no companions?*

This being his true thought, he went off alone with no retinue of monks.
First of all he sTayed where the chief disciples of the Great Adept Namkha
Gyatso called Tagla Orgyan and Chödrub, had formerly lived. This is a
hidden place of Padmasambhava at the foot of the rock called Norbü

Drag,[267] the small cave where the dakinis and guardians assemble. There he remained, reciting the seven- line prayer millions of times [and practicing] the profound path of guruyoga. He sTayed there for a long time practicing the yogas of Total Relaxation and Direct Leap. He also performed numerous offering rituals to purify his commitment. Then, on receiving [the understanding of] the symbolic signs of the dakinis, he disclosed the precious yellow manuscript containing the profound treasures he had previously received in the year of the Male Iron Rat (1840), and composed several secret meditative systems for attaining realization.

As he implemented the approach and became familiar with the practice according to the manuscripts, many marvelous signs appeared. Regarding the signs [of] mastery over self-generated instant presence, signs appeared which were visible to ordinary people. For example, when the Lord took hold of a dead tree, he made water flow from it. Also, while he was in his uncle Tagla's bedroom and it was time to go to the chapel, the door was blocked. Because he had attained the yogic power to control appearances, he stood there for a few moments and said to his own disciple Dampa Tendzin: "Open the door." As Tendzin moved towards the door, it opened by itself. And once, when he was living in the abbot's palace at Wachu, as he stood in front of a small yard where many plates and trays [full of barley] were stacked, they all fell to the ground. Nevertheless, the plates of barley and trays all landed face upwards, so not a grain was lost. [Seeing] this, Lama Orgyan and the others felt an unbreakable respect and faith. Similarly, when he was living in the monastic residence of his uncle Tagla, just as he was melodiously singing the [line in the] seven-line prayer[268] [declaring his] intention to become a protector of all beings without exception, he invited the Transcendent Wisdom Being (Jñanasattva) to visibly manifest from ethereal space. [The Wisdom Being appeared] as the natural rainbow-colored brilliance of the five wisdoms' natural iridescence. From the space surrounding the fivefold shining brilliance, [he] pointed to the Lord with his index finger. Tendzin, the fortunate faithful disciple, saw it all with his own eyes.

Then the Lord went east of the great sacred place [Lhang Lhang] to the small secret cave of the dakini at the foot of a crystalline stupa-shaped rock. [Although] it was hardly big enough to house a body, he remained there devoting himself to the instructions for the practice of Absorbing Elixir[269] of the Three Bodies independently, according to his own profound treasures. First, he remained in equanimity, each week [practicing] Absorbing Elixir of the Dharmakaya of the Dharmakaya, without any sustenance at all. Then, he practiced that of the Sambhogakaya of the Dharmakaya, taking only a dish of crystalline water. [While practicing] the Absorbing Elixir of the Nirmanakaya of the Dharmakaya, he placed a rasayana pill in the bowl of water and lived on that. He lived like this for three years. His understanding became the space of realization of the primordial purity; his meditation emerged continually as the spontaneous Clear Light. Having become free of desire for delicious food, he could sustain himself on crystalline water and rasayana pills. A cotton robe sufficed to cover his body, which naturally gave off a pleasant warmth.

After this, he practiced the Absorbing Elixir of the Mahasukha Sambhogakaya. In the Absorbing Elixir of the Dharmakaya of the Sambhogakaya, his sustenance consisted of a pill made of minerals, as well as of crystal clear water. In the Absorbing Elixir of the Sambhogakaya of the Sambhogakaya he used a pill made from the wanglag[270] plant and other medicines. With the Absorbing Elixir of the Nirmanakaya of the Sambhogakaya, he sustained himself with pills made of tsimen[271] and milk [diluted with] water.

At this time, a partridge and a small cat offered him edible flowers that blossomed near the meditation place. Bees made harmonious sounds and left sweet-smelling honey in a clay vessel placed before the Lord. Having attained clairvoyance and paranormal powers, he could climb rocky mountains with no difficulty at all.

Since the Protector Longchenpa had said that in order to realize contemplation as clairvoyant knowledge one has to stay on a venerable mountain, he followed this advice, and every week he received [from his previously mentioned companions] the three white offerings, pure butter, and other things. With the exception of a code made from the six-syllable mantra, he never mixed any other sound [with his practice]. From then on he lived only on the Absorbing Elixir of the Nirmanakaya. Occasionally he ate flowers and medicinal extracts. On other occasions, he lived on the three white offerings and butter, not mixing them with meat, alcohol, or garlic. From then on he never again ate meat or drank alcohol.

On another occasion, invisible to the others, the protector of the treasures Belugdrag and some other nyen[272] from the mountains came to stay for two or three weeks. Because he had attained the yogic ability to subjugate the apparent universe, carnivorous wild animals such as tigers, leopards, snow leopards, brown bears and such, all came before [the Lord] in a friendly and respectful manner. It makes us shout with joy how [closely] these exalted, marvelous actions compare to the widespread victorious activities of the Great Adept Tambhipa in India and of Sog Palgyi Yeshe in Tibet. Marvelous!

At that time, one by one the local spirits of the Dokham appeared before him, expressing their commitment to act according to the yogi's instructions. He urged them to protect the Buddha's teachings and to carry out virtuous actions to make all beings happier. He then composed many smoke-offering rites for each local spirit.

Then he went back to the dwelling place where he had lived before, and while he was staying there, his old mother came to see him, saying:

There you are all alone in that empty cave, without food or clothing.
What [past] behavior has matured into such a miserable situation?

He replied:

Living in my retreat place, I have always acted virtuously and
pursued a spiritual retreat. I have never sought the protection of a
monastery or benefactors.

This is all explained in *The Collection of Songs*.[273] I am not going to write more on this for fear [of going on for too long].

In verses:

> *Since time without reckoning, striving to be free,*
> *And adopting the earnest asceticism based on leaves and water,*
> *He obtained the essential nectar of peace, profundity,*
> *   and simplicity.*
> *May I be nurtured through the sieve of his transmission's*
> *   teachings!*

CHAPTER SEVEN
Acquisition of the Profound Treasures and the Beginning of Their Diffusion

🪷 The Lord and Lama Thegchog were with a pious benefactor to whom they had explained the practice of Cutting. Lama Thegchog said that during the night he had dreamt that the Lord was in the cave where he had formerly lived, and the lama had seen a sun with intensely bright rays of light shining from the cave's mouth, purifying all the darkness in the world. Although it was still dawn, in accordance with the ancient prophecy promulgated by the Great Adept Sherab Gyaltsen, and knowing full well that he was a sublime and excellent being, [Lama Thegchog] said to the Lord:

If you go to the temple of Chagdü and explain the instructions for the preliminaries to all the laypersons, masters, and monks, you will doubtlessly bring great benefit to all beings and to the Doctrine in this degenerate age.

Thus, time and again he was requested to take up the great drum of the Doctrine. Having made a commitment to do this, he went to the monastery for some months. He explained in detail the seven ordinary preliminary teachings of *The Vajra Heart of the Luminous Expanse* to both monks and laypersons, male and female, thus causing overwhelming compassion and the understanding of the ultimate sense to spring forth in the minds of many fortunate disciples.

The sublime yogi Thegchog served several true masters, including Dzaka Chogtrül Rinpoche. Having protected the initiations and reading transmissions stemming from authentic transmission lineages, [the Lord] received [from Lama Thegchog] the complete initiations and reading transmissions of the thirteen volumes of *The Gathering of the Guru's Intention*[274] cycle, which comes from the treasures of the indisputable Terchen Sangye Lingpa. Also, from the treasures of Terchen Ngadag Nyang Rinpoche,[275] he received initiations for all the extensive meditation practices of *The Gathering of the Sugatas of the Eight Transmitted Precepts*[276] cycle.

At this time, having received the possessions of a recently deceased devotee, he [commissioned] the engraving of the six-syllable mantra upon thousands of rocks as well as many repairs in the monastery. Also, he went to Gojam monastery at the request of the masters and monks who lived there. Having optimally sown the ordinary preliminary instructions among both lay practitioners and monks at the monastery and throughout the region, he greatly benefited them by [inspiring them to] cultivate virtue and renounce negative actions.

Guru Rinpoche, Knowledge Holders, and dakinis had miraculously sealed that place with numerous syllables and six-syllable mantras, but because nobody had heard about this, the Lord made them appear once again to purify the place by sprinkling water. On another occasion, at Yangshar Dragkar, he extracted particularly sublime sacramental pills from a treasure.

The Lord went again to the regions of Shangshi, Podzi, Drure, and Drewo and, when he entered a charnel ground on which there were corpses all around, non-human dark powers caused supernatural provocations to manifest. Because the Lord was established in the state of genuine contemplation of the unlimited and primordially pure natural state that is the uncompounded ultimate reality, he regarded [these manifestations] as a harmless dream, like an illusion emerging from the unceasing play of visions. He pacified the entire magical display of harmful intentions created by worldly dakinis and non-human spirits of unreal nature.

On this occasion, at the very instant when Orgyan Norbu, the lama of Tsokha, came to met the Lord, he saw that [the Lord] had three eyes. He then remembered a personal prophecy by Pema Nyinjed, the incarnation of a former siddha,[277] which said that seeing a Buddha in human form brings forth unbreakable faith.

One night when the Lord was in his tent with the flaps tied, many wild men and women began to sing and dance. This enraged the Lord who, although the tent flaps were tied together, passed right through them and chased the people away with a hail of stones. Therefore, due to his yogic discipline that inseparably blends the mind and its objects,[278] he is as magnificent as the former Pema Rigdzin, Sovereign of Adepts.

Returning to his former place of residence, he placed himself in the center of a great mandal-like plain, with the sacred place (Lhang Lhang) before him. With him were Taye, Tendzin, Kungyal, Chödrub, Gyurme, and Drure Tülku among many other fortunate disciples to whom he imparted, without limits, the nectar of the ordinary and special precepts which integrate the instructions of *The Unique Golden Syllable of the Dark Ultimate Essence*[279] and *The Vajra Heart of the Luminous Expanse.*

Once, from the venerable yogi Sönam Taye who possessed the complete initiations and reading transmissions of *The Eight Transmitted Precepts* cycle from the treasures of Nyang Rinpoche,[280] he received the initiations and reading transmissions of the nine volumes of this great tantric meditation practice.

At this time, each disciple built himself a small hut of stone and wood at the Master's place, and since then it has been known as the Dragkar retreat center.

How the Profound Treasures Were Brought to Light

On the way the profound treasures came to light, the inventory of the profound treasures of the Lord states:

An emanation of mine, resembling me, called Trülzhig Lingpa
  will appear as Vajra Khroda who subjugates the demons,[281]
  and he will emerge from the expanse of realization of ultimate
  Mind.
He will extract profound treasures from the center of the great
  rock [marked] with symbols.
Possessing the essential qualities of meditation along with
  certainty of vision,
He will be imbued with the yogic skill of spontaneous action.

In accordance with this, this excellent being, full of love and possessing yogic skill, in the year of the Female Fire Serpent (1857), at dawn on the tenth day of the tenth month, in a state in which sleep and the clear light are intermingled, had this experience:

His own mind manifested as instant presence[282] in the celestial
  space
At the summit of an eastern mountain embraced by sunlight.
Approaching the peak, to the right and the left,
Appeared a staircase of mother-of-pearl and golden lassos.
Inside the palace, on a great golden throne sat the Lotus-Born
  Lord,[283]
Surrounded by dakas and dakinis,
All smiling and looking happy.
The Lady of the dakinis, Vajrayogini,
Chanting many symbolic verses of the Vajra-Song, [said to him]:
"The moment has arrived for the profound treasures to appear."[284]

Having said this, the dakinis prophesied, through many symbolic words, the time at which the profound treasures would appear. Also, in the catalogue of the treasures [mentioned] above, it is written:

On the great rocky mountain, in the direction of the great holy
  place,
From the base of the rock that resembles a lion cub playing with
  its mother,
In the direction of the sky [at a distance of] eighteen dom[285] from
  the base,
Is found the lower door of the deep secret treasure chamber
Sealed by an immutable righthanded swastika bearing the letters
Ha, Ri, Ni, Sa.
In the direction of the sky [at a distance of] twenty-one dom
  from the base,
Is found the middle door to the deep and secret treasure
  chamber
Sealed by the mark of a phurbu[286] piercing an iron scorpion,
Bearing the symbolic syllables 'A' and 'Hum.'
In the direction of the sky [at a distance of] twenty-five dom
  from the base,
Is found the upper door to the deep and secret treasure
  chamber,
Sealed by an unchangeable visvavajra
And by the syllables 'Hri' and 'Hum.'

In the catalogue explaining the arrangement of the profound treasures,
[it says]:

Mingled with five kinds of precious objects,
[There is] a yellow manuscript in two volumes inscribed
  in molten beryl,
In particular, the sadhana of the wrathful Vajrakilaya.
[There are] one hundred and twenty-five statues and stupas,
Pills [made] from the flesh of a seven-times born brahmin,
[Whose ingestion] immediately brings liberation,
And a staff of Padma made of sandalwood.[287]

Deep within, the Lord thought:

Although I have persevered in the yogic skill that implies the total liberation of action and trod the supreme path that never searches for the Buddha elsewhere [than within oneself], I have no hope of attaining [enlightenment,] the supreme siddhi in this life. But since, due to the residual karma from the past, the great fortune of being a master of the deep treasures has fallen on me, it would be incorrect to be indifferent to the deep treasures of Guru Rinpoche.

Calling his disciples together before him, he described the pure visions emanating from the Clear Light and [his receiving of] the inventory of the treasures.

Then, the Lord and his disciples offered a ganachakra,[288] and on completing it they went to the foot of the great rocky mountain. There the disciples waited while the Lord, in a moment of intense meditative experience in which the objects perceived, the mind, and Dharmadhatu all intermingled in a single flavor, went directly to the edge of the mountain where there appeared, unaltered, the symbols on the door of the (treasure) chamber as described in the aforementioned treasure catalogue. There he ordered the guardians:

Hum, Hum, Hum!
Assembly of guardians of the outer, inner, and secret treasures,
You who have vowed to protect the teachings of the treasures for
*   one who in a previous life was Düdul Dorje Trolö,*
Remember that you are charged with the commitment to free
*   [the treasures]!*
The time has come for the 'father' Norbu to take them;
Give me the wealth of the profound secret treasures!

When the series of doors to the chambers were opened, an exquisite fragrance emanated, a shower of flowers fell, and many other marvelous signs appeared. In accordance with the inventory, [the Lord] brought out many profound treasures of Body, Speech, and Mind and took them to his disciples. Then the Lord used a rope to pull the disciples up to the door of the lower treasure chamber, and thus, filled with respect, they viewed the lower chamber.

On another occasion, these natural sounds resonated from a natural rock: "*Hum, Hum, Hri, Hri, Bam, Bam, Bhyo, Bhyo, Khrol, Khrol, Tri, Tri, Bswo, Bswo, Phat, Phat, 'Ur, 'Ur, Dir, Dir, Lhang, Lhang.*" They resounded for a long time and were heard by all the fortunate vajra disciples. This accorded with a prophecy symbolically spread by the dakini, which said that [the Lord] would receive the blessings of the Buddhas, have visions of yidams, be taken care of by the dakinis, be surrounded by the guardians and gods at his service, that demons would offer him their heart syllable, that guardians of the positive directions would be victorious and those of the negative directions defeated, that immense benefit would be generated for all beings thanks to the Doctrine, and that many disciples of the lineage and transmission of the Doctrine would gather around him.

How the Water Treasures Were Revealed

On the circumstances of revealing the treasures of water the Lord explained:

> At dawn on the thirteenth day, having raised a small tent on a rounded boulder resembling a mother-of-pearl elephant, while resting with my mind in a state of contemplation not fixed on any object or thought, I instantly saw in the depths, in the beautiful palace of the nagas,[289] the inconceivably [great] assemblies of the blue, white, yellow, red, and green dakinis who filled beautiful precious containers with nectars and offered them to me.

After two days, thinking that there really was a water treasure that was related to the boulder resembling a mother-of-pearl elephant, he hit it with his staff. From the mark of the blow, the water treasure—fragrant divine nectar—copiously flowed. Then, his disciples and some pilgrims, monks from the surrounding monasteries, and some Bönpo monks and lamas gathered there and, as they explained, the water had sprung from that desert ground, from that dry rock. They said that they had never before seen such particularly marvelous signs of realization, and they developed an unbreakable faith in the Lord, feeling that they had seen a true Buddha.

How the Golden Water of Dzambu Appeared

This is how the golden water of Dzambu appeared. When some servants from the monastery of Chagdü Orgyan Ling came [to invite him], the Lord and some followers set off for the monastery. A little later, during the night of the third day of the sixth lunar month, in a state in which sleep and the clear light are intermingled, the previously mentioned dakinis appeared, saying:

> *Just as we offered it to the Great Knowledge Holder of the past, Padma Jungne, now before you, venerable yogi, we offer the precious golden water of Dzambu in a pool of water treasures. Venerable yogi, accept it with love!*

In the morning, at sunrise, a brilliant rainbow settled between the monastery and the site of the water treasure. The Lord, understanding that in accordance with the prophesies of the mothers and wisdom dakinis there probably were some powerful gifts for public benefit, sent his disciple Rangdröl to that place, saying, "Go and fetch some water." The venerable Yogi Taye was then at that great retreat place with his disciples, and in the morning they all saw that the spring was full of [water] sparkling with golden [reflections], something they had never seen before. They said that this unique sign had appeared before them, an unsurpassable marvel. Rangdröl poured a bucketful of golden water into a skin and took it back [to the Lord]. On their arrival, when they looked at the water, most of it had turned into nuggets of gold. All the [images of] divinities in the chapels of the upper and lower parts of the monastery were blessed by having the water sprinkled on them, and in that very instant, the air and sky became filled with rainbows and a virtuous fragrance filled the air. Then the Lord returned to his dwelling and distributed the gold that had appeared among his many fortunate disciples, concealing a little as a hidden treasure to wipe out the decadence of the beings and of the land they inhabited. He also saved some for his monastery, Kalzang, to paint the ornaments adorning the divinities.

Moreover, when the venerable [Lord] went to uncle Tagla's monastery to give all the lamas, monks, and faithful the vow of the ascetic practice nyungne,[290] at dawn, in a state in which sleep and the clear light intermingle, the aforementioned dakinis appeared, saying:

Although the offering, the nectar of the water treasures
Is still drinking water,
When it is continually used by people of no commitment
Or by great sinners, the dakinis are upset.
In the past, the offering of many thousands of jars [of this water]
Caused the gate to lower births to immediately close
For anyone who merely touched it to his lips.

They said this, and disappeared.

The next morning, the Lord with Chödrub and many other disciples and laymen hurried to the pool at the retreat center. Guru Rinpoche appeared to the Lord, surrounded by an inconceivably great host of Knowledge Holders and dakinis. The vision was instantly absorbed within the Lord. Secretly entering into a meditative experience free from concepts, the Lord began writing on the boulder resembling a mother-of-pearl elephant, using his index finger as if the rock were made of butter. Laymen, monks and beggars all saw it with their own eyes. He inscribed the uncreated letter, the marvelous '*A*.' And thus, in accordance with the dakinis' prophecy, the Lord scattered grains in the spring, sealing it with invisibility for the future, while proclaiming the [dakinis'] warning.

What has been written so far is based on fragments of writings by the Master himself.

To go into more depth on the secret teaching, the cycle of *The Profound Doctrine: Self-Liberation that Encompasses Space:*[291] regarding the development stage, there is the extensive version of the stages of development and accomplishment called *Utterly Pure Self-Liberation,*[292] the middle version of these two stages, called *Primordially Pure Self-Liberation,*[293] and the abbreviated version, *Self-Liberation of Total Bliss.*[294] In the section of the *Heart Essence*—the concentrated essence of instructions of sutra and tantra—are the sadhanas of the hundred yidams, such as *The Adamantine Essence of the Definitive Sense: the Gathered Realization of the Three Roots.*[295]

The Lord copied the precious yellow manuscripts, and the scribe [for the final version] was Sönam Taye, the intelligent yogi of good family who composed the text from the nectar of [the Lord's] explanation.

On one occasion, the chief of Nyarong[296] summoned thirteen great lamas in the monastery of Zhiwa to preside over the placement of a consecrated vase[297] before a hundred monks, asking them:

> *Can you multiply these medicinal pills with your words of power? If nobody can, I shall multiply them with camphor and other precious substances.*

On hearing this, the lamas present said they could not do it. But the Lord said, "I will multiply them," and just as he said the words, the pills appeared in great abundance in the meditation room. Everyone saw the pills appearing by the zungthag,[298] and the chief of Nyarong felt happy, and gained sincere faith in the precious Lord.

On another occasion, a minister of the King of Nyarong was on the verge of death and invited the Lord to come to him. Because they had to arrive at night, some disciples, due the poor [visibility] along the road, set two butter lamps without a lantern on the ground to light the way. The wind blew hard but the lamps did not go out. If one thinks about these amazing facts [and sees how] they rival the wonderful feats of Pema Lingpa,[299] this deserves the celebratory cry: "Marvelous!"

In verses:

He is a Lord of Padmasambhava's profound treasures
Because, not depending on the duration of paths and levels,
He manifestly departed, miraculously, to the marvelous kingdom
of Vajrayana.
May I emulate this protector with his ocean of enlightened
actions!

CHAPTER EIGHT

How, Having Attained the Yogic Discipline That Contemplates the Coherence of all Teachings, He Established Numerous Fortunate Aspirants in Maturation and Liberation.

🌸 Adding to what was said above, once there arose in his mind the essential perspective that there is no contradiction among the doctrines, in this way he spread the nectar of the vast and profound teachings, beginning with his innumerable disciples, followers of the lineage. As Orgyan Rinpoche said:

> *It will be a more difficult task to benefit one single individual in the future than it is to benefit hundreds of sentient beings now.*

In accordance with this [prediction], there is now a great proliferation of the five degenerations and of malicious people whose intellect is full of erroneous ideas, who do not aspire to virtue and only carry out evil actions. Around here, people take care of their relatives and over there, they carry out perverse acts. To help those with [negative] accumulations, the main cause of [birth in] the almost unbearable Hell of Fire, one must seek a holy master who fulfills these criteria: to be erudite in the methods of the Victorious Ones and to personify compassion. Thus, the characteristics of a holy master are: first, for his own benefit, he must have fully accumulated wisdom and merit and have purified negativities as well as cultivated spiritual realization; then, for the benefit of other beings who are difficult to convert, he must not ignore the method of guidance enhanced by the four facilitators of conversion.[300] To [benefit] those minimally possessing the seed of liberation generated by previous purification, he must know the instructions of the gradual method that leads to the higher paths. He should likewise have an excellent intellect—the appropriate receptacle for Mahayana—and be very knowledgeable of the methods of personal and direct introduction into self-generated wisdom, the state of enlightenment that does not rely on future lives. Furthermore, he must protect beings, especially the needy and the humble, with his love. Having acquired a shield of patience and tolerance against those who harbor emotions of rivalry, attachment, and aversion, he does not show anger at evil actions. This is surely a real master with all the characteristics of a Noble One, a benevolent master. These are not absurd words inspired by the desire of some fool like myself! Excluding those whose vision is erroneous due to demonic intervention, those of refined intellect who possess the expansive eye of the Doctrine [will] honor [this kind of master] on their heads like a crown. As it says in the *Ornament of the Mahayana Sutra:*[301]

> *With a pacific master the discipline is complete pacification;*
> *He is especially powerful in virtue, and a holder of the tenth level;*
> *As he possesses supreme realization,*
> *He has great knowledge of the way to expound [the Doctrine].*
> *This loving being shows [us] the way to abandon sorrow.*

Thus, a master should possess the characteristics described in the scriptures.

The previously mentioned disciples from the monasteries of upper and lower Nyarong came to the holy master in order to become the fortunate receptacles for the nectar of knowledge, as did others such as Chogden, Özer, Jigme, Melong, Yengme, Gyurme, Alo, Chödrub, Ador, Samten, Lhachog, Lhündrub, Thogme, Mepön Wangyal, Rangjung, Kartra, Tashapa, Rangchag, and many hundreds more disciples, sons of his heart. He taught them consecutively, *The Vajra Heart of the Luminous Expanse, The Unique Golden Syllable of the Dark Yangtig,* and his own received treasure, the secret teaching *The Profound Doctrine: Self-Liberation that Encompasses Space.* Through retreats and according to their respective mental capacities, he instructed them in the ordinary preliminaries of the four thoughts that turn [the mind] away from samsara, the seven practices,[302] and so on. On [their] completion of the extraordinary preliminaries of rushen[303] which separate samsara and nirvana, he taught them the Total Relaxation of primordial purity and the spontaneously realized Direct Leap; all this was [taught] without limits, like an inexhaustible [flow of] nectar.

Also, at the request of his disciple Pechö, he gave direct instruction in the *The Instructional Text of the Red Pointing Mudra* and instructions on primordial Bön. Further, through *The Vajra Heart of the Luminous Expanse,* he gave the complete instructions of Inner Heat[304] and of the channels and winds. From his own treasure, *Self-Liberation that Encompasses Space,* he gave additional instructions on Inner Heat and on winds and channels as well as the initiation of the Thousand Buddhas and the great initiation of the *Peaceful and Wrathful Ones*[305] of Karma Lingpa. He also gave instructive advice for practicing the Clear Light in darkness.

In summary, this sublime being gave his own clothing and food to the poor without expecting anything in return. He dedicated totally and impartially to all beings the ocean-like virtues, a product of the two accumulations he treasured in his mind. He fully accepted in his heart all the suffering and wrongdoing caused by the ignorant illusions of non-realized beings. He constantly insisted that his disciples should renounce the selfish thoughts that cropped up in their minds, and instead cultivate the superior motivation of helping all sentient beings. He gave extraordinary importance to training the mind in the latter, as it is the main foundation of Mahayana. Thus, constantly insisting on these matters, he gave them instructions. Here are some of his verses:

> *Through the dedication of all [my] happiness to all beings,*
> *omitting none,*

> *May happiness fill space!*
> *Through the ripening [for myself] of all suffering without*
>   *exception,*
> *May the ocean of suffering be drained!*

Also,

> *May all the fruit I have obtained from instant presence,*
> *Ripen in the continuum of ignorant beings!*
> *Uniting within me all the darkness of ignorant beings,*
> *May it be purified in the ultimate dimension of the Wisdom of*
>   *instant presence!*

Such was his recitation of the dedication of merit on these occasions. On all occasions he always kept in mind the intention to benefit all beings.

The omniscient Tsongkhapa has said:

> *Understanding that all teachings contain no contradiction whatsoever and that all spiritual discourses serve as essential oral instructions, and joyfully apprehending the contemplation of the Victorious Ones provides protection even from the abyss of extreme negative actions.*

As the previous paragraphs make clear, this holy master had discovered in his mind the absence of contradiction in all the teachings of the Sugatas.

Also, subsequent to his solitary retreats, he disbanded the ties of dualistic perception of subject and object and he freed in the central channel the knot of the heart. When the omniscient Dharma King Jigme Lingpa was praying to the noble lady the dakini Vajrayogini, this secret treasure of realization of profound activity was revealed:

> *As you need not make efforts to study in the ordinary way,*
>   *be joyful!*

As sound and form are experienced as symbols and scriptures,
  be happy!!

Accordingly, the forms, sounds and thoughts—emerging as scriptures—are represented from beginning to end in [the Lord's] numerous vajra songs. [Most noteworthy are] the instructional songs praising the solitary mountain retreat, written for those who were [spiritually] born from the nectar of the Lord's word, including Kalden Küngyal, Tendzin, Pechö, and others, and [the song] for his disciple Dampa Tendzin on the moment of realizing the Three Bodies, the innate nature of mind:

Soar in the true condition of Dharmakaya, which is without base
  or root,
Practice according to instructions!
If you do not awaken in this life
I will feel disappointed!
Understand this, excellent son!

Thus, he advised.

According to the oral instructions of Tsungme Dagpo Rinpoche:

First: appetizing meat, the sinful food.
Second: tawny beer that drives men mad.
Third: the young adolescent virgin.
These are the three great poisons of the Dharma.
If you wish to practice the genuine Dharma,
Give up these three things.

The Lord dedicated [the following songs] to the assembled disciples: *The Obstacles Placed on the Path to Liberation for People who have Entered the Common Vehicle [of the Dharma]; The [Consumption of] Meat that Cuts Off Compassion at Its Root; The [Drinking of] Alcohol That is the Source of all Defects,* and *The Need to Renounce Young Women Who Are the Cause of the Breaking of Commitments.* To the venerable yogi lama Thegchog, to Pema and some others, he dedicated [the song] *The Advice on Remaining in the True Essence of the Nature of Mind, the Best Refuge of All.* Know that [all the songs] he sang on these occasions, such as *Dokhampa's Song of Feeling at Ease*—about the way to achieve stability in vision and meditation without partiality regarding practice or post-practice—are clearly compiled in *The Collection of Songs.*

To each of the fortunate disciples of his teachings who were already progressing at the level of Great Vajra Holders and to those who were able to fathom the necessity of evolving towards that path in the future, the Lord gave an exclusive name containing the word "dorje," telling them:

> *If you do not corrupt your commitments, by the power of the Vajra vehicle of mantras, we, father and sons, united in a single group, will attain enlightenment together.*

On some occasions even ordinary people heard [him say] this.

Also, when offered the goods of deceased devotees, even if these seemed to be treasure chambers containing all kinds of precious materials such as gold, turquoise, and coral, [the Lord and his disciples] would dismantle these riches on the spot and scatter them while reciting the mandal[306] offering to the assemblies of Bodhisattvas and the Buddhas of the ten directions. Again, if poor people in miserable condition with no hope of receiving anything were present, he would offer these riches to them. On other occasions, after offering the six-syllable mantra as well as all the valuables of the dying, he would tell them that all was illusion, even if wise neighbors and the nearby disciples could tell, on analyzing the circumstances, whether the dying person had been attached to riches or not.

In the same way, sometimes the riches offered by dying devotees, with the exception of rifles, financed the rock engravings of one hundred thousand six-syllable mantras. A rifle, even though it may have been the finest of hundreds and cost many dotse,[307] can never bring benefit, to say nothing of its having been used to harm the lives of sentient beings. Saying these words, he destroyed the weapons then and there, an extremely pure act.

Orgyan Rinpoche said:

Although my view is higher than the sky,
It is very accurate in distinguishing the cause, the fruit, and the
*   propensities of karma.*

According to this, his minute observation of the subtler karmic causes and their fruit was like a recitation from the *Sutra of the Hundred Karmas*. During this period the Lord went to a place called Pepung Thang to the right of the Great Holy Place (Lhang Lhang) and he blessed the earth, saying:

In the future, realized beings will come here.

Just as he had prophesied, due to the power the Great Orgyan's aspirational prayer and the concern of [the Lord], the supreme Refuge, this is what occurred.

One day some time later, the loving Protector and Lord of Compassion, the Lord of the Victorious Ones the fourteenth Karmapa Thegchog Dorje together with the third incarnation of the great pandita Situ Rinpoche—'He who has visited the five holy places [of Magadha]'— and the omniscient knower of the scriptures and reasoning, Kongtrül Yönten Gyatso, were invited by the chief of Nyarong to a valley called Ase Drongtul. At that time it was hard for the Lord to travel as he was suffering from rheumatism. Since it would have been unthinkable to hear of the Karmapa's arrival and not go [to see him], he worried all night long about his inability to travel. Then he dreamt that a qualified yogi appeared who, by sprinkling [water on] his body, caused a lot of pus and blood to flow from both his left and right foot. From then on [the Lord] felt neither fatigue nor any impediment to going or staying. Then the Lord and a couple of disciples went to meet [the Karmapa]. They offered all the materials of fruition: gold, silver, coral, tea, silk, and so on. In particular, intermingling his mind with that of the Karmapa, Lord of the Victorious Ones, and this being an appropriate circumstance for grasping the view of the inseparability of Mahamudra and Dzogchen, he offered the container[308] that had held his profound treasures. He received from the Karmapa the condensed instructions of Mahamudra. Further, from other reincarnations he received numerous sections of the teachings of the precious Kagyü tradition. To satisfy the desires of the Karmapa, the Lord offered some reading transmissions of his own treasures. The other lamas present offered a great initiation to the general public, among whom were the chief of Nyarong and his son. The Karmapa offered corporeal supports (images), vocal supports (instructions leading to Mahamudra), and mental supports (vajra and bell), as well as the skins of wild animals, silks, cotton, and many excellent sacred substances. The incarnation of Situ Rinpoche and others also made similar donations. After this, the Lord returned to the retreat center at Dragkar.

When the lamas convened to perform an annual ritual for the benefit of the chief of Nyarong, even though they had to come every year, they were presented with sublime offerings.

When the Lord and a pair of his disciples were on the road to upper Nyarong, listening to the continuous chant of [the cuckoo,] the Queen of Spring,[309] [the Lord] comprehended [the birdsong's meaning] that three sublime footprints of Vairochana, the great preceptor of the past, were [to be found nearby]. So he sent his superior Vajra disciples, such as Taye, to search [for them]. As they explained, they found the footprints. This is similar to [the incident in which] the glorious protector Nagarjuna and his disciple, as they heard the raven begin to call, comprehended the meaning of these sounds and thus discovered the path for establishing [beings] on the great level of the Noble Ones.

Also, in the monastery of Zhiwa a vase was to be consecrated,[310] and the Lord went there to act as the chief officiant. There he met Jigme, disciple of the venerable Damtsig Dorje, and received from him some reading transmissions of the *Heart Essence*.

He also went to the great auspicious ritual to benefit the chief of lower Nyarong, and thanks to the auspicious connection established through the great pure prayers of aspiration, when the Kalzang monastery was built, the chief offered him great quantities of provisions, materials, and food.

In response to the request of many of the faithful, he went to upper and lower Mekhog where he met the lama from Khane, Orgyan Phüntsog from whom he received various initiations and reading transmissions of the teachings of the Northern Treasures. According to the lama's intimate wish, the Lord offered him some initiations and reading transmissions from his own treasures. Since these were troubled times, the reincarnation of Tromge and his brother had settled there [in Mekhog]. The reincarnation, called Tsewang, offered this prayer to the Lord for his long endurance on earth:

Om swasti

Lord of Oddiyana, embodiment of the ocean of Precious Ones,
You who manifest the power to subjugate the three spheres of
*   existence,*
Let this excellent being who is committed to curing beings,
Remain for a hundred eons!
In this degenerate age, the practice of Dharma is as rare as a star
*   by day,*
And one who has realized the truth of the natural state is
*   even rarer.*
Thus, you are a siddha (as rare as) the Udumbara.
In this period when the five degenerations flourish,
You wear the armor of pure morality, the vows of virtue.
You are a bearer of the heroic accoutrements
Of the thirty-seven factors[311] leading to buddhahood.
Contemplating the equality and purity of all existence

When confronted by enemies,
You crush the armies of Mara to dust. This is marvelous!
In the garden of the pure vows of individual liberation
Blooms the beautiful flower of the bodhicitta of aspiration and
application
Due to the delight of contemplating liberation.
This delight gently waters the shoots of realization of the two
stages.[312]
By abstaining from meat and the blood of animals
Conditioned by the latencies of ignorance,
You show how the miracles of the Bodhisattvas
Refresh the mental continuum with great compassion and love!
As our masters say, drinking intoxicants is the domain of the
thirty defects.
Although the discipline of renunciation may be as light as dew on
grass,
It is the supreme Dharma of the sons of the Victorious Ones.
In times like these, many wish to harm the virtuous
Through criticism, calumny, and erroneous views.
The eight mundane dharmas are all fragile as a reed.
Who, if not you, can see their insubstantiality?
You accept only the humblest rank,
And [concealing] the gem of your ocean-like qualities,
You strive to act discretely, without display.
Without cultivating the pure code of conduct and bodhicitta,
One does not acquire a higher viewpoint, and covets religious
riches.
To attain this understanding, you have cultivated confidence in
[the certainty of] death
And abandoned wealth and material things.
You delight in generating this mental renunciation.
Sustaining yourself with the three white foods that delight the
Noble Ones,

And being a friend of tummo, the cotton robe that covers you
Is enough to keep you warm.
The great Noble Ones prescribed yogic asceticism
Sheltered in the palace of natural rock within the mountain.
The Lotus-born Lord—sovereign of the Doctrine of the Profound
    Treasures,
Antidote to the negative spirits of the five degenerations' disgrace,
Not forgetting his adamantine prophecy
Has charged you with the fundamental care of disoriented beings
And [ordained you] to bring them to the Dharma.
Now that the fruit of negative karma is ripening for all beings in
    Great Tibet,
Seeing their martyrdom that resembles the sufferings in the three
    lower realms,
May you make them all the object of your compassion!
Conflicts like these arise through illusion, hypocrisy,
And the power of desire and aversion.
By peaceful action is the mundane destroyed.
Fill the mental continuum of all beings with peaceful benevolence
And the seven riches of the Noble Ones.[313]
By the highest truth of the Unequivocal Jewel,
And the power of your pure and high intention,
Until [you] truly attain the nature of space,
May you, protector, realize the adamantine elements of the three
    secrets!

Thus he gave forth this offering.

Throughout that place he worked for the benefit of all beings, inciting people to cultivate virtue and abandon negativity, to recite the *mani* prayer, to spread the *jokhor*, carve mantras on the rocks, offer lamps, and save lives. In this way, when anyone—including monks from the region's nomadic monasteries—approached the chief of upper and lower Nyarong, the beneficial abandonment of negative acts and the cultivation of virtue were seen to occur [due to the Lord's proximity]. He received offerings as rich as a great king's treasures, objects pleasing to the senses such as gold, silver, turquoise, coral, and others, as well as horses, male and female dzo, yaks and their dams, tea, barley, butter, and so on. But he offered it all to sustain the monasteries, [to feed] helpless beggars, to free animals [intended for slaughter], and to carve the six-syllable and many other essential mantras on rocks. It is well known that out of all this, the only thing he kept for himself was a vessel full of tea.

To sum up the acts of this venerable being in the Land of Snowy Peaks, when we search through the riches in the biographies of possessors of yogic abilities whose sole mode is non-action, including [those of] the all-mighty Milarepa, the incomparable father and son of the Kadam tradition,[314] Gyalse Ngülchu Thogme, the Great Adept Melong Dorje, the Protector Longchen Rabjam, Ngari Pema Wangyal, Tsele Natsog Rangdröl, Trülzhig Wangdrag Gyatso, the Omniscient Jigme Lingpa, and so on, no difference can be found. Even if I, the disciples surrounding him, or any knowledgable person should examine [his life,] this can be easily understood.

In verses:

He offered the river of his effortless compassion
To those worthy of being trained,
The flock of swans who are
The fortunate ones endowed with faith and commitment.
He was the ruler of an ocean of scriptures, knowledge, and
    precepts.
May I be among the first disciples [to receive] the nectar of that
    time!

CHAPTER NINE

The Construction of the Temple as a Field of Merit for the Benefit of the Doctrine and Beings.

🌸 The Lord undertook the building of the new temple, un-contaminated by thoughts of the eight worldly dharmas that are linked to personal interest such as fame, earnings, desire, and so on. [He did this] to promote the flowering of the precious Doctrine of the Victorious Ones so that it should long endure, and so that beings afflicted by the five degenerations could obtain the cause that leads to liberation and become a field for the accumulation of merit. Previously in his youth, when he was in his uncle Tagla's monastery, Guru Rinpoche, the Knowledge Holders and the assembly of dakinis had appeared to him prophesying that in this very place he would build a temple that would greatly benefit all beings as well as the Doctrine. [The Lord] said that he had also had visions of a wonderful temple resembling the glorious monastic enclosure of Samye. He then put forth his intention in consultation with Lama Taye, the per-fect recipient of nectar, and some other venerable disciples. The disciples, sons of his heart, replied that the prophecies received by the Lord were undoubtedly authentic, and asked him how the monastery was to be built.

Then the Lord and all the disciples, being in favor, went to the monastery of his uncle Tagla. Because the Lord was certainly an authentic possessor of yogic skills whose sole mode is non-action, in terms of material wealth, food and donations—the conditions necessary for building the temple—he didn't even have the price of a brocade for a *jokhor*. But neither did that venerable being obstruct opportunities for obtaining riches, which appeared [as if from] the wish-fulfilling gem that satisfies all desires.

In the year of the Male Iron Monkey (1860), on the tenth day of the third lunar month, at the site of the monastery the Lord blessed the foundations by scattering flowers with the mandala of his hand. The disciples carried out ritual fumigation, sprinkled water and recited the *Nangzhi*, the *Nanggye*, and the *Tashi Tsegpa*.[315] At that moment marvelous signs miraculously appeared: the sky was filled with rainbows while in space, a hot auspicious sun glowed and a delicious perfume permeated the whole area.

On one occasion, the Lord defecated a little blood in which some relics, similar to mustard seeds, appeared and after two weeks some fortunate disciples obtained part of this. After that, some fifty disciples appeared from various monasteries. A group of people who came from the district of Shanglang Shis designed the foundation for the temple construction and built the temple walls. A faithful chief with a thousand men at his command [supplied] limitless food and riches and also [arranged for] the conditions favorable for building. The lama Dampa Taye took care of the food and supplies until the work was completed, and took on the great responsibility of acting as building foreman. From the beginning of the work until the end, the workers who persevered in their task were people who had a connection with the Lord, their names being: lama Küngyal, carpenter and bricklayer; lama Tendzin, woodcutter and mason; Kartra and Phüntsogs, responsible for transport; Rangchag, Kyeme, Kardön, and also five nuns, disciples of the master who carried wood and earth, and Kradön and Tsebum, the carpenters' supervisors. When heavy work such as laying the foundation was to be done, a group of men from Shangshi joined the Lord's disciples.

Thus, they spent five years building the first floor of the great main temple representing the Unfolding of the Realms of the Three Bodies, as well as the middle and upper floors, all of wonderful appearance. In the four directions of the main temple representing the Unfolding of the Realms of the Three Bodies, situated in the center are four chapels representing the four emanated realms, such as Abhirati.[316] These four chapels comprise the outer sanctuary, built like the immaculate unfolding of a celestial palace.

Then they started making the images of the divinities of the inner sanctuary, which were completed by the sculptors after two years' work. There were seven [sculptors] in all, including the horpa Lozang, master of clay modelling, Karma and Tharli from Nyarong, and four other sculptors. The supreme and truly holy refuge [the Lord] displayed a non-sectarian respect for all the precious teachings of the Victorious Ones with the aim of introducing the ultimate sense of realization, the essence of all teachings. As to the selection of the deities, because of his impartial respect for all the teachings in Tibet, the entire lineage of the kama and terma transmissions of the Nyingma order—school of the ancient translations—as well as the mandala and its corresponding deities, were represented. Also chosen were the entire line of masters from the oral transmission of Mahamudra and some divinities from the mandala. From the traditions of the later translations, the elucidator of the doctrine Sachen Künga Nyingpo and others of the lineage of the Path and Fruit of Realization were represented, as well as the great and venerable Tsongkhapa, the spiritual instructor who is a chariot of depth and breadth, and others from the lineage of the Gradual Path to Liberation as well as the mandala's divinity, Yamantaka.

He named the monastery Kalzang Sangye Chöling.[317] From two [conch] shells of different sizes they made two ineffable trumpets for the sound of essential mantras such as the six-syllable ones. According to the Lord's intention that scriptures of adepts and erudite writers from India and Tibet be brought [to Kalzang], among others the following were to be taken there: the precious *Kangyur* which is the support of the Words of the Victorious Ones, the *Tengyur*, the *Collected Tantras of the Nyingma order*, *The Seven Treasures of Longchenpa*, *The Nyingthig Yazhi*, *The Collection of the Treatises of Sakya*, and *The Heart Essence of the Great Expanse*. All these were works of the oral tradition and treasures of the Nyingma order and the new orders. Later, Lama Dampa Taye, who had heard the Lord's instructions, carried them out and brought these works to the monastery.

Also at that time, the faithful inhabitants of all regions who had fortunate karmic connections gradually came to serve the Lord, and because of this the lama went there, conferring great benefit.

Having set off for Zhagsar, [the Lord] stopped for the night at a place called Bendo Khog. At that moment, the guardian of the treasures gave him a treasure receptacle with a seal of many lotus flowers. After that, beginning with upper Bor, he visited the regions of upper and lower Kyowo, Khyala Nyinsub, upper and lower Tsochu and Ushag, as well as the monasteries of Zhidar, Chödrag, a Bönpo monastery, another Sakya, and Mathang monastery. On being requested for teachings by the lamas and monks, he taught them *The Peaceful and Wrathful Ones of the Three Bodies* from *The Self-Liberated Mind of the Peaceful and Wrathful Ones*[318] cycle, the brief preliminary instructions, and some initiations and reading transmissions of his own treasures. He also gave long life initiations to families of men and women, the practice for Cutting, the reading transmission of the Transference, and everything suitable for them. The transmission [and practice] of the Transference raised [the consciousness of] a white-haired old man. Throughout that country [the Lord] worked unimaginably to benefit all beings, inciting them to abandon negativity and cultivate virtue.

On visiting a lama named Sangye who was living in Adri, he received the initiation and reading transmission of Cutting of Künga Bumpa. He donated the objects offered [to him] on behalf of the deceased in aid of monasteries and as alms to beggars. He gave many riches for the construction of his temple to his two foremen Phüntsog and Kartra.

The Lord went to Nacha Dragkar, where he officiated in an extensive ceremony of offerings for strengthening the samaya.[319] Then, in response to individual requests, he had to go to Chaye, Ladam, Mare, upper and lower Drewo, Drure, and Bodzi. He fulfilled the hopes of the faithful with initiations and reading transmissions, and did a remarkable amount of good, teaching the abandonment of negativity and the cultivation of virtue. He gave alms to the beggars from the goods left by the deceased. Whatever came into the hands of the foremen was offered, as before.

Then, going into retreat at the old monastic residence of Dragkar, he founded [a retreat place with the name] Charkai Pemo. There were the fortunate disciples who had gathered before this venerable man for some time, such as the holy Mila Tharchin—who had great experience in the supreme intuitive understanding—Thugten, Chöden, Sönam, Lama Jinpa, Washül Palden Kyeme, Bön Karma, lama Akar, Ludrub, Könchog, Garwang, Ramjams, Ösel, Paljor, Orgyan, and others. He taught all these many fortunate disciples, giving them instructions, according to their individual needs, in *The Ultimate Essence (Yang tig)*, *The Vajra Heart of the Luminous Expanse, Mahamudra, The Self-Liberation that Encompasses Space,* and so on; the complete instructions of common and extraordinary teachings as well as the initiations of *The Gathering of the Guru's Intention*[320] and the two cycles of *The Eight Transmitted Precepts;* the instructions on channels and winds of Inner Heat; and the instructions on the Clear Light for dark retreat.

The disciple Melong, who had heard the Lord's teachings, the fortunate possessor of an unshakable faith who was constantly behind the feet of the lama —the Supreme Protector—became the recipient of the descent of the buddha mind, and set down in writing some auxiliary practices of the development and accomplishment phases of *The Self-Liberation that Encompasses Space* cycle, some notes on the sadhana of the *Hundred Yidams,*[321] and on many sections of the cycle of spiritual songs.

On one occasion, he who has no equal in the Three Worlds, the Knowledge Holder Mingyur Tenpai Gyaltsen, third incarnation of Drime Zhingkyong Gönpo, was invited by the chief of Nyarong to the Drongtö monastery. The Lord and numerous disciples went to see him. He offered a mandal and other abundant offerings, such as gold, silver, turquoise, and coral, silk, cotton, and wild animal pelts, as well as dzo and horses. In his presence they received detailed instructions on the seven preliminary [sections] of the *The Vajra Heart of the Luminous Expanse* teachings, the

common preliminary instructions, the reading transmission and instructions for the ritual of aspiration and application of bodhicitta as explained
by Gyalwa Götsangpa, as well as full initiations and reading transmissions
of *The Blazing Wisdom of the Guru*,[322] *The Peaceful and Wrathful Ones of
the Three Bodies*,[323] Amitayus, Garuda, Hayagriva, Vajrapani, *The Heart
Essence of the Great Expanse, The Gathering of the Knowledge Holders,
Yumka,* and so on. To satisfy the aspirations of the precious incarnation,
the Lord also offered some initiations and reading transmissions of his
own treasures. In this way, the gifts of the supports for Body, Speech, and
Mind were perfectly bestowed.

On another occasion, the king of Nyarong[324] together with numerous
officials and servants appeared in Dragkar on pilgrimage. The king said
to the Lord:

> *Unless you immediately manifest a sign of realization before my
> senses, anything they say about your rank as a great adept is nothing
> but talk.*

He also said to the other lamas:

> *He is known for his signs of realization, but no doubt he's just an
> impostor!*

Then the Lord, thinking to transform the negative feelings of the king and
his retinue into a little virtue, with the attitude that extinguishes illusory
perceptions in dharmata, went unhindered some twenty-five dom straight
ahead to the mirror-like base of a great rock. Reaching the slopes of the
rock, he left images in gold and silk and returned to his place. The [king's]
earlier offensive request to the lama caused a hundred different furious
roaring sounds to echo from the rock. The terrified king begged him:

> *Oh lama, it would be extremely benevolent of you to silence the
> dragon while I am here!*

Because the lama had achieved yogic mastery of the discipline governing appearances and the mind, he subjugated the dragon before him and, keeping his promise, the dragon remained silent for a week. Then the king, who was very impressed, said:

Lama, you are truly a Great Adept! Who needs to live painfully in an empty cave like this? I offer you land that produces a hundred thousand khal[325] of barley, horsehair cloth, and other goods required for a settlement, as well as a consort. Organizing a great settlement [of practitioners], you'll be acting for the benefit of all beings in lower Dokham.

The lama replied:

The king's donations are certainly great. But I, a humble person always living a solitary life on the mountain, have totally forgotten the pleasures of eating meat and drinking beer. Seeing, time and again, the sufferings in the lower realms of existence, I have completely lost interest in the eight mundane dharmas. Having meditated over and over on the illusoriness and impermanence of all things, I don't know how to make predictions regarding that which is considered permanent. For this reason, even if you give me the king's own daughter, a thousand ounces of gold, and ornaments, it is as if this were only a single mani mantra. I, a humble vagabond, have unlimited happiness. By doing anything for the benefit of the Doctrine and sentient beings, you obtain an unimaginable degree of happiness. By considering impartially and with pure vision the teachings of the Kagyü, Sakya, Gelug, Nyingma and Bön orders—whose flower-like guides do not allow themselves to be shackled by negative emotions—you establish doubt-free faith. Particularly, [you must] avoid [committing] any offense against the Buddha's Doctrine, as the karma of one who abandons the Doctrine is more like fire than like water, and there is no remedy anywhere. The maturing of our acts surrounds us, and there is no way to separate the one from the other. Even the power of merit [accumulated in] the four continents is like a dream. Everything composite resembles the ten metaphors for illusion.[326]

Thus he spoke.

Some time later, having invited the venerable Lama Künzang Jigme to the retreat place, he received the great initiation of *The Sutra of the Gathering of Realization of All Buddhas*[327] that summarizes the general meaning of all the vehicles. Later, in response to the requests of many of the faithful, he went to Zhagsar and later to Nacha Dragkar. At the instant he arrived at the sacred place, the lama surreptitiously disappeared without a trace. The monks searched everywhere but could not find him. Three days later the lama emerged from a cave at the holy place and his body shone so brightly that the eyes could not bear to behold it. He appeared with a silk-wrapped treasure receptacle in his hands. The fortunate people who saw him really perceived him as the supreme Pema Jungne or as Dorje Trolö.

After this episode, the chief of Nyarong invited the reincarnation Palden Chogkyi Langpo, great Sakyapa master of the Khön family, to the Zhiwa monastery. The Lord and a disciple went to see him and offered him gold, silver, wild animal pelts, and other sublime offerings. From him they heard the teachings in the Nyima Bepa style of the twenty-one Taras with initiations and reading transmissions of (each of) the separate sadhanas. [They] also [received] the initiation and reading transmission of the yidam Vajrasattva, the oral transmission and instructions on *The Path and Fruit of Bodhicitta*,[328] as well as the initiation and authorization for Sarvavid Vairochana. The incarnation of Sakya had a vision in which the Lord appeared as Guru Rinpoche. To satisfy the incarnation's wishes, the Lord offered him a couple of beneficial reading transmissions and gave him unsurpassable offerings, including a text on *The Path and Fruit.*

He then returned to his previous dwelling place. At a certain time, on the road to Drure enroute to lower Nyarong, was a rock with a spirit that was harmful to all beings. He picked up the rock with his hands and threw it. The spirit was subjugated by a vow. In many places he left imprints on trees, rocks, and so on, even using a spoon to write the six-syllable mantra on a rock. He also left many handprints and footprints.

Then there began a period of upheaval, caused mainly by the chief of Nyarong, who in Bugta confronted the chief of Derge, the chief of the five divisions of Hor, and the chief of Dzachukha. Many hundreds of men were imprisoned, and it was a time of great suffering. Using almost all the Lord's supplies and riches, the prisoners were fed and freed to return home. This was an act of great generosity because the supervisors of the Lord's possessions had [previously] been robbed. At this time, some venerable disciples gave all their goods and food to some of the poorest prisoners. As the Omniscient Jigme Lingpa said:

My mind, since infancy, contained compassion free from
falsehood.
Thus, this is greatly acknowledged in the story of my spiritual
liberation.

In this degenerate age, it is only the benevolent personal master who [sees to] the protection of beings through an equanimous compassion.

The Lord had earlier prophesied the inception of the war in Nyarong, as well as the future fall of the chief of Nyarong's capital. He had also prophesied how his benefactor[329] would be abused and how his death would occur. However, because I consider it unnecessary, I shall not write about it.

Then, those circumstances developed into a major conflict that resulted in the deaths of the chief of Nyarong and some of his sons. Hearing of this, moved by great compassion, the Lord recited the funeral liturgy, the Transference transmission, and many aspirational and devotional prayers. Due to the Lord's compassion and his commanding of his heir,

Lama Taye [to intervene,] the chief's general and his [other] sons were saved from death.

Then, the armies of central Tibet invaded Nyarong. The chief of Phug, Phunrabpa, and many Tibetan leaders went to see the Lord. He conferred many blessings and established spiritual connections with them all.

The following year there were many conflicts between the men of Nyarong and the Tibetans. The Lord went to the mountain to mediate the conflict, and the Phunrabpa official, who had been promoted to governor of Amdo, offered the Lord a container of twenty-five khal of barley and some three hundred good rifles. Even though these rifles' value in dotse was over three hundred silver ingots, he had them destroyed there and then.

In the prophetic index of the profound treasures, it is written:

*[Among] the three characteristics [of body, speech, and mind] and
other qualities of the Precious Lord of the Doctrine, [is that of being]
a leader of one hundred and eight Great Adepts.*

In accordance with this prophecy, afterwards the Lord of these teachings, the unsurpassed physician who heals through the Doctrine, manifested the ocean of his protective actions by bestowing the gift of a precious command with a big golden seal, and said:

*By the power of this aspirational prayer, may the relations between
the old and the new traditions be without sectarianism, and may
the conditions for the permanence of the Doctrine of the Victorious
Ones be forever established!*

He then reconciled many groups and chiefs who had been at loggerheads for some time. At that time, the governor and various other opposing groups—former enemies—were reconciled. [The Lord] went to a place in Nyarong called Gyazur, and arrived at a newly congregated monastic community. Blessing the earth, he assigned it the name Sangag Dechen Chöling monastery in Kharkyawa. He also founded a new temple for nuns, which he called Temple of Tsogyal. Thus, he named a new monastery and new temple. He left many supports [for practice] in the two monastic enclosures. He prophesied that later these two places would flourish greatly. He then returned to his own monastery.

Then, he went to meet a person whose realization equals that of the king of adepts in India, the fourth incarnation of Dzogchen Pema Rigdzin, called Jigme Chökyi Wangchug, also known as Mingyur Namkhai Dorje whose name resounds throughout the three worlds like the great drum [of the deities]. Some sixty disciples went with the Lord and offered all kinds of precious materials including several kinds of brocade, ornamental costumes for the deities, as well as tea, horses, and dzo. Those who had recently lost a family member asked the Lord to send the deceased to a pure dimension, giving him the person's name in writing. Then, Mingyur Namkhai Dorje Rinpoche, having conferred the common preliminaries of *The Heart Essence of the Great Expanse* and *The White Path to Liberation*,[330] offered the long version of the instructions. Mingyur Namkhai Dorje and Khenpo Kalden made notes on the instructions and gave the reading transmission of the common instructions of *The Transcendent Wisdom Master* and the practice of the channels and winds of Inner Heat, as well as for the cycles of *The Gathering of the Knowledge Holders, Yumka, Blazing Hayagriva-Garuda*,[331] *The Unification of the Threee Jewels*,[332] and his own treasure, *The Pure Vision of the Powerful Guru Raksha Garland of Skulls*,[333] giving the complete initiations and reading transmissions. To satisfy Rinpoche's desire, the Lord offered him some of the minor texts of his own treasures.

Later he met one who had obviously attained realization and supreme knowledge, Paltrül Rinpoche, who told him:

Sublime being, I have heard of your feats and, in this degenerate time, you are certainly a coherent Bodhisattva with everything that this implies. I think it would be favorable to expound to you the text Guide to the Bodhisattva's Way of Life.[334]

He gave the fifteen [chapters] of *Guide to the Bodhisattva's Way of Life*, as well as the reading transmission of *Chanting the Names of Manjushri*.[335] That incarnation, the Sovereign of Realization of Knowledge, offered the Lord the following long life prayer and auspicious verses:

> *Thanks to the power of the Lotus Born, the immortal essence of all the Victorious Ones,*
> *And of the immeasurable mandala of the magical deities of long life, as well as the dakas, dakinis, and guardians,*
> *May this excellent representative of Padma live a long life!*
> *By your marvelous signs of realization,*
> *Valiant savior of these arrogant and difficult beings,*
> *You are the only protector of the savages to be converted in this degenerate age.*
> *May your lotus feet stay firmly on the Vajra throne!*
> *[May you] establish the purest vision in those who have erroneous vision,*
> *And transform the accumulation of the ten kinds of wrongdoing through the glory of the ten virtues!*
> *May you have a long life, unique benefactor who gloriously bestows*
> *The splendid golden age, putting an end to the age of conflict!*
> *Further, in these immense countries of Jambudvipa,[336]*
> *May all pure Masters of the Doctrine of the Victorious Ones,*
> *And all who support its diffusion and teachings, live long!*
> *May the precious Doctrine of the Victorious Ones spread and flourish!*

Thus, this sublime spiritual master offered a long life prayer.

Later, having gone to Gangtrö to draw out some profound treasures [hidden] in the elements of nature, he made some drawings of the signs of the treasures on the rocks. At the same time, in the temple at that place he had immeasurable pure visions. Specifically, going to the glorious mountain of Chamara,[337] he met the excellent sovereign of the Knowledge Holders, Orgyan Thötrengtsal (Padmasambhava). As he had obtained a transmission of the teachings of unimaginable power as a blessing, [in his mind] there appeared the mind treasure, *The Tantra of the Melodious Song of the Vajra*[338] that knows no limits.

Then, Mingyur Namkhai Dorje offered him his hat, a monk's shawl and a cushion, as well as supports for body, speech, and mind, and other unsurpassable offerings, saying:

> *Sublime being, both you and I are inseparable from the totality of*
> *pure dimensions.*

And thus speaking, their minds intermingled in a single state. Then they invited Lama Tsültrim Dragpa, the master who was an expert in the *Kangyur* and with him, in a relaxed way they gradually read through it from the beginning. [As a result,] laymen and religious people in the area greatly increased their avoidance of negativy and cultivation of virtue.

In keeping with the needs of the monasteries and of the pious laymen in the surrounding area who requested his services, [the Lord] went to visit Horkhog valley—all the hills of the Dre riverbed—and from Rongpatsa he went slowly on to Beri, Dangthog, and Kardze. Thus, he gave long life initiations, commentaries on the Doctrine, the reading transmission of the practice of Transference and the practice of Cutting, and he purified the place. Everyone's spiritual practices favoring the abandonment of negativity and the cultivation of virtue were strengthened. The goods of the deceased were used in support of all the monasteries and as alms for the beggars.

While he was living in the region of Kardze monastery he had a good encounter with the incarnation of Zigyab Rinpoche from whom he received some teachings, including the initiation of the Medicine Buddha and the reading transmission of *The Hundred Deities of Tushita*.[339] With a piece of Chinese copper[340] he had been given that was valued at sixty ounces of silver, he made an incense burner decorated with the glorious endless knot, 'that which has six angles.'

Thus, having crossed the great river [of Kardze], thanks to his supernatural powers, he left footprints. Such are the wonders of his yogic deeds, identical to the acts of past masters such as Guru Rinpoche and the Great Adept Virupa, which occur upon the acquisition of the supreme view.

Then, in the valleys of upper Nyarong, he went to Zhiwa and Harpang where he gave initiations and established spiritual links, brought about the abandonment of evil and the cultivation of virtue, provided supports for the faith, and made donations to the poor, as previously described.

When he arrived at Zhiwa, he made a prophesy regarding the young heir and prince, called Sögyal:

He has an excellent system of energy channels, and without doubt
he is an emanation. He should therefore follow me [as a disciple],
which will certainly help both the Doctrine and all beings.

He then gave abundant initiations and blessings. The boy later became the indisputable and venerable great tertön who opened the hundred doors of profound treasures, Lerab Lingpa.[341]

He then went to the monastery of Zilha Bum and predicted the building of the new convent of Nyinchar while blessing the foundations of the [future] temple.

On reaching a region called Delong, he sTayed in a green meadow adorned with flowers and surrounded by a pleasant wood, a place possessing many positive qualities for a solitary retreat. There he received from the preceptor of the canonical texts, Tsültrim Dragpa, the complete reading transmission of the precious *Kangyur* of the Victorious Ones as well as for the twenty-five volumes of the transmission lineage of the *Tengyur*. Further, from the repa[342] Namdröl Dorje, he heard the preliminaries of the *Heart Essence* and the yantra yoga of channels and winds. From lama Künzang Jigme he received the reading transmission of *The Profound*

Innermost Essence of the Guru[343] and *The Profound Innermost Essence*[344] of Longchenpa.

During this period, the Lord conferred the instructions for the preliminaries in detail to his new disciples, among whom were Gangshar, Zhidröl, Thugchog, Gagme, Künzang, Dagleg, Trinle, Gyaltsen, Palzang, and numerous lamas from upper and lower Nyarong.

Although the disciples close to Drubchen Rinpoche[345]—Togden Dampa Palden and the bhikshu[346] of noble vows, Sönam Gyaltsen—had no need to follow another lama, on seeing the qualities of the Lord's works they were convinced he was a real Buddha. From then on they sought to be close to him.

On one occasion, the Tibetans and the people of the Tongkor region entered into conflict. Thus, the Lord had to go to Tongkor to pacify the conflict. As there was a great place of pilgrimage devoted to the Lords of the Three Families,[347] he went there on pilgrimage and performed a purification ritual. [The inhabitants] of the villages and monasteries throughout the region felt an insuperable faith and abandoned negativities and cultivated unparalleled virtue.

Later, after the Lord had returned to his own monastery at Kalzang and consecrated the temple, he presided over an assembly convened for the celebration of the 'consecration of the Vase' ritual, authenticated by two teachings: *The Self-Liberated Mind of The Peaceful and Wrathful Ones* and that of his own treasure, *Self-Liberation that Encompasses Space*. Due to the powerful waves of blessings, the holy pills [contained in the Vase] were scattered all around.

He also invited to the monastery the eminent scholar from Ogön, Lama Sherab Gyaltsen, to give concise instructions on the *Guhyagarbhatantra* and on *The Profound Inner Meaning*[348] by the Lord Rangjung Dorje.[349] When the Lord invited the khenpo of Dzogchen monastery, Sherab Tharchin, the latter gave the reading transmission of the complete *Collected Tantras of the Nyingma*,[350] as well as access to the practice of the Peaceful Deities and the instructions on Gyalse Shenphen Taye's *Six Topics of Knowledge*.[351]

On another occasion, servants from the monasteries of Öphung and Dechen came to ask the Lord if he could come to preside over a consecration of the Vase. He went and consecrated the Vase in the two monasteries and bestowed many initiations, thus establishing spiritual connections with all who came from the region and the monasteries.

He did numerous beneficial deeds for all beings, such as when he [responded to] his intense desire to repair the ruins of the previous residence of Gyalse Dorje Chöwang, the monastic enclosure of Samten. On his way home, he arrived by chance at Gojam monastery and consecrated the site of the new main temple.

After he had returned to Kalzang to stay, at a certain time there appeared rainbow-colored spheres of light[352] of varying brightness in the sky, as well as an immense circle of light surrounded by four smaller ones in [each of] the four directions. All the monks and lamas saw these excellent signs, a marvel that had never been seen before. The Lord and some of his disciples such as Kalden and Taye had visions of the Thousand Buddhas of the Glorious Eon. The Lord composed a hymn to each of the names of the Buddhas of the Glorious Eon. It consisted of several parts, including the sections of salutation, offering, confession of negativities, rejoicing in virtue, requesting the spinning of the wheel of Dharma, requesting the enlightened ones not to pass on to nirvana, and unparalleled dedication of the root of all virtue toward the attainment of total realization, all in the style of the Dharma treasures and of pure visions.

On that occasion Karma, Rinchen, Loden, Rangrig, Chagdrel, and Ango came to the Lord as new disciples. Other disciples already known to the Lord, such as Tülku Rigdzin, Kalzang, Sempel, Künga, Kündröl, and many others were like sons to him. To them he transmitted the preliminary instructions in full detail. Having named Rangrig—linked to the most profound of the Lord's teachings—his spiritual heir, he showed him a prophecy regarding the future treasures [he would discover]. Later, Rangrig became a great and venerable treasure finder, having acquired mastery on the mind treasure, *The Secret Treasury of the Realization of Samantabhadra*.[353]

Shortly thereafter, the carpenters' and painters' work in the temple mentioned above was finished. Then, having completed the three mandalas —the extensive, the medium and the concise—of *The Profound Doctrine: Self-Liberation that Encompasses Space,* under the Lord's supervision, the painter Adön began work on the tsakali[354] for the method of the medium mandala. Later, following the precise instructions given to him by this doctrine's holder Dzatrül Rinpoche,[355] using his extensive spiritual vision, the same painter completed [the tsakali] of the extensive method, and so on.

In verses:

The ocean that gathers the river of his impartial compassion
Is like the treasure of the naga king, perfect in its one hundred
*   qualities.*
May the one who possessed the cloud of the precepts' essential
*   nectar,*
This Lord of the rain that matures and liberates, take care of me!

CHAPTER TEN

How, Having Destroyed Fixation on Illusory Vision, He Remained in Experience Free From Action.

From then on, the Lord no longer held any concepts nor was he attached to mundane phenomena. At times he remained in a state free from action under all circumstances, making no distinction between day and night. He sometimes went to join children at play, behaving just like one of them. In the same way, at times he covered himself with a blue robe and joined the assembly of practitioners, while at other times he went naked. Sometimes when he gave teachings, his voice was like that of an old man. At other times, he sang his songs of spiritual experience.

Many fortunate people watched as neither sunlight nor lamps could cast his shadow. At times he seemed transparent, and some disciples who carried him on their backs from his dormitory to the monastic enclosure felt as if he weighed no more than an article of clothing. Many fortunate spiritual heirs who were attending him, like Taye and Melong, witnessed how the Lord's speech was not contaminated by ordinary values.

After some time, the Lord and many disciples left their monastery of Kalzang and travelled towards some monasteries at Nyagshi, having been invited there by other disciples. He bestowed many initiations and established spiritual connections. Later on, he consecrated the main chapel of Zhagnying Samten monastery. From upper Trom, many of the faithful sent servants who begged for his presence. There he gave an initiation for long life and established many spiritual links. He had an excellent meeting with two incarnate lamas from Tromge, both the older and the younger. He also met Ngawang, surrounded by hundreds of sublime yogis.

Because the greatly learned [holder] of supreme knowledge Dzatrül Rinpoche Künzang Nampar Gyalwa lived in Trom, [the Lord] went there with his disciples and had an excellent meeting with him. [The Lord] asked the precious incarnation for a long life initiation and a spiritual connection. To please him [in return], the Lord gave him some initiations and reading transmissions of his own treasure, and he offered him the empowerment for the volume of Dharma treasure. Thanks to his pure prayer, their minds were joined in a single state. On asking the excellent incarnation for the initiation [for long life], the Lord held a very brilliant mandal with a relief in the center but no border to limit it. There was therefore no way of keeping the offerings on the mandal; nevertheless, he arranged the piles of rice and many precious materials in heaps almost a cubit high. Because of this, the omniscient incarnation fused his mind in a single state [with the Lord's], forging a fortunate interdependent connection through which [Dzatrül] became the holder of the Lord's doctrine.

Later, moving to lower Trom, he had an excellent meeting with the incarnation Adzom and his uncle.[356] In particular, he united his mind in a single state with [the mind of] Drugtrül Rinpoche,[357] the practitioner of the yoga of secret mantra.

In lower Trom they sTayed in a place called Serzhung where a practice camp had been established for a retreat. When the powerful, erudite adept lama Lungtog arrived, they had a good meeting. From this venerable lama [the Lord] heard the explanation and meaning of the sutra known as *The Commemoration of the Three Jewels* and the abbreviated form of the *Guide to the Bodhisattva's Way of Life* by the great son of the Victorious Ones, Shantideva. Later, at the retreat place at Kharkhog, he received from the same lama the abbreviated form of *The Transcendent Wisdom Master* written by the Knowledge Holder Jigme Lingpa [containing] the guiding instructions for the section on Ati Yoga, the pinnacle of all vehicles. Because this venerable lama was very close to Jigme Lingpa in the transmission lineage, he pleased the Lord who dearly longed for the waves of blessings perpetuated uninterruptedly through the human lineage.

To his closest disciples including Sarbu, Kartsen, Lode, Kalden, Tsultrim, and so on, as well as to some hundreds of disciples from upper and lower Trom, [the Lord] offered instructions for the preliminaries as well as for the Inner Heat belonging to the systems of winds and channels.

In response to the request of the old lama Namkha, Drugtrül Rinpoche, and the incarnation Ngawang, he offered the lamas, the assembly of monks, and thousands of laymen and women an initiation [that opens the doors] to all the vehicles, that of the *Sutra of the Gathering of Realization of All Buddhas*, as well as the initiations and reading transmissions of the *The Self-Liberated Mind of the Peaceful and Wrathful Ones*, of the twenty-one Taras from the treasure of Künzang Düdjom, and [of] the cycle *Self-Liberation that Encompasses Space*, the treasure that he had received. He exhorted them all to practice and to abandon negativities, thus bringing unimaginable good to all beings.

At that time, the Lord felt great kindness toward a novice called Ngawang Tendzin, who was from the Tatrom assembly, and gave him excellent advice, saying:

> *You are an emanation, and you will work excellently for the good of all beings.*

Later, confirming this prophecy, [the novice] became Thutob Lingpa, a great incarnate treasure finder with supreme authority over the extensive and profound treasure chamber.

After this, the Lord and many disciples went to visit Drubthob Rinpoche, a master whom they had met in the past, and they had an excellent reunion. They requested numerous initiations and reading transmissions, including [the one for] *Yumka, the Queen of Total Bliss*. The Lord said that due to certain circumstances, he would call the conscious principle of a recently deceased person into the base of a skull cup. And doing as he said, while he was sustaining it, the skull cup rose into the air and the vajra that the lama was holding in his hand also rose higher and higher, flying off into the sky. It is likely that the deceased person's consciousness, remaining in a concrete form, was at the bottom of the skull cup because the Lord moved it, focusing instant presence on the corpse[358] by the special system of the yogis of Total Perfection, in harmony with the explanations in the secret tantras.

The Lord returned to his residence [Kalzang] to remain for a time. In response to the request of the incarnation from Dragmar and his own disciple, the monk Sönam Gyaltsen, he went to Dragmar monastery and met with the precious incarnation. He gave explanations on meditative systems of realization, consecrated the three principal kinds of cult objects,[359] and gave initiations and numerous doctrinal explanations. He also gave initiations and established spiritual links, officiated in Cutting practices and gave the reading transmission of the Transference to many religious people and laymen from the surrounding area who had great faith in him. He benefited all beings by inciting the cultivation of virtue and the abandonment of negativity, and the tireless cultivation of generosity towards the poor.

Later, he was invited to the two monasteries in the Garje district, and on arriving at Khangbu monastery he had a positive encounter with Khyenchö Chökyi Chenyang Tülku Rinpoche. [The Lord] offered extensive explanations of the meditative systems mentioned above, as well as the initiations and consecrations of the three cult objects. The local chiefs treated him very well. To both monks and laymen he offered long life initiations, spiritual links, and reading transmissions of the Transference and the Cutting practices. Having felt a great aspiration imbued with faith, they all became beneficially inclined to cultivate virtue and abandon negativities.

He then went to Tsophu, the monastery of one of his masters, Drubchen Rinpoche,[360] where he had a pleasant meeting with the chief Nyima and with lamas and monks in general. Before the remains of Drubchen Rinpoche, he recited the prayer of seven branches to gather the accumulations [of merit and wisdom], did the meditation and recitation of guruyoga, and then bestowed the gift of the four initiations. Because all the disciples and laymen of the area were filled with an unsurpassable faith, enormous benefit was achieved for all beings through the abandonment of the negative and cultivation of the positive. The Lord offered many riches in support of the doctrine of this lama, who had been his protector. Returning once more to Tromkhog, he had a good meeting with the tertön of Serpa, Garwang Drodül Lingpa and they exchanged initiations and teachings, uniting their minds in a single state.

Later, while staying in a monastery in the valley called Samu, he conferred the instructions for the preliminaries to the previously mentioned disciples as well as to Sarbur, Rangzhag, Dzinme, Chödrub, Tharchin, Gyurme, Nyima Tsering, and others. The Lord said:

Understanding that ordinary thoughts are our own unfolding
Is the great joy of self-liberation free from error.
He who remains naked in the state of great bliss
Is the yogi who possesses great happiness.
In the state of transcendent wisdom, which is happiness and bliss,
The song of happiness goes, "ki li li!"
And the dance of the state of self-liberation, bliss, and emptiness
  resounds!

And also:

To know that Transcendent Wisdom is our self-manifestation
Is the great bliss of self-liberation without meditation.
He who remains naked in the state of great bliss
Is the yogi who possesses great happiness.
In the state of Transcendent Wisdom that is happiness and bliss,
The song of happiness goes, "ki li li!"
And the dance in the state of self-liberation, bliss, and emptiness
  resounds!

His glorious throat expressed these joyful songs of yogic experience, accompanied by vajra laughter.

After these events, his body manifested a serious illness. He ate nothing for three weeks, and told his closest disciples:

> *I am entering the space of peace. Visions of groups of spiritual*
> *heroes and yoginis appear*
> *[before me], coming from the pure field of Orgyan Khangdrö Ling*
> *to welcome me.*

Then, the closest disciples, including Togden Dampa Palden begged him:

> *Out of compassion for all beings in general who have no protection,*
> *and for your disciples here congregated in particular, we beg you to*
> *give up [the idea of dying].*

In response to their many sobs and groans, [the Lord] said to them:

> *Do not despair. I shall remain for another year or two.*

His body remained alive for three half-years. This act of dominion over life and death resembles the story of the accession to nirvana of the Victorious One from the past [Buddha Shakyamuni] when he accepted the request of his lay disciple Chanda to remain for a few more months.

In verses:

> *Splendid wish-fulfiling gem of magnificent virtue,*
> *He accomplished at once the hopes of sentient beings*
> *And the transcendence over day and night*
> *By his total contemplation, beyond ordinary mind.*
> *May I be protected by this ruler of beings!*

Chapter Eleven

How He Transmitted His Spiritual Testament, in the Form of Advice, to His Vajra Disciples.

The Sovereign Daka of the Adepts [the Lord], said:

With pure vision, everything is a harmonious friend. What sense is there in binding oneself with the rope of suffering? Remaining constantly in the unique state and distancing oneself from the conceptual mind, without attachment to the objective sphere, this is the life of the bodhi.

He acted in accordance with his speech.

The Lord, accompanied by all those fortunate disciples who practiced the nectar of his teachings, stopped at a place called Kharkhog near the rock at Drichung Kowo, which is an ancient place where Rinchen Lingpa had discovered treasures. Practitioners such as the [Kathog Situ,] scholarly Lord of the Adepts and incarnation from the monastery of Kathog, along with his disciples as well as the sublime Lama Lungtog, arrived like a string of ducks on a lotus lake in order to meet the Lord. They were ardently searching for precious and profound spiritual precepts. They were given initiations, reading transmissions of different sections of the teachings and, in particular, the profound essential instructions of the Section of the Precepts. On this occasion, [Kathog] Situ Rinpoche offered this prayer for the Lord's long life:

Om siddhu nha

Self-Generated Lotus (Padmasambhava) and the sixty masters,
With the aim of spreading the Doctrine of Ati that transcends
*   concepts,*
The summit of the nine vehicles,
You show yourselves as yogis with plaited hair and white robes.[361]
Approaching you with compassionate intent,
I beg that those trapped by ordinary philosophical reasoning,
Attached to acts of training and discipline, who only see through
*   speculation,*
May all directly experience the self-generated Transcendent Wis-
*   dom*
By being introduced to the Primordial Protector [Samanta-
*   bhadra]!*
Bodhicitta has no birth or death.
The sterile confines of ignorance lead to future deviation.
May the excellent hero who has conquered the four demons of his
*   own vision*[362]
Remain among us without resorting to the Victorious Ones' great
*   method*
Of leaving for the Dharmadhatu!
Further, being so dissatisfied by the essence of words, names, and
*   superficial writings*
Inadequate against the deception caused by illusion,
I beg you to act, free from increase or decrease, beyond all mun-
*   dane acquisition,*
And [pray] that your mandala of the ornaments of Body, Speech,
*   and Mind*
Remain until the realization of all beings!

That was the prayer he offered.

Then he offered instructions on the preliminaries, on Inner Heat, channels and winds, and other teachings to the previously mentioned disciples such as Sangphur, Wangchug, Geleg, Karma, Rinchen, Thogme, Kyondrel, Jigdrel, Gyapön, Chödrag, and so on. To these same disciples and by means of the written instructions of *The Transcendent Wisdom Master*, he bestowed the introduction for the direct discovery in one's own condition of the manifest Wisdoms and Bodies, in the present moment that is free from dependence on future lives. He thus conferred the precepts of the Buddhas, the unparalleled profound instructions of the Total Perfection.

He also advised each of his disciples:

Whether I die or whether I remain, you must now abandon once and for all the senseless illusory actions, the appearance of virtue that is actually based on the eight worldly dharmas, the senseless discussions that fall into dogmatism and, within yourselves, an intention to help others that is made up of nothing but empty words and is thus an incomplete compassion. [All this] would result in a cause of Buddhahood [about as significant] as the tip of a hair.
Abandon senseless, illusory action!
Behead the eight worldly dharmas!
Base yourselves on your own practice experiences!
Do not discuss vision and meditation with others!
Let great compassion infuse your mental continuum!
Fulfill the most important aspirations of the old man, who is me, myself!
Do good for yourselves and for others!
Make no mistakes! Make no mistakes!

He repeated this endlessly. Giving a staff to each of his new disciples, he advised them:

> *Do not act according to the common black illusion that attends the*
> *objects of the six aggregates of consciousness.*[363] *If you cannot maintain*
> *the presence of the knowledge of your own mind, and you feel like*
> *moving, strike your leg! If you feel like working, strike your hand!*
> *If you feel like speaking, strike your mouth!*

Thus, generating the strength of heart that does not fall into disquisitions on theoretical views or meditation, the Lord imparted much nectar-like advice. Just as is described [in the life] of the protector of times past, Longchenpa—who, on meeting the Adept Kumaradza was subject to many exhausting circumstances due to the siddha's instructions, never staying in one place for more than two or three months—in the same way, having [at last] reached the monastery of the former master Kathogpa Jetsün Changchub Palwa in the country called Tselha Wangdo, master and disciples sTayed for some time. His new disciples, the omniscient and compassionate incarnation Tendzin Norbu and the incarnation of Chophu gathered before him. In accordance with their aspirations, he conferred the initiations and reading transmissions of sections of the teachings and the unparalleled essential instructions for one hundred profound precepts. Then, the Lord received a revelation in the form of a mind treasure, of the sadhana of mind, *Self-Liberated Instant Presence*[364] consisting of the meditative system of realization of the tutelary deity Hayagriva-Vajrapani; the outer meditative system of realization, *The White Lotus Garland,*[365] and the secret meditative system of realization, *The Gathering of the Awareness Holders,*[366] all belonging to the *Peaceful and Wrathful Ones* cycle.

On one occasion, the Lord, holding in his hands all the riches [bequeathed by] a deceased follower of the teachings, said, "All this should be used to print the general teachings of the path of the Sugatas," and gave it all to the monastery of Kathog. At a certain time, asking all his disciples to gather before him, he said:

> *It is certain that I shall not be here much longer, so you must practice*
> *as I have been teaching since long ago, and make no mistakes.*

Calling each one to him, he gave definitive instructions to each according to his motivations and faculties, giving many introductions into the
profound meaning. Later, they went to a valley called Nyin where they
sTayed for several months. The Lord and his disciples made many ritual
offerings to repair the samaya. In *The Precious Treasury of Qualities*,[367] it
is written:

> *Like the [clinging] vines so common in the dense jungles*
> *   of Malaya,*
> *If you follow [a master], commit yourself to follow him faithfully,*
> *As if he were a fragrant sandalwood tree in the damp woodlands.*

Consequently, even if an individual with negative actions, like a butcher,
came before this holy person, the simple act of attending the precious
nectar of his teachings on the preliminary instructions would produce in
his mental continuum an elevated impulse towards renunciation, and he
would become a person motivated solely by the practice of bodhicitta and
realization. All knew this. Similarly, if one examines and observes how
the spiritual activities were carried out to benefit all beings, [one will see
that] they were not produced by selfish desires caused by ignorance, but
were carried out according to the indications intentionally set out by the
Victorious Ones to illustrate the deceptions into which humans fall. [This
capacity] pertains to the area of realization, [illuminated] by the vast and
pure eye of the Dharma.

In verses:

> *He exhibited the uncontrived conduct of one hundred rays of*
> *   light,*
> *Removing the sphere of accumulation of darkness*
> *Caused by illusory concepts.*
> *May I become a suitable disciple of the supreme vehicle*
> *As taught by that Protector,*
> *And be a light-giver through the supreme and marvelous vehicle!*

Chapter Twelve

Examining the Authoritative Texts of the Supreme Vehicle; How He Integrated His Body Into Space.

🌸 There, in the presence of the sublime Lord, disciples from far and near as well as the faithful, piously and respectfully asked him which personal deity was suited for practice aimed at avoiding obstacles in life and [promoting] longevity; [they asked him to explain] what their previous lives had been like and what their future ones would be like. The Lord replied:

In past lives you have accumulated the corresponding virtues and negativities. Therefore, you have the bodily marks and moles on the upper and lower body, and these are permanent. In the next life you will become this or that, and I told you long ago with which deity of realization [you are connected]. All of you should check where you have moles on your upper and lower bodies and how they indicate a long or short life. Regarding the personal yidam, it is the one toward which you feel the most faith and devotion. It is like discerning the characteristics of kyurara[368] by holding it in your hand and observing it.

Out of respect, the disciples were afraid to write down [his advice], and so I cannot write any more on this matter. However, you must know that you can find information on the succession of births in other [writings].

Then, on the new moon day of the peaceful month of nirvana—the Vaisakha month—in the year of the Water Monkey (1872) called Angkira, the Lord pitched a little tent and entered it. Telling his disciples to come, he asked them to rest and to meditate on the support [of faith] above the crown of their heads, and he instructed them as follows:

> *In all your lives, may you never be separate from a perfect guru,*
> *And continually enjoying the glory of the Doctrine,*
> *May you fully achieve the qualities of the levels and paths [of*
>   *realization]!*
> *May you quickly attain the level of Vajradhara!*

And also:

> *Now each of you must go to his own place. I am going to sew up the*
> *entrance to the tent and let no one approach for one week.*

In keeping with the Lord's instruction, each disciple sadly went to his own place. Then, the day after the week was up, they honored the tent where the Lord lived by performing prostrations. On opening it they found—in the place where the lama had rested—his clothes, cushion, the hair from his head, and his fingernails and toenails. Of the mandala of his body, nothing remained. Then, when the disciples erupted in a chorus of desperate lamentations, a rainbow appeared, and its light filled the sky.

At this time, the disciples who had excellent cognition and all those who were truly sons of his heart, saw him in visions or during sleep where, bestowing his word upon them, he gave them great confidence in the supreme teachings.

In particular, in that period Trülzhig Changchub Lingpa[369] appeared to the Knowledge Holder Kusum Lingpa—also known as Gyalse Rigpai

Dorje—and recognized him as a son of Transcendent Wisdom and, unifying the knowledge of the vast expanse of profound, sublime Teachings, he bestowed these words:

The refined nectar of the adamantine heart of Ati is found nakedly
in the matchless Upadeshas I exhorted you [to practice], excellent son!

Saying this while remaining [suspended] in space before him, he displayed the threatening mudra with his right hand on the crown of Kusum Lingpa's head, to seal the act of concealing within him the secret treasure comprising the interpretation of the symbolic code of the dakinis. From this instant, Kusum Lingpa attained the realization of the kingdom that totally transcends concepts. He became free from the trap that seizes the dualistic phenomena of samsara and nirvana. Without exception, the visual appearances, sounds, and thoughts perceptibly emerged as the mandala of the three secrets [body, speech, and mind]. The key points of the vehicle of total liberation were inserted into his mind while the creative energy of Knowledge and Transcendent Wisdom blazed forth. Thus, the qualities of spiritual realization and abandonment [of negativities] were brought to light.

After a few days had passed, the Lord of the family [of realized ones] Trülzhig Lingpa, appeared in person and showed him a precious yellow manuscript about a cubit long containing several types of symbolic writings of the dakinis. He said, "Son, do you know this?" Although Gyalse Rigpai Dorje did not know it fully, he did have some idea [of symbolic writing]. The Lord, placing his right thumb on [Gyalse Rigpai Dorje's] head, said:

May the realization that interprets the symbolic writing of the
dakinis merge into your consciousness, my son. A Phat!

Immediately after saying this, the Lord looked to his right where the Queen of the dakinis Ekajati was, and saying, "Give that which I have proclaimed, fully and with no omission, to the son of my heart!" he disappeared into space as if he were a rainbow. At dawn the next day the atmosphere was filled with iridescent light and appearances of numerous auspicious and marvelous signs. [This knowledge] having been activated by the Lady of the Mantras (Ekajati) through the symbols self-generated in dharmata, a master copy of the interpretation of the dakinis' code was created, which was ultimately found in its entirety in one of the Lord's treasures, the collection of rituals of spiritual actions of *Hayagriva-Vajrapani: the Self-Liberation of Dharmata.*[370] It is also found among the Lord's secret sadhanas, for example, in the many sections dedicated to the blessings of the mind treasures.

This marvelous account accords with that used by Garab Dorje, the Lord who transmitted the Excellent Vehicle, and with [those of] the majority of realized Knowledge Holders who embraced fortunate disciples with the Body of Transcendent Wisdom.

Going further into the latter, I must add that from the ultimate point of view of primordial purity of Total Relaxation, the concrete nature of the physical body is purified, or rather, reintegrated into the elemental particles, as occurred at the departure of Pang Mipham Gönpo and others; this point becomes a lovely elixir for the heart of the fortunate. Marvelous!

In brief, this sublime being, maintaining the severe asceticism undertaken in the past, became free in the state beyond mental fixation, overcoming the reckoning of virtue and sin; he cultivated impartial compassion and united phenomena and mind in a single flavor. Having liberated attachment to food and clothing, water and a simple cotton robe were enough to sustain his body. In sunlight or lamplight, his body did not cast a shadow. His excrement and urine did not smell bad, and his body was as light as cotton. He crossed great rivers and rocky mountains with no difficulty; he possessed the extraordinary ability to know other people's minds. All these are the unmistakable marks of mastery of the paths of Total Relaxation of primordial purity and the four spontaneous visions[371] of the Total Perfection, as established by reasoning and scripture. In *The Blazing Relics,*[372] it is written:

...in the field of visible experience, just as an aspiration travels through a mountain unhindered, [the realized being] is able to descend into the depths of the earth or [stand on the surface of] the water without sinking.

Also, in the tantra of the Total Perfection, The Self-Manifesting Instant Presence,[373] it is written:

His body is like cotton, broad and of good complexion, with no grey hair or wrinkles; the hair and nails cease growing

...

Having always told the truth, anything said is beneficial to others.

....

Wrong words are never spoken; the diversity of the Dharma is spontaneously expressed.

...

Having cultivated the mind, neither food nor clothes are necessary; samadhi is established for months and years and the attention is focused on the dance of the inner winds. Purified by the thought of future death, attachment to actions has ceased; having given rise to a limitless compassion, negative emotions do not arise in his mental continuum.

Similarly, the Protector Longchenpa wrote:

At the level of Reaching the Culmination of Instant Presence[374] that is somewhat like an elephant who has fallen into the mud,[375] absolutely everything, including rocky mountains, becomes diaphanous transparency, without obstruction. His voice, as melodious as that of a small Kumbhanda [spirit], fluently expresses Dharma verses whenever he speaks. The mind, like someone recovered from an infectious disease, is immune to the recurrence of the karmic traces that cause good or bad thoughts to arise. When the Extinction in

> *Dharmata[376] is reached, the body, like a corpse in a charnel ground,
> would not show fear even if a deadly executioner should appear. The
> voice resembles an echo, and because the things said are not seized,
> others' words are repeated. The mind, as the inhabitant of a country
> shrouded in mist, always being in its place—the immeasurable
> space of reality—has transcended the projection and recollection of
> memories and thoughts.*

This quotation coincides with what was previously written.

Then Kyabgön Gyurme Tsewang Chogdrub, Yangsi Tsewang Rigdzin Gyatso, Dzapön Pema Tendzin and their disciples, lama Namkha,
Chöjung, Thubten, the entire community from Washül Tatrom, Drugtrül
Rinpoche, and all the the Lord's disciples present performed a great offering ritual to venerate the lama.

The spiritual heir, Lama Taye, as well as Jigme, Tendzin, Ludrub,
Palden, Gangshar, and many other of the Lord's direct disciples came from
many different places and, meeting at Kalzang monastery, they built a stupa
in the mahabodhi style, complete with all its [special] characteristics and
made of precious materials and gilded bronze. It contains the Lord's hair,
his clothes, fingernails and toenails, his vajra and phurbu, sacramental
substances and dozens of pill-relics of the Tathagatas, along with hair,
clothing, nasal blood,[377] and medicinal substances blessed by incarnate
masters and disciples—followers of the three practices that lead to nirvana— the numerous adepts of India and Tibet. Also placed inside were
yellow manuscripts, supports for body and mind, ritual substances, and
blessed medicines found in the places where treasures were discovered by
the five great incarnate treasure finders. As supports for the word, hundreds
of dharani for extending the presence [of the Doctrine], inner, outer, and
secret tantras of all traditions, writings on precious materials, hundreds
of propitiatory rituals for activating the indications of the treasures, the
Prajñaparamita in one hundred thousand verses and in eight thousand
verses, the meditative system of realization of *The Blazing Wisdom*[378] and
others, every one an ineffable support for voice. There are also [images of]

complete series of deities, entire lots of rich offerings including a couple of bronze cauldrons filled with clarified butter, tea, barley, butter, silk, cotton, arms, and so on, and many other articles of abundance that had been offered.

Drugtrül Rinpoche, the sublime yogi Namdröl Dorje, and many other noble people carried out the consecration ritual, fulfilling all the requirements.

In verses:

He manifestly dissolved the wheel of his emanation-body
In the primordially liberated space of total emptiness.
This marvel spread into the three worlds like a delicious feast.
May I quickly achieve the high level of this sovereign guru!

1. Padmasambhava's image in Derge Gonchen.

2. Katbog monastery.

3. Fresco of Düdul Dorje, Kathog monastery.

4. Fresco of Longsal Nyingpo, Kathog monastery.

5. Yogis from Kathog doing three year retreat.

6. *Stupa dedicated to Pema Düdul, erected at the site where he realized the Rainbow Body.*

7. *Gendun Shedrub Phelgyeling monastery in Nyagrong Dzong.*

8. *Lama A kha, Kalsang Gyatso, abbot of Gedun Shedrub Phelgyeling and one of the lineage holders of Pema Düdul's transmissions.*

9. *The mountain sanctuary of Lhang Lhang. In the center is Kalzang monastery, built by Pema Düdul.*

10. Main hall, Kalzang monastery.

11. Stupa containing the relics of Pema Düdul, temple of Kalzang.

12. Stupa containing the relics of Rangrig Dorje, chief disciple of Pema Düdul.

13. The rock of Lhang Lhang.

14. *Fresco of Pema Düdul surrounded by his most important disciples, Kalzang.*

15. *Lama Nyidar displaying a stone bearing Pema Düdul's footprint.*

16. Pema Düdul's staff.

17. Low relief of Avalokiteśvara found as a treasure (gter ma) by Pema Düdul.

18. One of the caves in Lhang Lhang mountain from which Pema Düdul brought the treasures to light.

19. *Prayer flags at the mouth of Lhang Lhang's main cave.*

20. *One of the caves in which Pema Düdul spent years in meditation.*

21. Village of Khangtseg where Pema Düdul spent his childhood.

22. *View from the caves.*

APPENDIX I

Index of Texts Belonging to the Profound Doctrine (zab chos) Called Self-Liberation That Encompasses Space (Zab chos mkha' khyab rang grol)

VOLUME I

1. 'Chi med kun bzang padma 'byung gnas kyis: skyes rabs rnam thar mdor bsdus bkod pa las: bka' thang gang shar rang grol rin po che: snang srid gsal ba'i mkhyen gsum me long dbyings: dri med nyi zla 'od zer:
2. rJe grub dbang 'khrul zhig byang chub gling pa'i rnam thar nyung bsdus kyi gsol 'debs /
3. sPros bral nam mkha'i rdzong ba'i zhal gtams las/ don dam rang zhal bla mar gsol 'debs /
4. mKha' khyab rang grol gyi zab khrid sangs rgyas myur lam las/ blo ldog rnam bzhi'i bsdus khrid ngag 'don rgyun khyer /
5. bKa' gsang zab chos mkha' khyab rang grol las: tshom bu 'bum phrag mngon par sangs rgyas pa'i: zab khrid sngon 'gro'i ngag 'don rgyun khyer ni: skad cig sangs rgyas myur lam rang grol:
6. bKa' gsang zab chos _____: gang gi sngon 'gro skyabs sems rim pa:
7. _____: bskyed rdzogs 'khor 'das rnam dag rang grol:
8. _____: bskyed rdzogs 'khor 'das ka dag rang grol:
8.1. _____: mngon bskyed rab 'byams ye shes rgya mtsho/225

Volume 2

5. bKa' gsang zab chos mKha' khyab rang grol las: ma rig mun gling nang 'khrul bgegs tsho gsal: bden brjod byin rlabs nyi ma 'bum 'char zhing: 'dre bdud chos skur gyur ba'i man ngag: 129
6. bKa' gsang _____: dbang bshad kun snang rang grol: 133
7. bKa' gsang_____: dbang bskur spros bral 'khor 'das rang grol:157
8. _____: dbang bzhi bskur thabs bsdus pa: 201
9. bKa' gtad bden tshig smon pa rdo rje'i chings zhes bya ba:207
10. Zab chos mkha' khyab rang grol las: ma bsgom sangs rgyas chos lnga:211
11. _____: man ngag sku gsum bcud len 'ja' lus rdo rje'i sku brnyes:219
12. bCom ldan rta phag chos nyid rol pa yi: las byed ma rig mun sel ye shes nyi ma rang shar: 243
13. bCom ldan rta phag chos nyid rol pa las: dkyil 'khor spyi bstod dngos grub char 'bebs:311
14. bCom ldan rta phag chos nyid rol pa las: bskul pa mkhyen brtse'i dal ster: 319
15. bCom ldan_____: smad las stong chen klong yangs gzung 'dzin rang grol: 329
16. bCom ldan_____:gtor bzlog khro bo rol pa: kun rtog gyul rgyal: 339
17. rTa phag chos nyid rol pa las: zur mda' man ngag gsang thig:351
18. dPal chen po rta phag he ru ka'i don dbang 'dod 'jo'i bum bzang skal bzang skyes bu smin byed bdud rtsi'i chu bo: 355
19. rTa phag chos nyid rol pa'i dmar chen gtor bzlog gi rim pa khrigs su bdebs pa kun rtog yul ngor bzlog pa'i 'khrul 'khor. 381
20. mkha' khyab rang grol rdzogs chen snying thig las: kun bzang thugs sgrub rig pa rang grol: 425
21. mKha' khyab rang grol rdzogs chen snying thig las: btags grol phung po 'ja' lus rang grol: 447
22. _____: phyag 'tshal nyams chags sdig sgrib rang grol: 455
23. _____: phyag 'tshal nyams chags sdig sgrib rang grol: 469
24. _____: skong ba 'khrul 'khor rang grol dngos grub dpal gter: 475
25. _____: zhi khro'i thugs sgrub skong ba rig stong rang grol: 489

26. Thugs sgrub rig pa rang grol gyi dkyil cho ga gag don gsal ba'i sgron me bhugs so. bkra shis par shog. 497

27. Zhi khro'i thugs sgrub rig pa rang grol gyi gnas lung gi cho ga: 571

28. mDo sngags bka' 'dus mkha' mnyam rang grol las: sangs rgyas sgrub pa mkha' mnyam rang grol: 587

29. _____: thub dbang sgrub thabs rnam mkhyen sangs rgyas: 599

30. mDo sngags bka' 'dus snying gi thig las: thub pa'i mdzad pa bcu gnyis kyi dbang bskur: 605

31. _____: ye shes sman bla'i thugs sgrub nyon mongs nad 'joms: 617

32. _____: gsang bdag thugs sgrub gza' gnyan klu 'joms nag po: 623

33. _____: khyung sgrub yang thig gcig dril: 625

34. _____: rje btsun sgrol ma'i thugs sgrub 'de klong yangs pa: 627

35. _____: rje btsun sgrol ma'i sgrub pa 'khor ba rang grol. 633

36. _____: rje btsun 'phags ma'i dbang bskur 'khor ba yongs sgrol: 643

37. _____: rjes cho ga mtshams sbyar dri med nyi zla'i phreng ba: 651

38. mDo sngags bka' 'dus mkha mnyam rang grol las: gter srung mkha' 'gro sde lnga'i gsang sgrub mchog gi dbal ster: 659

39. _____: gter srung mkha' 'gro sde lnga'i mchog gsol yang thig snying po: 661

40. _____: gsol 'debs dang 'brel ba'i gtor bsngo bsdus ba: 663

41. mDo sngags bka' 'dus snying gi thig le las: chu gtor tshogs gnyis rgya mtsho: 665

42. _____: dkar gsur zag bral ye shes kun khyab: 675

43. mDo sngags bka' 'dus mkha' mnyam rang grol las: 'gro kun ma lus rigs drug gnas 'dren: 677

44. _____: dpal rdo rje sder mo'i nad gdon 'dul ba: 691

45. _____: dpal rdo rje sder mo'i rgyal nad dang 'gag gri 'dul ba: 693

46. _____: dpal rdo rje sder mo'i sa gri 'dul ba: 695

VOLUME 3

VOLUME 4

1. bKa' gsang zab chos mkha' khyab rang grol las: ma bsgom sangs rgyas 'pho ba'i zab lam: 785
2. _____: 'pho ba rig pa rang grol: 787
3. _____: brgyud gsum brgyud 'debs 'pho ba'i rim pa: 789
4. _____: ma bsgom sangs rgyas 'pho ba'i zab lam: 791
5. _____: zab mo don gi tshogs 'khor 'khor 'das gdod nas rang grol: 815
6. Phyag rgya chen po mkha' khyab rang grol gnyis: ya mtshan zab khrid nyi zla kha sbyor gyi: rgyun khyer 'phags lam rnam mkhyen shing rta: 829

VOLUME 5

1. bKa' gsang zab chos mkha' khyab rang grol las: rtsa rlung mchog gi grub chen gyi gsol 'debs: 393
2. _____: rtsa thig rlung sbyang ngag 'don rnam dag nyi zla'i dkyil 'khor: 395
3. _____: rtsa thig rlung sbyang gi rtsa tshig mchog gi grub chen: 401

Bibliography

WORKS IN TIBETAN

Jigme Lingpa ('Jigs med gling pa).
    kLong chen snying thig, vols 1–4
    In *Rin chen gter mdzod chen mo*, vols. 106–109, edited by
        the Venerable Dingo Chentse (Dil mgo mkhyen
        brtse) Rinpoche
    Paro, Bhutan: Kyichu monastery, 1978

Padma Düdul (Padma bdud 'dul)
    Nyag bla padma bdud 'dul gsung 'bum
    Nyag rong redaction
    Kathog Monastery (xylography)

Sherab Özer and Jangchub Gyatso (Shes rab 'od zer and Byang chub rgya
mtsho)
    Shar rgyal ba bskal bzang dgon gyi byung ba rags bsdus
    Chengdu: Si khron mi rigs dpe skrun khang, 1996

Tapiritsa/Nangsher Lodpo (Ta pi hri tsa /sNang bzher lod po)
'Od gsal sems kyi me long
    In *Zhang zhung snyan rgyud: History and Doctrines*
        of Bon po Nispanna Yoga
    New Delhi: Satapitaka Series, vol. 73, 1968

Yeshe Dorje (Ye shes rdo rje)
    Nyag bla padma bdud 'dul gyi rnam thar dang mgur 'bum
    Chengdu: Si khron mi rigs dpe skrun khang, 1998

————————.

    Nyag bla padma bdud 'dul gyi rnam thar dang mgur 'bum
    In *The Collected Revelations of Nyag bla Padma bdud 'dul* (*Nyag bla
        padma bdud 'dul gsung 'bum*), vol. 0780
    Scanned from the Nyag rong redaction
    Cambridge MA: Tibetan Buddhist Resource Center (TBRC)

Khetsun Sangpo (mKhe brtsun bzang po)
    Biographical Dictionary of Tibet and Tibetan Buddhism
    In *The rNying-ma-pa Tradition*
    Dharamsala: Library of Tibetan Works and Archives, 1973

Translations and General works

Achard, Jean Luc. *Les testaments de Vajradhara et des porteurs-de-science*. Paris: Les Deux Océans, 1995.

_____ . *L' Essence perlée du secret. Recherches philologiques et historiques sur l'origine de la Grande Perfection dans la tradition rNying ma pa*. Turnhout, BE: Brepols, 1999.

Aguilar, Oriol. "Byang-chub rgyal-mtshan y su época. Un estado de la cuestión sobre la ascensión de la dinastía Phag-mo gru-pa," in *Boletín de la Asociación Española de Orientalistas*, XXVIII, pp. 111–113. Madrid, 1992.

(Endnotes)

1   Allione, Tsultrim. *Women of Wisdom*. London: Routledge & Kegan Paul, 1984.

Aris, Michael, and Aung San Suu Kyi, ed. *Tibetan Studies in Honour of Hugh Richardson*. Warminster, UK: Aris & Phillips, 1980.

Aris, Michael. *Hidden Treasures and Secret Lives: A Study of Pemalingpa and the sixth Dalai Lama*. London: Kegan Paul International, 1989.

Asanga: see Rahula, Walpola, 1980.

Baroetto, Giuseppe. *L 'Insegnamento esoterico di Padmasambhava. La collana delle visioni*. (translation of *Man-ngag lta-ba 'i phreng-ba* by Padmasambhava). Merigar: Shang Shung Edizioni, 1990.

Bechert, Heinz. "The date of the Buddha reconsidered," in *Indologica Taurinensia* 9, 1982: pp. 29–36.

Beyer, Stephan. *The Cult of Tārā*. Berkeley, Los Angeles and London: University of California Press, 1978.

Bischoff, F.A., and Hartman, Ch. "Padmasambhava's invention of the phur-bu." Ms. Pelliot tibétain 44. In *Études tibétaines dediées à la mémoire de Marcelle Lalou*. Paris: Maisonneuve, 1971: 11–28.

Blondeau, Anne Marie. "Le Lha-´dre bKa´-thang," in *Études Tibetaines dédiées à la mémoire de Marcelle Lalou*. Paris: Maisonneuve, 1971: pp. 29–126.

_____. "Analysis of the Biographies of Padmasambhava according to Tibetan Tradition: Classification of the Sources". In Aris, M. and Aung San Suu Kyi, 1980.

_____. "Las religiones del Tíbet," in *Las religiones constituidas en Asia y sus contracorrientes* 1, no. 21 (First French edition in La Pléiade, 1976). Madrid, 1981.

Bosworth, B.A. *Alejandro Magno*. (Spanish version, 1996). Cambridge: Cambridge University Press, 1988.

Bouillier, Veronique. "Des prêtres du pouvoir: Les yogī et la fonction royale," in *Prêtrise, pouvoirs et autorité en Himalaya*. V. Bouillier and G. Toffin, ed. Paris: Éditions de l´École des Hautes Études en Sciences Sociales, 1989.

Briggs, G. W. *Goraknath and the Kanphata Yogis*. London: Oxford University Press, 1938.

Burnell, James. "The Lives of Indian Buddhist Saints: Biography, Hagiography and Myth," in *Tibetan Literature: Studies in Genre. Essays in Honor of Geshe Lhundup Sopa*. José Ignacio Cabezón, and Roger R. Jackson, ed. Ithaca, New York: Snow Lion, 1996.

Conze, Edward. *The Large Sutra on Perfect Wisdom* (with the divisions of the *Abhisamayālankāra*). Berkeley: University of California Press, 1975.

Corbin, Henri. *El hombre y su ángel.* (First French edition, 1983). Barcelona: Destino, 1995.

Chandra Das, Sarat. *Tibetan-English Dictionary.* (First edition, 1902). Kathmandu: Ratna Pustak Bhandar, 1985.

Chang, Garma C.C., trans. and annot. *Six Yogas of Naropa and Teachings on Mahamudra.* Ithaca, NY: Snow Lion Publications, 1977.

Chögyal Namkhai Norbu. *Dzogchen e Zen.* Arcidosso: Shang Shung Edizioni, 1989.

_____. *The Six Vajra Verses.* Compiled by Che-Ngee Goh. Singapore: Rinchen Editions, 1990.

_____. *El cristal y la via de la luz.* Compiled by John Shane. Barcelona: Kairós, 1996.

Chögyal Namkhai Norbu and Clemente, Adriano. *The Supreme Source: The Kunjed Gyalpo, the Fundamental Tantra of Dzogchen Semde.* Ithaca, NY: Snow Lion Publications, 1999.

Dargyay, Eva M. *The Rise of Esoteric Buddhism in Tibet.* Delhi-Varanasi-Patna: Motilal Banarsidass, 1979.

Davidson, Ronald M. "The *Litany of Names of Mañjuśrī,*" in *Mélanges Chinois et Bouddhiques. Tantric and Taoist Studies in Memory of R.A. Stein,* vol. 20. Brusssels: Éditions Steickmann, 1981.

_____. *Indian Esoteric Buddhism: A Social History of the Tantric Movement.* New York: Columbia University Press, 2002.

Dezhung Rinpoche. *The Three Levels of Spiritual Perception.* Jared Rhoton, trans. Boston: Wisdom Publications, 1995.

Dorje, Gyurme. *Tibet Handbook with Bhutan.* Bath: Footprint Handbooks, 1996.

Dowman, Keith. *Sky Dancer: The Secret Life and Songs of the Lady Yeshe Tsogyel.* London: Routledge and Kegan Paul, 1984.

Dudjom Rinpoche, Jikdrel Yeshe Dorje. *The Nyingma School of Tibetan Buddhism: its Fundamentals and History.* Gyurme Dorje and Matthew T. Kapstein, trans., ed., and annot. Boston: Wisdom Publications, 1991.

Eliade, Mircea. *Histoire des croyances et des idées religieuses 2: De Gautama Buddha au triomphe de christianisme.* Paris: Éditions Payot, 1978.

Evans Wentz, W. Y. *The Tibetan Book of the Great Liberation.* Sardar Bahādur and Lama Sonam Senge, trans. London: Oxford University Press, 1954.

——————————. *The Tibetan Book of the Dead.* Lama Kazi Dawa Samdup, trans. London: Oxford University Press, 1957.

——————————. *Milarepa ou Jetsün-Kahbum: Vie de Jetsün Milarepa.* Lama Kazi Dawa-Samdup, trans. Paris: Éditions Maisonneuve, 1985.

Gell, Andrew. *The Anthropology of Time.* Oxford/Providence: Berg Publishers, 1992.

Guenther, Herbert V. *The Life and Teaching of Naropa.* London: Oxford University Press, 1963.

——————————. *Wholeness Lost and Wholeness Regained: Forgotten Tales of Individuation from Ancient Tibet.* SUNY Series of Buddhist Studies. Albany, NY: State University of New York Press, 1994.

——————————. *The Teachings of Padmasambhava.* Brill's Indological Library, vol. 12. Leiden-New York-Köln: Brill, 1996.

Gyaltsen, Shardza Tashi. *Heart Drops of Dharmakaya: Dzogchen Practice of the Bön Tradition.* Ithaca, NY: Snow Lion Publications, 1993.

Gyatso, Janet. "Signs, Memory and History: a Tantric Buddhist Theory of Scriptural Transmission," in *Journal of International Association of Buddhist Studies* 9, no. 2(1986): 7–35.

_____. *Apparitions of the Self: The Secret Autobiographies of a Tibetan Visionary.* Princeton, NJ: Princeton University Press,1998.

Haar, Erik. *The Yar-lung Dynasty.* Copenhagen: G.E.C. Gad, 1969.

Hanna, Span. "Vast as the Sky: The Terma Tradition in Modern Tibet," in *Tantra and Popular Religion in Tibet.* Geoffrey Samuel, Hamish Gregor, and Elisabeth Stutchbury, ed. New Delhi: Aditya Prakashan, 1994: 8–19.

Ingo Lauf, Detlef. *L 'Heritage du Tibet.* Berne: Kümmerly and Frey, 1973.

Jackson, David. *Enlightenment by a Single Means.* Vienna: Der Österreichischen Akademie der Wissenschaften, 1994.

Kapstein, Matthew T. "The Strange Death of Pema the Demon Tamer," in *The Presence of Light: Divine Radiance and Religious Experience.* M.T. Kapstein, ed. Chicago and London: University of Chicago Press, 2004: 119–156.

Karmay, Samten G. "The rDzogs-chen in its Earliest Text: A Manuscript from Tun-Huang," in *Soundings in Tibetan Civilization.* M. T. Kapstein and B. N. Aziz, ed. New Delhi: Manohar, 1985: 272–282.

_____. *The Great Perfection: A Philosophical and Meditative Teaching of Tibetan Buddhism.* Leiden: Brill, 1988.

Kongtrul Lodrö Taye, Jamgön ('Jam mgon kong sprul blo gros mtha' yas). *Myriad Worlds.* Translated and edited by the Translation Committee of Kalu Rinpoche. Ithaca, NY: Snow Lion Publications, 1995.

Lamotte, Étienne. *Histoire du Bouddhisme Indien.* Louvain: Publications de l'Institut Orientaliste, 1958.

Lavastine, Philippe. "Tri-varga (les trois valeurs)," in *Actes du Colloque International de Cering-LaSalle*, July, 1973.

Levi, Sylvain, trans. and ed. *Mahāyāna-sūtrālamkāra*. 2 vols. Paris: Bibliotheque de l'École des Hautes Études, 1907 and 1911.

Lipman, K. and Norbu, N., trans. and comm. *Primordial Experience (rDo la gser zhun) by Mañjuśrīmitra*. Boston & London: Shambhala 1987.

Longchenpa (kLong chen rab 'byams pa). *You Are the Eyes of the World (Byang-chub kyi sems kun-byed rgyal-po 'i don khrid rin-chen sgru-bo)*. Lipman, K., and Norbu, N., trans. and comm. Novato: Lotsawa, 1987.

Mañjuśrīmitra. See Lipman, K. and Norbu, N., trans. (1987).

Macdonald, Arianne. "Préambule à la lecture d´un rGya-bod Yig-tshang," in *Journal Asiatique*, Paris: Imprimerie Nationale, 1963.

Macdonald, Arianne, ed. *Études tibétaines dédiées à la mémoire de Marcelle Lalou*. Paris: Adrien Maissonneuve, 1971.

Masefield, Peter. *Divine Revelation in Pali Buddhism*. London: George Allen & Unwin, 1986.

Moses, Stephane. *El angel de la historia*. Madrid: Editorial Cátedra, 1997.

Nyoshul Khenpo. *Natural Great Perfection*. Surya Das, trans. Ithaca, NY: Snow Lion Publications, 1995.

Orofino, Giacomella. *Contributo allo studio dell´insegnamento di Ma gcig Lab sgron*. Naples: Istituto Universitario Orientale, 1987.

Padma bdud 'dul. *Il canto dell' energia*. Chögyal Namkhai Norbu and Enrico dell' Angelo, trans. Arcidosso: Shang shung Edizioni, 1989.

Prats, Ramón. "Some Preliminary Considerations Arising from a Biographical Study of the Early gTer-ston," in *Tibetan Studies in Honour of Hugh Richardson*. "Proccedings of the Internationalseminar on Tibetan Studies (Oxford, 1979). Editors Michael Aris & Aung San Suu Kyi. Warminster, 1980.

_____. *Contributo allo studio dei primi gter-ston*. Naples: Istituto Universitario Orientale: vol. 17, 1982.

_____. "The aspiration prayer of the ground, path and goal: an inspired piece on rdzogs chen by 'Jigs med gling pa," in *Orientalia Iosephi Tucci Memoriae Dicata*. Rome: Istituto Italiano per il Medio ed Estremo Oriente, 1988.

Rahula, Walpola, trans. and comm. *Le compendium de la super-doctrine (philosophie) (Abhidharmasamuccaya) d'Asaṅga*. Paris: Publications de l'École Française d'Extreme Orient, vol. 78, 1980.

Reynolds, John M. and Norbu, Namkhai. *Self-Liberation through Seeing with Naked Awareness*. New York : Station Hill Press, 1989.

Reynolds, John M. & Norbu, Namkhai. *The Golden Letters*. Ithaca, NY: Snow Lion Publications, 1996.

Rodríguez Adrados, Francisco. *Asoka, edictos de la ley sagrada*. Barcelona: Edhasa 1987.

Roerich, George N. *The Blue Annals: the Stages of the Appearance of the Doctrine and Preachers in the Land of Tibet*. (First edition, 1949). Delhi: Motilal Banarsidass, 1979.

Ronis, Jann. "Powerful Women in the History of Degé: Reassessing the Eventful Reign of the Dowager Queen Tsewang Lhamo (D. 1812)," in *Revue d'Études Tibétaines* no. 21 (October 2011): 61–81.

Samuel, Geoffrey. *Civilized Shamans: Buddhism in Tibetan Societies*. Washington, DC: Smithsonian Institution, 1993.

Samuel, Geoffrey, Hamish Gregor & Elisabeth Stutchbury, ed. *Tantra and Popular Religion in Tibet*. Delhi: Aditya Prakashan, 1994.

Schopen, Gregory. *Bones, Stones, and Buddhist Monks: Collected Papers on the Archaeology, Epigraphy, and Texts of Monastic Buddhism in India*. Honolulu: University of Hawai'i Press, 1997.

Silburn, Lilian, ed. *Tch'an-Zen: Racines et floraisons*. Paris: Hermès, Éditions des Deux Océans, 1985.

_____. *Śivasūtra et Vimarśinī de Kṣemarāja*. Paris: Publications de l'Institut de Civilisation Indienne (vol. 48), 2000.

_____ and Padoux, André. *Abhinavagupta: La lumière sur les tantras. Chapitres 1 à 5 du Tantrāloka*. Paris: Publications de l'Institut de Civilisation Indienne et Collège de France, 2000.

Smith, G. "*Introduction*," to *The Autobiographical Reminiscences of Ngag dbang dpal bzang, Late Abbot of Kah thog Monastery*. Sonam Topgay Kazi, ed. Delhi: Jayyed Press, 1969.

_____. "*Introduction*," to *Kongtrul's Encyclopaedia of Indo-Tibetan Culture*. Lokesh Chandra, ed. Delhi: International Academy of India Culture, 1970.

Snellgrove, David. *Indo-Tibetan Buddhism: Indian Buddhists and their Tibetan Successors*. London: Serindia, 1987.

_____. *Four Lamas of Dolpo*. Kathmandu: Himalayan Book Seller (first edition 1967), 1992.

Snellgrove, D. & Richardson, H. *A Cultural History of Tibet*. Boston and London: Shambhala (first edition 1968), 1992.

Stein, Rolf A. *Vie et chants de 'Brug-pa Kun-legs le yogin*. Paris: Maisonneuve et Larose, 1972.

_____. *La civiltà tibetana*. Torino, IT: Giulio Einaudi Editore, 1986.

Tartang, Bradburn &Yeshe De. *Masters of the Nyingma Lineage*. Crystal Mirror Series (vol. 11), Berkeley: Dharma Press, 1995.

Templeman, David. *Tāranātha's Life of Kṛṣṇācārya/Kāṇha*. Dharamsala: Library of Tibetan Works & Archives, 1989.

Thondup, Tulku. *Hidden Teachings of Tibet*. London: Wisdom Publications, 1986.

_____. *Buddha Mind*. New York: Snow Lion Publications, 1989.

_____. *Masters of Meditation and Miracles*. Boulder and London: Shambhala, 1996.

Tucci, Giuseppe. *Minor Buddhist Texts*. First Italian edition, 1956. Delhi.Varanasi-Patna-Madras: Motilal Banarsidass, 1986.

_____. *The Religions of Tibet*. First German edition, 1970. London: Routledge and Kegan Paul, 1980.

Valby, Jim, trans. *The Great History of Garab Dorje, Manjushrimitra, Shrisingha, Jnanasutra, and Vimalamitra*. Arcidosso: Shang Shung Edizioni, 2002.

Van Schaik, Sam. *Approaching the Great Perfection: Simultaneous and Gradual Methods of Dzogchen Practice in the Longchen Nyingtig*. Boston: Wisdom Publications, 2004.

Wangdu, Pasang and Diemberger, Hildegard. *dBa' bzhed: The Royal Narrative Concerning the Bringing of the Buddha's Doctrine to Tibet*. Vienna: Österreichischen Akademie der Wissenschaften, 2000.

Watson, Burton, trans. *The Vimalakirti Sutra*. New York: Columbia University Press, 1997.

Wayman, Alex. *The Buddhist Tantras: Light on Indo-Tibetan Esotericism.* Delhi: Motilal Banarsidass, 1973.

—————————. *Yoga of the Guhyasamājatantra.* Delhi-Varanasi-Patna: Motilal Banarsidass, 1977.

Notes

1 Tibetan words are written in phonetic transcription in the text, but in the notes are transliterated using the Wylie system. Sanskrit words in the text are without diacritical marks, while the correct IAST orthography is found in the notes.

2 This PHD thesis, whose title is *El loto de Nyag rong. Un estudio sobre la vida de Nyag bla Padma bdud 'dul y su transmisión del conocimiento,* was presented in the Departament d'Antropologia Social i Cultural at the Universitat Autònoma de Barcelona, in November 2005.

3 *rJe bla ma 'khrul zhig byang chub gling pa'i rnam thar skal lzang dga' ba'i bdud rtsi'i sprin tshogs,* in *Nyag bla pad ma bdud 'dul gyi rnam thar dang mgur 'bum,* published by Si khron mi rigs dpe skrun khang, Chengdu, 1998.

4 *mKha' khyab rang grol.*

5 I wish to express my gratitude to Adriano Clemente, main translator of Chögyal Namkhai Norbu's works, for giving me the opportunity to study these volumes in May 2004.

6 I interviewed these two masters during my travels in Kham during May and June, 2005.

7 Also known as Lhan brag and Shang lang.

8 *gter ston*: discoverer of spiritual treasures (*gter ma*).

9 *kha byang.*

10 These are: his miraculous birth in Lumbini, illumination under the tree in Bodhgāya, first sermon in the Deer Park at Sārnāth, and his death at Kuśinagara (also known as Kāsia).

11 See Snellgrove (1987), p. 6, note 4.

12 These songs, known under the generic names of *vajragīti, caryāgīti,* and *dohā,* fall within the great Indian tradition of mystical experience expressed in poetic language.

13 On Tāranātha's *rGya gar chos 'byung,* see Burnell (1996). The biography of Nāropā was translated by H.V. Guenther, in Guenther (1963).

14 See Gyatso (1998), pp. 114–115.

15 See Guarisco (1986).

16 See Templeman (1989).

17 These three biographies, of which there are several versions, relate the lives of the three first patriarchs of the Total Perfection. See Thondup (1996) and Valby (2002).

18 Tib. *rtogs brjod;* Skt. *avadāna,* and Tib. *rnam thar;* Skt. *vimokṣa.*

19 Janet Gyatso brilliantly stresses this aspect in her *Apparitions of the Self.*

20 outer: (*phyi'i rnam thar*); inner: *nang ba'i rnam thar;* secret *gsang ba'i rnam thar;* most secret: *yang gsang ba'i rnam thar.*

21 *thob yig:* repertoire of received teachings; *gsan yig:* teachings heard.

22 James Burnell Robinson, in his study on the biographies of the eighty-four *mahāsiddha* of Abhayadatta (in Cabezón, J.I. & Jackson, R.R., 1996) considers that the hagiographical texts can be interpreted in three ways: as history, as a hagiography, or as myth. These three approaches are not mutually exclusive, each one being faithful to its particular character. The historical aspect provides the objective historical facts present in the biography; the hagiographical approach presents information on the transmission and the religious reality surrounding the text; and the mythical aspect studies sacred events which, while not scientifically verifiable, are of essential importance to the nature of the text. Interesting parallels between this *etic* vision and the *emic* view of the tradition (with its division into inner, outer, and secret biographies) could be drawn.

23 *rang gi rnam thar.*

24 *mgur.*

25 Oral communication by Chos rgyal Nam mkha'i nor bu.

26 *mgur 'bum.*

27 *mnyams mgur.*

28 Nyi zla kun mdzas.

29 'Khrul zhig gling pa.

30 Published by Si khron mi rigs dpe skrun khang, Chengdu 1998.

31 Ye shes rdo rje: *Nyag bla padma bdud 'dul gyi rnam thar dang mgur 'bum*. In *The Collected Revelations of Nyag bla pad ma bdud 'dul* (*Nyag bla padma bdud 'dul gsung 'bum*), volume 0780. Scanned from the Nyag rong redaction, Tibetan Buddhist Resource Center.

32 Information provided by the *mkhan po* bSod nams bstan pa.

33 *ris med*.

34 On the *khams pa* resistance and warriors, see Shakabpa (1984), chapters 18–19. For a historical description, see Peissel (1972).

35 The two sons of dPal 'khor btsan (881–911), Nyi ma mgon and bKra shis brtsegs, continued to hold power in different zones. The kingdom of Guge and Purang in western Tibet was founded by the former, and some parts of central Tibet became controlled by the latter. Their descendants patronized the reintroduction of institutional Buddhism in those parts of the country.

36 See Aguilar (1992), on the kingdom of the Phag mo gru pa.

37 See Samuel (1993), Part One (pp. 39–139).

38 See Shakabpa (1984), chapter 9.

39 *nyag rong gi bla ma*.

40 *nyag*: the Yalong, tributary of the Yangtse.

41 *bri chu:* the Yangtse.

42 In 1914, plenipotentiaries from the British Empire, Tibet, and China met in the Indian city of Simla to establish a treaty to put an end to this litigation and define the relationship between Tibet and China. The treaty was finally signed by the Tibetan and British plenipotentiaries, but not by the Chinese, who claimed sovereignty over all of Tibet. In this treaty, the Tibetan Government renounced the Province of Amdo and the eastern part (to the east of the Yangtse) of the Province of Kham, which came, nominally, to belong to China. However, the effective control of Chinese administration was not stabilized until the invasion of 1950.

43 Another part of the traditional territory of Kham to be annexed to Yunnan Province was the Autonomous Tibetan County of Dechen.

44 Some of the facts on Nyarong are gleaned from the guide to Tibet, *Tibet Handbook with Bhutan* by Gyurme Dorje (1996).

45 *gnas*: equivalent to the Sanskrit *pīṭha* or *kṣetra*, 'sacred place' which in most cases are places of pilgrimage. Western bibliography on this subject is abundant. Pilgrimage sites and other sanctuaries of the holy Tibetan geography have been dealt with in detail by Toni Huber, Katia Buffetrille, Span Hanna, Anne-Marie Blondeau, and Alex McKay among others.

46 The geomantic science (*sa dpyad*) in Tibet holds an importance similar to that of fengshui in China.

47 *sa bdag, the'u rang, btsan, gnyan, bstan ma:* classifications of spirits, which are even more numerous at the local level.

48 The practice of Absorbing of Elixirs (Tib. *bcud len;* Skt. *rasāyana*) is described in detail in the biography, but not the composition of the *bcud len,* which is explained in the texts revealed by Pad ma bdud 'dul.

49 *mchod rten:* also used to designate an internal element of a temple such as a metal container decorated with gems and ornaments.

50 Vairocana, one of the first monks to be ordained in Tibet, was a disciple of Śrī Siṃha in India and Padmasambhava in Tibet. He was exiled to eastern Tibet after being falsely accused of the attempted to seduction of dMar rgyan, one of the Emperor's wives.

51 The fifth Dalai Lama, Ngag dbang blo bzang rgya mtsho, also patronized the rNying ma pa order. He was a rDzogs chen practitioner with a spiritual relationship with gTer bdag gling pa of sMin grol gling monastery, and he helped in the expansion of the rNying ma pa in Khams.

52 Particularly in the case of the rNying ma pa order, the monasteries in the kingdom of sDe dge were, from the seventeenth century on, the order's most active in Tibet. These monasteries were Kaḥ thog rdo rje gdan, dPal yul, Zhe chen, and rDzogs chen. With the exception of Kaḥ thog, founded in the twelfth century, those named were founded in the seventeenth and eighteenth centuries. See Smith (1969).

53 'Jigs med gling pa (1730–1798). On this master see Gyatso (1998), Van Schaik (2004), and Thondup (1996).

54 *kLong chen snying thig.*

55 In fact, when the Queen travelled to central Tibet in 1788, she was not yet dowager and her husband, the King Sa dbang bzang po also went to meet 'Jigs med gling pa. Sa dbang bZang po died two years later.

56 *rNying ma'i rgyud 'bum.*

57 dGe rtse 'gyur med tshe dbang mchog grub (1761–1829).

58 Tshe dbang rdo rje rig 'dzin, also known as sDe dge yab chen (1786–1842).

59 In Smith (1969), pp. 12–13. On Queen Tsewang Lhamo, see this same article and also the more recent of Jann Ronis (2011) pp. 61–81, where a more updated description of the Queen's life and reign is portrayed.

60 'Jam dbyangs mkhyen brtse'i dbang po (1820–1892).

61   The 'Five Tertön Kings' (*gter ston rgyal po lnga*): Nyang ral nyi ma 'od zer, Guru Chos dbang, rDo rje gling pa, O rgyan gling pa, and 'Jam dbyangs mkhyen brtse'i dbang po, all considered emanations of the King Khri srong lde'u btsan, a disciple of Padmasambhava.

62   The Transmission of the Seven Currents (*bKa' babs chu bo bdun*) gathers the main transmission modes in the rNying ma pa order.

63   *sa gter.*

64   *yang gter.*

65   *dgongs gter.*

66   *dag snang.*

67   See the works on the rNying ma pa tradition by Tulku Thondup, especially in Thondup (1986) and (1996).

68   'Jam mgon kong sprul blo gros mtha' yas (1813–1899).

69   *Rin chen gter mdzod.*

70   mChog 'gyur gling pa (1829–1870).

71   Shar rdza bkra shis rgyal mtshan (1859–1934).

72   'Jigs med phrin las 'od zer (1745–1821).

73   mDo mkhyen brtse ye shes rdo rje (1800–1866).

74   rDza dpal sprul o rgyan 'jigs med chos kyi dbang po (1808–1887).

75   Khang brtsegs mgon po: literally, 'protector,' or patron, of Khang brtsegs.

76   bDe klong rgyal nya thang.

77   The paternal line, called *rus rigs* (lit. 'line of the bone') in many cases also indicates affiliation with a specific clan.

78   sTag bla pad ma ma ti (1591–1637). About this master, see Tarthang, Bradburn and Yeshe De, (1995), p. 234 .

79   *sku drag.*

80   *khral pa.*

81   *dud chung.*

82   *grong pa.*

83   For a general description of the social division, family ties, and inheritance, I have used Samuel, G., (1993).

84   Biography, chapters 7 and 9.

85   *'dul ba.*

86   For the dream, elaboration and practice of *jo 'khor*, see chapter 4 of the biography.

87   The prophetic statements (Tib. *lung bstan*; Skt. *vyākṛta*) are collected in the first chapter of the biography.

88 *Zab chos mkha' 'khyab rang grol.*

89 'Khrul zhig gling pa, lit. 'destroyer of illusion.'

90 *rje* or *rje nyid.*

91 In *gZhan stong mkhas lan seng ge'i nga ro.* For an excellent translation of these passages of Mipham's text and also passages of Pad ma bdud 'dul's biography, see Matthew T. Kapstein, "The Strange Death of Pema the Demon Tamer," in Kapstein, M.T., ed., *The Presence of Light: Divine Radiance and Religious Experience* (2004).

92 The complete name of the temple is bsKal bzang sangs rgyas chos gling.

93 For the history of bsKal bzang dgon pa and the evolution of the temple, see *Shar rgyal ba bskal bzang dgon gyi byung ba rags bsdus*, by Shes rab 'od zer and Byang chub rgya mtsho.

94 See Evans-Wentz (1985).

95 See Guenther (1963).

96 For a good study of the master-disciple relationship in Sufism, see Corbin (1995).

97 *rdo rje slob dpon:* 'vajra master.'

98 The first great attempt in Tibet to harmonize monastic vows with the ethics of Mahāyāna and the *samaya* of tantrism was the work of Sa chen kun dga' rgyal mtshan, *sDom gsum rab dbye.* There later appeared other approaches to the subject, such as the *sDom gsum rnam nges* by mNga' ris pan chen pad ma dbang rgyal.

99 The tantric commitments (Tib. *dam tshig;* Skt. *samaya)* model different attitudes ranging from intention through ritual aspects, and may vary according to the particular tantra or level of understanding.

100 This is the case of Atiśa, who asserted this opinion in his *Bodhipathapradīpa.*

101 Mantra practitioner (*sngags pa*), or yogi (*rnal byor pa*) can be applied also to a monk or nun, but usually refers to lay practitioners.

102 The practice of *gcod*, revealed by Ma gcig lab sgron, was integrated into all Tibetan religious traditions.

103 *ban chung.*

104 The male novice monk (Tib. *dge tshul;* Skt. *śrāmaṇera*) has to respect ten fundamental precepts.

105 I must express my gratitude to Jann M. Ronnis, who helped me in the interview with the *mkhan po*, translating his discourse in *nyag rong skad*, a dialect that I could not fully understand.

106 Information obtained in Kaḥ thog, May, 2005.

107 Such is the case in the biographies of the yoginis Ye shes mtsho rgyal and Ma gcig lab sgron. On the first, see the translation of the biography revealed by sTag sham nus ldan rdo rje, in Dowman (1984); on the second, see Orofino (1987) and Allione (1984).

108 *gsang bdag:* 'Lord of the Secrets.'

109 Information obtained in Kaḥ thog in May, 2005.

110 The Rainbow Body (*ja' lus*), along with the Great Transference (*'pho ba chen po*) is the supreme realization attained through the practice of Total Perfection. Both are accomplished through the total integration and self-liberation of the practitioner's constituents in the primordial Base, manifesting a body whose elements have reverted to their true nature: light.

111 The 'Place of Attainment of the Rainbow Body' (*ja' lus sgrub sa*) is located in the small valley of sNyin, some 10 km from the village of Ba rong and about 60 km east of dPal yul.

112 The explanations of practices and doctrines are presented as notes throughout the biography.

113 In the process of 'maturation' (*smin*) the practitioner develops the capacity to realize the four kayas through the Four Initiations; 'liberation' (*grol*) is obtained through practicing the instructions that concretize and apply the wisdom transmitted in the initiations.

114 *byin rlabs:* considered very important to further the capacities of the practitioner.

115 The integration of Total Perfection doctrines and cycles in the bKa' brgyud order was reinforced when the third Karmapa Rang byung rdo rje (1284–1339) became a holder of Total Perfection transmissions. Rang byung rdo rje was a disciple of the master Kumārarādza who received the *Bi ma snying thig* teachings from Me long rdo rje and established a rDzogs chen practice lineage in the bKa' brgyud order based on his own cycle, the *Karma snying thig*. See Tartang, Bradburn, and Yeshe De (1995).

116 The rNying ma pa system is structured in nine soteriological levels. In ascending order, first there are the three vehicles based on the *sūtra*: the vehicles of the early disciples (*Śrāvaka*), of the lonely Buddhas (*Pratyekabuddha*), and of the Bodhisattvas. Next are the outer tantric vehicles: *Kriyātantra, Caryātantra,* and *Yogatantra*. Then there are the three uppermost, the most sublime, the inner tantric vehicles: *Mahāyoga* (*rnal 'byor chen po*) and *Anuyoga* (*rjes su rnal 'byor*) are transformational systems; *Atiyoga* (*shin tu rnal 'byor*) is the vehicle of self-liberation, or rDzogs chen (Total Perfection).

117 It is possible that Dung ral gling pa is the same as the sixth O rgyan rin po che, named bDud 'joms dung ral gling pa. The O rgyan rin po che lineage of lamas is related to dPal yul monastery in Khams.

118 See chapter 3 of the biography.

119 lCags mdud o rgyan gling.

120 See the above section: *Spiritual Tradition in Eastern Tibet.*

121 Mi 'gyur nam mkha'i rdo rje (1793–1870).

122 rDzogs chen padma rig 'dzin (1625–1697) was from Khams. He received teachings and initiations from many masters such as Karma chags med, gTer chen bdud 'dul rdo rje, and the fifth Dalai Lama, among others. At the request of the fifth Dalai Lama, he founded the retreat center of bSam gtan chos gling in the Ru dam valley in Khams, which later became the rDzogs chen monastery. See Tarthang, Bradburn and Yeshe De (1995), and Dudjom Rinpoche (1991), pages 736–737 and p. 817.

123 *Bi ma snying thig.*

124 *mKha' 'gro snying thig.*

125 The *Dag snang gu ru raksha thod phreng rtsal.* On the affiliation of this master with the transmission lines of the various *snying thig,* see Thondup (1996), pp. 35–37. On his life, idem pp.175–178, and Tarthang, Bradburn and Yeshe De (1995).

126 sNyo shul lung rtogs bstan pa'i nyi ma (1829–1901).

127 See the above section, *Spiritual Tradition in Eastern Tibet.*

128 *Ye shes bla ma:* section of the *kLong chen snying thig.*

129 'Jigs med rgyal ba'i myu gu (1765–1843), the main disciple of 'Jigs med gling pa.

130 The other lineages are: Zhing skyong, dGe rtse, rMor tsha, dGon snying, dBon po, and 'Brug grags dgon lag. See Smith (1969), p. 6.

131 Theg mchog rdo rje (1798–1868).

132 Dus gsum mkhyen pa (1110–1193).

133 *Rin chen gter mdzod.*

134 On Kong sprul, see Dudjom Rinpoche (1991), pp. 859–868, and Kongtrul Lodrö Taye, Jamgön (1995), pp. 15–35.

135 Padma nyin byed dbang po (1774–1853). The biography erroneously informs us that this is the third Si tu.

136 *rtsa ba'i bla ma.*

137 Total Relaxation (*khregs chod*) and Direct Leap (*thod rgal*) are the two yogic phases in the *man ngag sde* section of Total Perfection.

138 *kLong gsal rdo rje snying po.*
139 See Sangpo (1973). In 1991 I translated this brief biography, a first approach to this subject.
140 See chapter 5 of the biography.
141 *chos bdag.*
142 On the Holder of the Doctrine (*chos bdag*), Tulku Thondup Rinpoche in *Hidden Teachings of Tibet* explains that there are two kinds, the principal one and the lesser one. The principal one receives the mental order (*gtad rgya*) from Padmasambhava during the period when the treasure is hidden in order to protect it for a future time. While not having this same experience, the lesser one would still have been identified by the omniscient Padmasambhava who, empowering him through prophecy and devotional prayer, facilitates his future appearance as a Holder of the Revealed Doctrine. See Thondup (1986).
143 sTag bla pad ma mati (1591–1637).
144 Gar dbang zhig po gling pa (1524–1588). On this *gter ston*, see Tartang, Bradburn, and Yeshe De (1995), pp.234–235.
145 On Rig 'dzin klong gsal snying po (1625–1692), see Tartang, Bradburn, and Yeshe De (1995), pp. 253–254.
146 See chapter 9 of the biography.
147 See the beginning of chapter 7 of the biography.
148 *thugs kyi sras.*
149 *bLa ma'i dgongs pa 'dus pa.*
150 Lama A kha is one of the contemporary holders of Pema Düdul's teachings.
151 Information obtained through interviews with those two lamas in Khams, May 2005.
152 Information provided by mkhan po bSod nams rten pa of Kaḥthog.
153 Rang rig rdo rje, alias Rig pa'i rdo rje, Nyag bla rang rig, or as *gter ston*, sKu gsum gling pa (1847–1903).
154 See chapter 9.
155 See chapter 12.
156 See Tarthang, Bradburn, and Yeshe De (1995), p. 358. According to the mkhan po bSod nams bstan pa, Ran rig rdo rje married a girl belonging to the Khang gsar family.
157 gTer ston bSod rgyal, with the *gter ston* name Las rab gling pa(1856–1926).
158 mThu stobs gling pa(1858–1914).

159 A 'dzom 'brug pa 'gro 'dul dpa bo rdo rje, also known as Rig 'dzin sna tshogs rang grol (1842–1924). About A 'dzom 'brug pa, see Thondup (1996), pp. 228–229, and Tarthang, Bradburn, and Yeshe De (1995), pp. 335–337.

160 Kun mkhyen pad ma dkar po (1526–1592).

161 The *Transcendent Wisdom Master (Ye shes bla ma)* is the main section on rDzogs chen instructions in the *kLong chen snying thig (The Heart Essence of the Great Expanse)*.

162 *rtsa lung.*

163 The name of the monastery is bKhra shis dung dkar 'khyil, which I had the privilege of visiting in 1994. A 'dzom sgar, 'the settlement of A 'dzom,' is its popular name.

164 Chos rgyal Nam mkha'i nor bu was recognized as an emanation of A 'dzom 'brug pa by dPal yul karma yang srid rin po che and by Zhe chen rab 'byams Rin po che when he was two years old. See Norbu (1996).

165 'Brug sprul rin po che.

166 Nyag bla byang chub rdo rje (1826–1961 or 1978).

167 *Chos nyid rol pa'i glu.* This song has been translated by Chögyal Namkhai Norbu and Enrico dell'Angelo in Padma bdud 'dul (1989).

168 A gyu mkha' 'gro rdo rje dpal sgron (1838–1953).

169 Oral communication by Chögyal Namkhai Norbu. The master.disciple relationship between Padma bdud 'dul and A gyu mkha' 'gro is also mentioned in the latter's biography, in Allione (1984).

170 See Allione (1984), p. 245.

171 See chapter 4 of the biography.

172 See chapter 8.

173 See chapter 8; not to be confused with Kaḥ thog Si tu, who did belong to the rNying ma order.

174 See chapter 9.

175 See chapter 8.

176 See chapter 9.

177 See chapter 9.

178 *rJe bla ma 'khrul zhig gling pa'i rnam thar skal bzang dga' ba'i bdud rtsi'i sprin tshogs.*

179 Knowledge Holder (Tib. *rig 'dzin;* Skt. *vidyādhara*) is one of the epithets, along with Great Adept (Tib. *grub thob chen po;* Skt. *mahāsiddha*), used in esoteric Buddhism as a title for enlightened masters.

180 The masters and disciples concerning whom I have obtained information are marked with an asterisk. They are discussed in the introductory section on *Masters and Disciples.*

181 *mDo sde bskal bzang.*

182 Tib. *chu srin:* a kind of dragon living in the depths of the ocean.

183 *gtor ma:* figures made of dough that serve a sacrificial function in rituals. Here the text refers specifically to *bshos bu,* little tormas made of butter.

184 As is explained later on in the biography, this would be his usual name.

185 The Plain of Treasures (*gter mdzod thang*) is probably the meadow situated in front of the rocky peak of Lhang Lhang.

186 Another name of Padma bdud 'dul.

187 This quantity of days corresponds with the forty-nine days of the intermediate state (*bar do*), the existence experienced by a being between his death and rebirth.

188 *dzo:* cross between a yak and a cow.

189 *tsha tsha:* molded clay sculptures, usually placed around *stūpas* or sacred places. These may be made to benefit the dead, sometimes by mixing their ashes with the clay.

190 *rma khog:* a mythical land that also appears in another of Pema Düdul's dreams later in this same chapter. As is shown in the above passage, it is like a parallel dimension bound to the human world through karmic debt.

191 *gla sgang* (in the text *gla dgong*): *cyperus,* a medicinal herb.

192 *nim pa: azadirachta indica,* a medicinal tree.

193 *mon bu:* a medicinal herb.

194 *chu rus, rtsug pa* and *sngo sdum* (or *ldum*): different kinds of green herbs.

195 *zho:* a monetary unit.

196 *gya ma:* a unit of weight, approximately half a kilogram.

197 *do tshe:* Chinese monetary unit of silver, equivalent to fifty *srang* of Tibetan currency.

198 *dre:* a mesure of capacity, approximately one litre.

199 *Zhi khro bag chags rang grol:* belongs to the *Zhi khro dgongs pa rang grol* cycle discovered by Karma gling pa. In the *Zhi khro* cycles, based upon Anuyoga-style transformation practices, the yogi self-generates as a divinity and visualizes his inner *cakras* as the *maṇḍala.* This practice, particularly the cycle discovered by Karma gling pa, (fourteenth century), the *Zhi khro dgongs pa rang grol* with his section *Bar do thos grol chen mo* can be applied to benefit the dead.

200 *Phung po gsum pa'i mdo.*

201 *rDo rje gcod pa.*

202 *Om mani padme hum:* the six-syllable mantra of Avalokiteśvara.

203 *gto:* generic designation for rituals for exorcism and prosperity.

204 *kumutala:* a nocturnal lilac.

205 Palchen Pema Dragpo (*dpal chen pad ma drag po*): a wrathful manifestation of Padmasambhava.

206 *rDo rje gro lod:* one of the Eight Manifestations of Guru Padmasambhava (*gu ru mtshan brgyad*). The other seven manifestations are: *Gu ru pad ma 'byung gnas, Gu ru shakya seng ge, Gu ru nyi ma 'od zer, Gu ru seng ge sgra sgrog, Gu ru mtsho skyes rdo rje, Gu ru padma rgyal po,* and *Gu ru blo ldan mchog sred.*

207 five degenerations: the degeneration of the vision, emotions, circumstances, lifespan, and capacities.

208 These verses are from the *Byang chub sems dpa'i spyod la 'jug pa* (the *Bodhisattvacaryāvatāra*) of Śāntideva (oral information from Chögyal Namkhai Norbu).

209 This refers to the practice of choosing the *yi dam,* in which a flower is thrown on the *mandalas.*

210 *chur ba,* is a kind of curd extracted from milk.

211 *mDo sde las brgya pa.*

212 *mDo dran pa nyer bzhag.*

213 Ancient Indian coins.

214 *rgya bo:* literally, 'beard,' in this context a reference to the faded color of the aging dog's muzzle.

215 The text reads *nyag khog,* possibly an error for *nyag rong.*

216 Lantsha (*lany dza*) is an ornamental script developed in the eleventh century from the Nepalese Ranjana script. It is used for writing in the Sankrit language, especially in the titles of translated texts and for mantras, both in books and mural paintings.

217 *star bu:* the *hippophae rhamnoides,* a medicinal bush.

218 *gri kug:* a curved knife used in rituals, and one of the major symbols of the wisdom *dākinī.*

219 *thod pa:* a cup made from a human skull, containing nectars, associated with tantric deities and used in tantric rituals.

220 Padmasambhava.

221 *rJe btsun sgrol ma'i snying thig.*

222 *lan dza* and *warthu:* two ornamental styles of calligraphy for Sanskrit language.

223 Tib. *phyag rgya;* Skt. *mudrā:* symbolic hand gestures made during tantric rituals.

224 Mahākaruṇā, 'The Great Compassionate One:' an epithet for Avalokiteśvara, the Bodhisattva of universal compassion.

225 *jo 'khor*: a great prayer wheel, which is spun resting on the ground while the *ma ṇi pa* (the religious specialist dedicated to this practice) chants the *mantra* and explains teachings or hagiographies to the public, usually in the street or marketplace where people gather.

226 *'das log*: people who are 'back from beyond,' that is, who have had a *postmortem* experience. Generally, this experience consists of a series of visions of states beyond death; these visions are explained by the *'das log*, who thereby acquire a certain spiritual charisma.

227 *le'u bdun pa*: prayer to Padmasambhava in seven lines, believed to have been composed by Padmasambhava himself.

228 The *Treasures from the North* (*byang gter*) comprise the totality of the revealed texts of Rig 'dzin rgod ldem 'phru can (1337–1408), discovered at Zang zang lha brag and other places. Up to our epoch, The *Treasures from the North* tradition has mainly been transmitted through the rDo rje brag monastery in central Tibet, one of the six main monasteries of the rNying ma pa order.

229 *Kun bzang dgongs pa zang thal*: the main *tantra* in the *Treasures from the North*. See previous note.

230 The *maṇi* is the *mantra* of Avalokiteśvara, Lord of Compassion, referred to in this passage by another of his names, Thugs rje chen po, Skt. Mahākaruṇā). The *siddhi* mantra is one of those associated with Padmasambhava.

231 *mthar do*: a formula of confession, used when one is obliged to eat the flesh of an animal killed on the same day.

232 *mna' sdig*: another formula of confession.

233 The four thoughts are: the difficulty of obtaining the precious human birth, death and impermanence, the power of the law of cause and effect (karma), and the suffering of conditioned existence (*saṃsāra*).

234 The act of Taking Refuge (*skyabs su 'gro ba*) in the Buddha, his teachings, and the community of believers is the central ritual for becoming a Buddhist. For one who is already a Buddhist, it is a return to the true sense of the teachings.

235 The text reads *nor lugs*, probably an error for *nor lug*, meaning cattle in general.

236 mDo mkhyen brtse ye shes rdo rje (1800–1866).

237 *rig 'dzin 'dus pa*: a practice belonging to the *kLong chen snying thig* cycle. It is one of the tantric practices in the section on meditative realization, consisting of the internal practice of the male peaceful aspect.

238 *yum ka bde che rgyal mo*, or *'queen of bliss:'* another *sādhana* belonging to the *kLong chen snying thig* cycle, which belongs to the Knowledge Holders group of *sādhanas*, but in the female peaceful aspect. *Yum ka* is a manifestation of Ye shes mtsho rgyal, consort of Padmasambhava.

239 *Ye shes bla ma:* the text of rDzogs chen instructions in the *kLong chen snying thig* cycle.

240 *Kīlaya (Phur pa):* one of the most important *yi dam* of the inner tantras, practiced particularly in the rNying ma and Sa skya orders. *Kīlaya* is the aspect of Enlightened Activity (*'phrin las*) in the *Eight Sādhana Teachings* (*Grub pa bka' brgyad*) of Mahāyoga.

241 *zangs mdog dpal ri:* The paradise of Padmasambhava, the Glorious Copper-colored Mountain.

242 *rJe 'bangs:* the Lord (Emperor Khri srong lde'u btsan) and the other Tibetan disciples of Padmasambhava, who were the emperor's subjects.

243 This possibly refers to his uncle's spiritual treasures.

244 Rin chen gling pa (1295–1375), a *gter ston* who discovered the cycle *rDzogs chen gcig chod kun grol chen po.*

245 Tib. *bde bar bshegs pa'i snying po;* Skt. *sugatagarbha:* similar to *tathāgatagarbha,* the 'Buddha-nature.'

246 The Three Jewels (*dkon mchog gsum*): Buddha, Dharma, and Saṃgha or monastic community.

247 *rgyal po, the'u rang, rgyal 'gong, srin mo:* several classes of earthly spirits who sometimes create obstacles for the practitioner.

248 *shang lang:* another name for the mountain of Lhang Lhang.

249 Tib. *rnga yab gling;* Skt. *cāmara:* the western subcontinent where the Glorious copper-colored Mountain, Padmasambhava's dwelling, is found.

250 *'jig rten chos brgyad:* pleasure at gaining something and displeasure at not gaining it; happiness and sadness; fame and disgrace; praise and blame.

251 The four visions (*snang ba bzhi*) are the four visionary levels of *thod rgal* practice.

252 *kLong gsal rdo rje snying po:* a *gter ma* cycle discovered by Klong gsal snying po (1625–1692). This cycle is one of the specialities of Kaḥ thog monastery.

253 Total Relaxation (*khregs chod*) and Direct Leap (*thod rgal*) constitute the two main levels of practice in the *Man ngag sde* section of Atiyoga. The first leads to the realization of Primordial Purity (*ka dag*) and the second, to the Spontaneous Presence (*lhun grub*) manifesting as light of wisdom, which brings on the realization of the Rainbow Body (*'ja' lus*).

254 The Transference practice (*'pho ba*) is one of the yogas of the Accomplishment stage of the tantric path. Consisting of the transference of consciousness into a pure dimension, it is to be applied particularly at the moment of death.

255 *sNying thig ma bu*: the *sNying thig ya bzhi* cycle, the most ancient collection of texts on the thought and practice of the *Man ngag sde* section of Total Perfection. It contains two original sections, one from Vimalamitra and the other from Padmasambhava, and three additional sections consisting of kLong chen pa's exegesis. Vimalamitra's section, named *Bi ma snying thig*, is linked to seventeen tantras. Padmasambhava's, the *mKha' 'gro snying thig*, is linked to the *kLong gsal* tantra. kLong chen pa's exegesis on the first part (Vimalamitra's) is named *bLa ma yang tig*; the second exegesis is the *mKha' 'gro yang tig* (Padmasambhava's); and the general exegesis is the *Zab mo yang tig*.

256 sMin gling gter chen, alias O rgyan gter bdag gling pa (1634–1714): the most important rNying ma pa master of the seventeenth century. Disciple and master of the fifth Dalai Lama, gTer bdag gling pa kept alive the practice and study of the *bKa' ma* and many other cycles of tantric teachings. He wrote commentaries on the three internal sections of the rNying ma tantras, but he is particularly known for his own revealed treasures, among them the *A ti zab don snying po*. Lo chen dharma śrī (1654–1717), his brother and disciple, shared with him the direction of sMin grol gling monastery founded under the protection of the fifth Dalai Lama. A highly erudite monk, he was celebrated for his exegeses of canonical texts, especially for his commentary on the *Gūhyagarbhatantra*, the *gSang bdag zhal lung*.

257 bDud 'dul gling pa: a *gter ston* who died during the Dzungar invasion of Tibet in 1705. He discovered a treasure centered on the practice of Tārā and other teachings on Vajrakīlaya, but many of his *gter ma* are now missing.

258 kLong gsal snying po (1625–1692): a great *gter ston* whose treasures encompass most of the esoteric practices of the rNying ma tradition. He worked in association with bDud 'dul rdo rje (1615–1672), and both revitalized the spiritual practice in Kaḥ thog monastery. He discovered the cycle *kLong gsal rdo rje snying po* that became a specialty of Kaḥ thog monastery. This cycle was transmitted many times to Padma bdud 'dul, who in turn transmitted it to his disciples on several occasions.

259 Ratna gling pa (1403–1479): a master important in rNying ma history for his revitalization of many of this order's teachings, some of which had come close to extinction. He compiled one of the first versions of the *rNying ma rgyud*

'bum, the canonical collection of the old order tantras. Furthermore, he was a great *gter ston* who discovered twenty-five treasures on diverse subjects.

260   *kLong chen snying thig.*

261   Tib. *phyag rgya chen po*; Skt. *mahāmudrā:* the 'great symbol': the realization attained through tantric practice as defined by the new orders of Tibetan Buddhism (*gsar ma*). As the final fruit, it signifies the liberation of the yogi in the ultimate reality, the radiant luminosity that is inseparable from bliss and emptiness (*bde stong gi 'od gsal*) of indivisible nature *(dbyer med).* Although it is usually conceived of as the fruit of the two tantric phases (*bskyed rim* and *rdzogs rim*), there is also a *Mahāmudrā* that is not based on the path of transformation, but is similar to *rDzogs chen.* This last system is followed principally in the bKa' brgyud pa orders.

262   Tib. *bde bar gshegs pa;* Skt. *sugata:* 'one who has arrived at a state of beatitude:' usually used as a synonym for *Buddha.*

263   Lha lung dpal gyi rdo rje, disciple of Padmasambhava who, after killing the apostate king gLang dar ma, went to eastern Tibet.

264   *Yang tig nag po 'bru gcig:* a *gter ma* teaching discovered by Dung mtsho ras pa phyi ma in the fourteenth century. As its name indicates, this teaching belongs to the Yang ti level of rDzogs chen. The Yang ti is considered the most profound system of Total Perfection teachings.

265   *Khrid yig dmar mo mdzub tshugs:* a cycle on tantric and rDzogs chen practices of the New Bön tradition (*bon gsar*). Composed by Kun grol grags pa (b. 1700), this cycle was also widely diffused among rNying ma practitioners.

266   Padmasambhava.

267   Here there appears a note in brackets, possibly added by the editor: "On somebody's asking about the house of A mya, this one known as sTag bla Chos 'grub rgya mtsho comes from the A mya monastic household originating from the lineage of sons and spiritual descendants of the lamas of the sacred place of Lhang brag."

268   *tshig bdun ma'i gsol 'debs*: seven-line prayer to Padmasambhava.

269   The Absorption of Elixir (Tib. *bcud len;* Skt. *rasāyana*) consists of fasting accompanied by the ingestion of small quantities of mineral and vegetable substances, with the aim of purifying the psychophysical constituents. This is normally done in retreat in combination with other yogic practices. As we can see from the text, there are variations in the degree of fasting and in the quality of the elixir.

270   *dbang lag:* the *orchis latifolia.*

271 *rtsi sman:* medicines made with oils and essences.

272 *gnyen:* a type of nature deity.

273 *mGur 'bum:* a collection of songs of the experiences (*nyams mgur*) of Padma bdud 'dul, which follows his biography. The title is *Nyams mgur skor skal bzang thar lam 'god pa'i phrin las,* in Dorje (1998).

274 *bLa ma'i dgongs pa 'dus pa:* a *gter ma* cycle revealed by Sangs rgyas gling pa (1340–1396). He discovered the treasure in a cave in the Tsa ri mountains, the sacred sanctuary in southeast Tibet. He also found some parts of this cycle in his native region of Kong po. The *gter ma* consists of thirteen volumes.

275 Nyang ral nyi ma 'od zer (1124–1192).

276 *bKa' brgyad bde gshegs 'dus pa:* a *gter ma* cycle revealed by Nyang ral nyi ma 'od zer, centered on the eight meditative practices of the Mahāyoga.

277 In the text: *si dhu.*

278 *snang sems ro gcig 'dres pa:* literally, 'intermingles apparent objects and the mind in a single flavor.' It should be noted that 'single flavor' (*ro gcig*) is one of the terms defining the experience of contemplation in *Mahāmudrā,* where it designates one of the four yogas of the tradition of sGam po pa.

279 *Yang tig nag po gser gyi 'bru gcig:* the *gter ma* cycle discovered by Dung mtsho ras pa phyi ma in the fourteenth century.

280 *The Eight Transmitted Precepts* (*bka' brgyad*) are the meditative practices of realization (*sādhana*) of the Mahāyoga. Here this refers more specifically to the *gter ma* cycle discovered by Nyang ral nyi ma 'od zer (1114–1192), *The Gathering of the Sugatas of the Eight Transmitted Precepts* (*bKa' brgyad bde gshegs 'dus pa*).

281 rDo rje khro bo lod is a *yi dam* associated with Padmasambhava, being one of his eight manifestations (*guru mtshan brgyad*). This entire line refers to Padmasamhava's declaration of Pema Düdul as his emanation.

282 *rig pa;* Skt. *vidya:* one of the key terms in Atiyoga. Whereas in other levels of Tibetan Buddhism it signifies knowledge in general, intellect, or even reasoning, in rDzogs chen parlance its meaning is more subtle. As Chögyal Namkhai Norbu asserts, *rig pa* is not the Primordial Base (*gdod ma'i bzhi*), but the recognizance of the presence of this Base. Thus, this same master translates *rig pa* as "instant presence," because it is the non-dual cognizance that embraces all phenomena, being recognized by the practitioner in the instant, present moment.

283 Padmasambhava.

284 In this fragment there are references to the inner channels according to rDzogs chen.

285 *'dom:* a unit of measurement, corresponding to a fathom, measured by the extension of the arms.

286 *phur bu:* three-sided ritual dagger associated with the practice of Vajrakīlaya.

287 Tib. *tsan dan;* Skt. *tsandana.*

288 *tshogs 'khor:* 'circle of accumulation (of offerings):' a tantric ritual consisting of offerings of food and drink, which are also consumed by the participants.

289 Tib. *klu;* Skt. *nāga:* underground or water spirits.

290 *smyung gnas:* a practice of fasting and prayer lasting for one day or longer. During this practice, ten vows must be observed.

291 *Zab chos mkha' khyab rang grol.*

292 *rNam dag rang grol.*

293 *Ka dag rang grol.*

294 *bDe chen rang grol.*

295 *rTsa gsum dgongs 'dus nges don rdo rje snying po.*

296 As was made clear to me by the *mkhan po* bSod nams bstan pa, the chief mentioned here—and throughout the biography whenever *nyag dpon* is mentioned—refers to mGon po rnam rgyal, the rebel chief who dominated a large area of eastern Tibet.

297 *bum sgrub 'dzugs:* probably refers to the burial of a chalice filled with consecrated pills (*ril bu*) and other relics in order to empower the place.

298 *gzungs thag:* a cord of six colors tied to a *vajra* placed on a vase containing pills or relics. The cord comes out of the *bum pa* (vase), and is held by the officiants while the substances are consecrated. The story suggests that the pills spontaneously emerged from the chalice.

299 Padma gling pa (1445–1521): the great *gter ston* who was mainly active in Bhutan. The comparison alludes to Padma gling pa's discovery of a physical *gter ma* in Me 'bar mtsho lake in Bhumthang valley, where he dropped into the lake with a lighted torch that was still burning when he emerged from the depths with the treasure.

300 These are: generosity, peaceful words, coherent conduct, and giving appropriate teachings.

301 *mDo rgyan.*

302 *yan lag bdun pa:* performing postrations, confessing wrongdoing, making offerings, rejoicing in others' virtue, urging the teaching of the Dharma, beseeching the Master not to depart into *nirvāṇa,* and dedicating merit.

303 *ru shan:* practices belonging to the *Upadeśa* (*Man ngag sde*) level of rDzogs chen. These practices are aimed at distinguishing ordinary mind from the nature of mind, symbolized respectively by *saṃsāra* and *nirvāṇa* in the formal name of the practice.

304 The practice of Inner Heat (*gtum mo*) is an important discipline of the Accomplishment Phase in the tantric path. As such, it is one of the Six Yogas of Nāropā (*Na ro chos drug*), and its aim is to develop the experience of the heat linked to the sun's energy, producing the enhancement of bliss (*bde ba*).

305 See n. 191, above.

306 *maṇḍal:* an offering arranged (geometrically, as in a deity *maṇḍala;* Tib. *dkyil 'khor)* on a round plate-like base generally representing the entire universe with all its most valued and auspicious contents.

307 *rdo tshad:* a monetary unit.

308 *sgrom bu:* the vessel that contains the hidden scriptures or objects.

309 The cuckoo sings at the beginning of spring, hence this epithet.

310 This refers to the burial of a relic-filled container. See the previous chapter.

311 *byang phyogs so bdun:* thirty-seven factors to be cultivated on the path to enlightenment, including the Four Applications of Mindfulness (*dran pa nyer bzhag bzhi*), the Four Perfect Renunciations (*yang dag spong ba bzhi*), the Four Bases of Miraculous Power (*rdzu 'phrul gyi rkang pa bzhi*), the Five Capacities of Total Enlightenment (*rnam byang dbang po lnga*), the Five Powers of Total Enlightenment (*rnam byang gi stobs lnga*), the Seven Branches of Enlightenment (*byang chub yan lag bdun*), and the Eightfold Noble Path (*'phags lam yan lag brgyad*).

312 The two stages of the tantric path are the Development Stage (*bskyed rim*) and the Accomplishment Stage (*rdzogs rim*). The first is mainly concerned with the development of the visualization of the deities and *maṇḍalas* and the recitation of the mantras, while the second works on the subtle level of channels, cakras, and winds. The union of the two stages leads to *Mahāmudrā.*

313 The seven riches of the Noble Ones: faith, generosity, discipline, learning, modesty, sense of shame, and introspection.

314 The two masters who began the bKa' gdams pa lineage, Atīśa (982–1054) and his disciple 'Brom ston pa rgyal ba'i 'byung gnas (1005–1064).

315 All these texts are *dhāraṇis* (formulae similar to mantras), the recitation of which is said to produce auspicious conditions.

316 *Abhirati:* the Kingdom of True Bliss, the Buddha-field of Akṣobhya.

317 sKal bzang sangs rgyas chos gling.

318 *Zhi khro dgongs pa rang grol:* the *gter ma* discovered by Karma gling pa in the fourteenth century, better known by its abridged name, *Kar gling zhi khro.*

319 *Tshogs bskang rgya chen.*

320 *bLa ma dgong 'dus.*

321 *Yi dam brgya rtsa.*

322 *Guru ye shes rab 'bar:* a tantric deity associated with Padmasambhava, also present in Padma bdud 'dul's *gter ma* (information from Chögyal Namkhai Norbu).

323 *sKu gsum zhi khro:* the practice of the Peaceful and Wrathful Deities in the *Zhi khro dgongs pa rang grol* cycle of Karma gling pa.

324 This probably does not refer to mGon po rnam rgyal, the chief who dominated Khams at this time and who was a fervent disciple of Padma bdud 'dul. It may refer to another aristocrat whose power would be limited by the dominion of the previously mentioned chief.

325 *khal:* a unit of volume equivalent to 25 pounds.

326 The ten metaphors for illusion include the image of the moon on water, reflections in a mirror, the castle of the *gandharvas,* and others.

327 *Dus pa mdo* or *mDo dgongs pa 'dus pa:* considered to be the most important of the four root tantras of the Anuyoga.

328 *Lam 'bras:* the essential the path in the Sa skya tradition. Combining *sūtra* and *tantra,* it was introduced into Tibet by the master Gayādhara in the eleventh century, who transmitted the teaching to 'Brog mi Lo tsa ba, the founder of the Sa skya order.

329 The text reads *mchod yul* (recipient for offerings), but I think this is an error for *mchod yon* (benefactor, donator of offerings). This entire passage refers to mGon po rnam rgyal, who died in a fire when his citadel was under siege.

330 *Thar lam dkar po.*

331 *rTa khyung 'bar ba:* the *sādhana* based on a *heruka* that unifies the aspects of Hayagrīva (*rta mgrin*) and Garuḍa (*Khyung*). It belongs to the *kLong chen snying thig* cycle, specifically to the section on the wrathful male Wisdom Holders.

332 *dKon mchog spyi 'dus:* discovered by Rig 'dzin 'ja' tshon snying po (1585– 656) at Hom 'phrang (in the Kong po region), it consists of a *guruyoga* practice centered on Padmasambhava as the unification of all masters. This cult developed greatly among rNying ma and bKa' brgyud practitioners.

333 *Dag snang gu ru raksha thod phreng rtsal.*

334 *Byang chub sems dpa'i spyod la 'jug pa:* the *Bodhisattvacaryāvatāra* of Śāntideva.

335 Tib. *'Jam dpal mtshan brjod;* Skt. *Mañjuśrīnāmasaṃgīti:* a canonical text much appreciated in the Tibetan Buddhist tradition. It consists of a canticle describing Mañjuśrī's atributes and his *maṇḍala* in a manner that rNying ma pa masters consider to be akin to rDzogs chen knowledge. This text belongs to the *samādhi* chapter of the tantra, *The Net of Magical Illusion* or *Māyājāla* (*sGyu 'phrul drwa ba*), the main tantra of the *Mahāyoga.*

336 *Dzam bu'i gling:* according to *mahāyanā* cosmology, the southern continent of our world, comprising India and other countries.

337 Tib. *rNga yab;* Skt. *Cāmara:* an island in the southwest where the Glorious Copper Mountain (Zangs mdog dpal ri), the dwelling of Padmasambhava, is located.

338 *rDo rje'i sgra dbyangs kyi rgyud.*

339 *dGa' ldan lha brgya ma:* the *guruyoga* practiced primarily in the dGe lugs pa order, centered on the order's founder Tsong kha pa blo bzang grags pa (1357–1419).

340 *rgya rag:* may signify either a type of copper from China or India, or a kind of liquor (*a rag*) from one of those countries.

341 Las rab gling pa: also known as gTer ston bsod rgyal or Nyag bla bsod rgyal (1856–1926). This important *gter ston*, who was master and disciple of the thirteenth Dalai Lama, lived in sKal bzang monastery after Pad ma bdud 'dul's departure.

342 *ras pa:* literally, 'he who wears a cotton robe.' This is an epithet for certain yogis (most notably Mi la ras pa), generally of the bKa' brgyud pa order, and refers to their austere dress.

343 *bLa ma yang tig:* kLong chen pa's commentary on the *Heart Essence of Vi-malamitra* (*Bi ma snying thig*).

344 *Zab mo yang tig:* kLong chen pa's general commentary on the *Four Heart Essences* (*sNying thig ya bzhi*). This last cycle assembles the *upadeśa* traditions linked to Vimalamitra and Padmasambhava.

345 'Gyur med chos dbyings rang grol, root master of Padma bdud 'dul.

346 *bhikṣu;* Tib. *dge slong:* a fully ordained monk.

347 The Lords of the Three Families (*rigs gsum mgon po*) are Avalokiteśvara, Mañjuśrī, and Vajrapāṇi of the Lotus, Buddha, and Vajra families respectively.

348 *Zab mo'i nang don.*

349 Rang 'byung rdo rje (1284–1339): the third Karma pa.

350 *rNying ma'i rgyud 'bum.*

351 These are: the five aggregates, the eighteen spheres of the senses, the six senses and their objects, interdependent origination, the power of discerning what is and is not, and the four Noble Truths expounded by the Buddha.

352 *thig le.*

353 *Kun tu bzang po'i dgongs pa'i gsang mdzod.*

354 *tsa ka li:* small paintings representing individual deities, offerings, and so on, which are displayed during tantric initiations.

355 Dza sprul Kun bzang rnam par rgyal ba was the Holder of the Doctrine (*chos bdag*) of the treasure of Padma bdud 'dul, as is explained in the next chapter.

356 The text reads *khu dben,* a mistake for *khu dbon,* 'uncle and nephew'.

357 Another epithet for the incarnation of A 'dzom, better known as A 'dzom 'brug pa sNa tshogs rang grol.

358 The text reads *bam po,* a mistake for *bam ro* (corpse).

359 *rten gsum:* images to represent the Body, scriptures to represent the Voice, and *stūpas* to represent the Mind, all of which are supports of the three enlightened aspects.

360 This is 'Gyur med chos dbyings rang grol, his root master, who had evidently died.

361 This refers to the appearance of the *tantrika,* or lay tantric practitioner.

362 This is an allusion to the name *bdud 'dul,* 'he who has subjugated the demons.'

363 *tshogs drug:* the consciousness of each of the five senses, plus the mental consciousness.

364 *Thugs sgrub rig pa rang grol.*

365 *Phyi sgrub pad dkar phreng ba.*

366 *Rig 'dzin 'dus pa.*

367 *Yon tan rin po che'i mdzod:* a text written by 'Jigs med gling pa on the characteristics of the path of realization.

368 This may refer to the medicinal herbs *amalaki (phyllantus emblica)* or *myrobalan (emblica officinalis).*

369 Here Padma bdud 'dul is called by his *gter ston* name, 'Khrul zhig byang chub gling pa,' which also appears in the title of the *rnam thar.*

370 *rTa phyag chos nyid rang grol.*

371 The Four Visions (*snang ba bzhi*): the four levels of practice in the Direct Leap (*thod rgal*) yoga, the most elevated practice in rDzogs chen.

372 *sKu gdung 'bar ba:* one of the seventeen tantras of the *Most Secret Cycle (yang gsang)* in the *Man sngag sde* section of Ati Yoga, which is one of the auxiliary tantras (*yan lag gi rgyud*).

373 *Rig pa rang shar:* another one of the seventeen tantras of the *Man sngag sde* section, and an explicative tantra (*bshad rgyud*).

374 *rig pa'i tshad phebs:* the third level of the Four Visions (*snang ba bzhi*), in which the visionary experiences are most highly developed.

375 This simile refers to the profound evenness and stillness experienced in this state.

376 *chos nyid zad pa:* the last level in the Four Visions, in which the practitioner is totally reintegrated into the true nature. The culmination of this level leads to the realization of the Rainbow Body (*'ja' lus*).

377 *shang* (*shangs*) *mtshal:* blood from the nose.

378 This most likely refers to the *Blazing Wisdom of the Guru* (*Gu ru ye shes rab 'bar*).

Index

About the Author

Yeshe Dorje was a direct disciple and contemporary of Pema Düdul and was probably among the thirteen disciples given the name Dorje who were considered to be his spiritual sons.

About the Translator

Born in Barcelona in 1965, Oriol Aguilar received his PhD in cultural anthrolopogy from the Universitat Autònoma de Barcelona in 2005. Focusing on religious studies, particularly the Buddhism of Tibet, he studied Tibetan language in Barcelona and Paris (École Pratique des Hautes Études) and trained in translation with the Shang Shung Institute. He met Chögyal Namkhai Norbu in 1987, and since 1998 has collaborated with Shang Shung Publications as a member of the International Publications Committee (IPC) of the Dzogchen Community on the publication, particularly in the Spanish editions, of the teachings of Chögyal Namkhai Norbu, including translation of Tibetan texts.